Materialien für den bilingualen Unterricht
Geschichte

Invitation to History

Volume 1:

From the American Revolution
to the First World War

Cornelsen

Materialien für den bilingualen Unterricht: Geschichte
Invitation to History
Volume 1: From the American Revolution to the First World War

Erarbeitet von
Annegret Weeke, Düsseldorf

Didaktische Mitwirkung:
Manfred Wildhage, Braunschweig

Redaktion: Dr. Christine Keitz, Marc Proulx
Karten und Grafik: Dr. Volkhard Binder, Berlin
Illustrationen: Gabriele Heinisch, Berlin; Thomas Binder, Magdeburg
Umschlaggestaltung: Klein & Halm Grafikdesign, Berlin
Layout und technische Umsetzung: werkstatt für gebrauchsgrafik, Berlin

www.cornelsen.de

1. Auflage, 1. Druck 2006 / 06

Alle Drucke dieser Auflage sind inhaltlich unverändert und können im Unterricht nebeneinander verwendet werden.

Druck: GRASPO, Zlin, Tschechien

ISBN-13: 978-3-06-064263-2
ISBN-10: 3-06-064263-X

Inhalt gedruckt auf säurefreiem Papier aus nachhaltiger Forstwirtschaft.

Preface

Invitation to History is your new book for the bilingual history class. Its nine thematic units cover the period of the "long" 19th century, that is, the time from the American Revolution to the First World War. In each unit you'll find the following elements:

Texts and Timelines

give you an overview or introduce you to the thematic unit. Words with an asterisk * are important history terms listed in the unit revision pages and explained in the Glossary of terms (see Appendix, pp. 124–127).

Sources

for your work: secondary sources, written primary sources, cartoons, portraits, statistics, photographs, maps and paintings. They are numbered throughout in each unit.

S 5 Tobacco exports from Virginia, 1616–1775 (in pounds)

Year	Tobacco exports
1616	2300
1617	20,000
1618	50,000
1622	60,000
1626	300,000
1639	1,500,000
1700	20,000,000
1775	100,000,000

History skills

introduce you to the work of historians. They give you strategies and tools for analysing the different kinds of sources.

Key terms and Biographies

These boxes give you further information on history terms or key personalities.

Biography

Thomas Jefferson

Jefferson – a lawyer and wealthy plantation owner – was born in Virginia in 1743. The "Declaration of Independence" from 1776 (S 14) was mostly written by him. His ideas of self-goverment and the natural rights of the people influenced the Declaration. In 1801 Jefferson became President of the United States and retired from office in 1808. He died in 1826.

New vocabulary

All numbered words[1] are explained or translated on the same page.

Tasks

In each unit you'll find different kinds of tasks which help you to understand an event or development, for example

- by **organizing information** in charts and diagrams to simplify and summarize information, making it easier to understand and remember (see Appendix, pp. 142–143).
- by **making connections:** tasks to critically question an historical interpretation, to draw comparisons or to relate historical events and developments to the present.
- by **doing extra research:** tasks that tell you to do some **Extra research** – in a German history book, in an encyclopaedia, on the Internet, or in any other reference material. Present your results as a PowerPoint presentation or in any other form.

Activate your English

These boxes will help you to write and speak about historical topics.

Activate your English

Agreeing or disagreeing

In my opinion/view ...
I'm of the opinion that ...
I think it is right because ...
The source can serve as evidence because ...
I agree (very much) with the idea because ...
I disagree (entirely) because ...
I don't think so because...
I can't accept that because ...

Unit revision

At the end of each unit there are activities to revise key events, key terms and personalities, as well as history skills and vocabulary.

Appendix

The Appendix gives you a glossary of history terms, a glossary of biographies, an English-German vocabulary list, a historical dictionary and examples of the types of charts and diagrams used in ***Invitation to History.***

Contents

Unit 6 Germany on its way to an industrial society

Unit 7 German unification – Unification "by blood and iron"?

Unit 8 Europe in the age of imperialism

Unit 9 The First World War, 1914–1918

Appendix

Unit 1

The American Revolution

1.1 The settlement[1] of North America

S1
Cornelius Wytfliet, Map of America, 1597

Native Americans

The first American immigrants, more than 20,000 years ago, were wanderers: hunters and their families following animal herds from Asia to North America, across a land bridge where the Bering Strait is today.

When Spain's Christopher Columbus discovered the New World in 1492, probably about 1.5 million Native Americans* lived in what is now the United States. Because he thought that the place where he landed – San Salvador in the Bahamas – was India, he called the Native Americans "Indians"*.

During the next 200 years, people from Europe followed Columbus across the Atlantic Ocean to explore America, set up trading posts[2] and found colonies[3] (see p. 12). Native Americans suffered[4] greatly when they came into contact with Europeans. Violent conflicts over land, along with alcohol and Old World diseases[5] to which Indians had no immunity, reduced their numbers to about 350,000 in the United States by 1920. Some tribes disappeared altogether. Today they number about two million (0.8 per cent of the total US population).

Many US place-names are Indian words, including the states of Massachusetts, Ohio, Michigan, Mississippi, Missouri and Idaho. Indians taught Europeans how to grow crops[6] that are now well known throughout the world, such as corn, tomatoes, potatoes and tobacco. Canoes, snowshoes and moccasins are among the Indians' many inventions.

1 settlement *Besiedlung*
2 trading post *Handelsstation*
3 found a colony *eine Kolonie gründen*
4 suffer *leiden*
5 disease *Krankheit*
6 crop *Feldfrucht*

European settlers[1] in North America

The English founded their first permanent colony* (Jamestown) in Chesapeake Bay in 1607. The French followed with their own colony, Quebec, in 1608, and soon after the Dutch began to settle in the region that became present-day New York. Within another generation, the Plymouth Company (1620), the Massachusetts Bay Company (1629), the Company of New France (1627), and the Dutch West India Company (1621) began to send thousands of colonists to North America: the French built up large territories along the Saint Lawrence River, the Dutch along the Hudson River, and the English in Virginia and Massachusetts.

Why did the settlers come?

Religious groups such as the Puritans* and the Quakers felt that they had to leave England because they were not allowed to practise their religion freely. The most famous group, the Pilgrim Fathers*, left Plymouth on board the *Mayflower* and arrived at Cape Cod Bay, Massachusetts, in November 1620. The hope of finding gold and treasure[2] attracted explorers and adventurers. Pamphlets[3] encouraged new emigrants and described America as a paradise. Thus Englishmen, Frenchmen, Germans, Scots, Irishmen, Dutchmen and Swedes crossed the Atlantic Ocean in search of rich, fertile[4] lands and a better life in the colonies.

Only a few colonists could finance their trip for themselves and their families to make a start in the New World. In many cases, their transportation was paid for by ship captains, merchants[5] and landowners who needed workers. In return, immigrants had to work as unpaid and unfree labourers[6] (called indentured servants*), usually for four to seven years. It has been estimated[7] that half the settlers living in the colonies south of New England came to America under this system.

S2 ***Nova Britannia: Offering most excellent fruites by Planting in Virginia,* by Robert Johnson, pamphlet, London 1609**

1 settler *Siedler*
2 treasure *Schatz*
3 pamphlet *Broschüre, Prospekt, Streitschrift*
4 fertile *fruchtbar*
5 merchant *Kaufmann*
6 labourer *Arbeitskraft, Arbeiter*
7 estimate *schätzen*

S 3 William Bradford, author of *History of Plymouth Plantation*, 1630

William Bradford, one of the leaders of the group of Pilgrims known as the "Pilgrim Fathers", described their hopes and fears before sailing to the new land in his book History of Plymouth Plantation:

The place we had thoughts on were some of those vast and un-peopled countries of America. Although fertile, they are without civilized inhabitants. This idea [to go to those places] caused many doubts and fears among us. Some objected[1], saying that the length of the voyage[2] was such as the weak bodies of women and old people would never be able to endure[3]. And once there we should be in never ending danger of the savage[4] people, little different from wild beasts, who not only kill men, but torment[5] them in the most bloody manner[6] that may be imagined. We agreed that the dangers were great, but though they were likely, yet they were not certain. And all of them, through the help of God, by strength and patience, could be borne[7] and overcome.

William Bradford, History of Plymouth Plantation (1630), in: David D. Hall (ed.), Puritans in the New World, Princeton University Press, *2004, from: www.pupress.princeton.edu/chapters/s7738.html, 10 September 2005. Abridged and simplified by the author.*

1 **a** Photocopy the text on pp. 6–7 and underline all the important information on the settlement of North America (Who, what, where, when, why and how?).
b Draw a map of the North American continent. Then label[8] the map with lines, arrows and brief information on the settlement: e.g. draw a line to the place where Columbus landed. Label it with San Salvador. Note down the date of his landing.

2 In note form, write down information on the Pilgrim Fathers and the Puritans from the text on pp. 6–7 and from the Glossary, pp. 124–127. Your notes should answer the questions: Who, what, where, when, why and how?

3 **a** Translate the title in S 2.
b Discuss the author's reasoning for writing the pamphlet. Who do you think he wrote it for?

4 **a** Find information on William Bradford (see S 3 and Appendix, p. 128), and organize the information in a mind map (see Appendix, p. 143).
b Note down in a bulleted list[9] the Pilgrim Fathers' hopes and fears before sailing to America (S 3).

5 Be a textbook author: Use the excerpt[10] from Bradford's account[11] (S 3) and write three sentences for a history textbook on the Pilgrim Fathers' view of the Indians in North America.

6 In US high school textbooks you may find sentences like: "The early European settlers expected to find an empty wilderness." Do you think Bradford's account (S 3) can serve as evidence[12] for this statement? Why or why not? Discuss in class (see **Activate your English**).

7 Organize the section "The settlement of North America" in an event map. For an example of an event map, see Appendix, pp. 142–143.

8 **Extra research:** Give a PowerPoint presentation on Christopher Columbus (see S 1, the person in the top left-hand corner).

Activate your English

Agreeing or disagreeing

In my opinion/view ...
I'm of the opinion that ...
I think it is right because ...
The source can serve as evidence because ...
I agree (very much) with the idea because ...
I disagree (entirely) because ...
I don't think so because...
I can't accept that because ...

1 object to sth. *einwenden*
2 voyage *journey, trip*
3 endure sth. *etwas ertragen*
4 savage *wild*
5 torment sb. *jdn. quälen, foltern*
6 manner *way*
7 bear – bore – borne sth. *etwas ertragen*
8 label *beschriften, kennzeichnen*
9 bulleted list *Aufzählung (mit Aufzählungszeichen am Zeilenanfang)*
10 excerpt *Ausschnitt*
11 account *Bericht*
12 evidence *Beleg, Beweis*

1.2 Involuntary[1] immigrants

Shiploads of unfree labourers

The first black Africans were brought to Virginia in 1619, just 12 years after the founding of Jamestown. In the beginning, many were seen as "servants"[2] who could earn their freedom just like the white indentured servants*. In 1664, however, the colony of Maryland declared that all blacks and their children in the colony would "serve for life". Virginia soon followed the example. From then on, more and more black slaves* worked on the booming tobacco plantations[3] in Virginia and Maryland instead of white indentured servants. Although some slaves lived as household servants in the Middle Atlantic and New England colonies, the majority of slaves worked on the cotton[4] and rice plantations in the southern colonies of Virginia, Maryland, South Carolina and Georgia.

S4

A tobacco plantation on the title page for the 1788 commentary of the US Constitution

S5 **Tobacco exports from Virginia, 1616–1775 (in pounds)**

Year	Tobacco exports
1616	2300
1617	20,000
1618	50,000
1622	60,000
1626	300,000
1639	1,500,000
1700	20,000,000
1775	100,000,000

S6 **Slave population of Virginia, 1619–1860**

Year	Number of slaves	Number of total population	Percentage of enslaved
1619	20	1000	2.0
1625	23	1232	1.8
1648	300	15,000	2.0
1670	2000	40,000	5.0
1700	8000	58,000	13.7
1750	120,000	231,000	51.9
1800	339,796	807,557	42.1
1820	411,886	938,261	43.9
1840	431,873	1,025,227	42.1
1860	472,494	1,219,630	38.7

S 5, S 6: www.slaveryinamerica.org/history/hs_es_tobacco_slavery.htm; www.economics.ucr.edu/papers/papers03/03-12.pdf; www.eh.net/encyclopedia/?article=wahl.slavery.us, 10 September 2005.

9 Explain the difference between indentured servants and slaves (see the text).

10 **a** Present the development of the number of slaves (S 6) and of the tobacco exports from Virginia (S 5) in two line graphs.
b Write a paragraph describing the development of the number of slaves in S 6.
c Write a paragraph comparing the number of slaves and the percentage enslaved in S 6.

11 **a** Describe the development of tobacco exports from Virginia in the 17th and 18th centuries (S 5).
b Compare the growth of the tobacco exports (S 5) with the development of slavery (S 6) and draw conclusions[5].

Activate your English

Talking about statistics

Figures increased[6] / rose / went up ...
There was an increase / a rise in ...
Figures decreased/dropped/fell ...
There was a decrease/drop/fall in ...
Figures remained steady ...
to rise sharply/dramatically/slightly/ gradually
to rise by ... per cent / by 100,000

1 involuntary *unfreiwillig*
2 servant *Diener*
3 plantation *Plantage; landwirtschaftlicher Großbetrieb in warmem Klima, der sich auf die Erzeugung eines Produktes spezialisiert*
4 cotton *Baumwolle*
5 draw conclusions *Schlüsse ziehen*
6 increase *steigen, (an)wachsen*

Evaluating sources

Primary sources versus secondary sources

Historians use primary sources[1] to get as close as possible to what actually happened during an historical event or time period. William Bradford's description of the Pilgrims' hopes and fears[2] (S 3, p. 8) is an example of a primary source. However, historians also use secondary sources[3]. For example, the text on p. 6 is a secondary source. Every historian who writes a textbook uses primary sources as well as secondary sources.

What is the difference?

In the simplest sense, primary sources are texts or other materials produced during the time in history which you are studying.
Secondary sources are materials
– produced by people in a later period;
– which use primary sources as evidence and examples;
– which often express an opinion or an argument about a past event or time period.
Magazine articles from December 1989, for example, are primary sources for the study of the German unification[4] in 1989–1990. But any book or magazine article or movie published or released much later about the unification is a secondary source.

S 2 *Nova Britannia: Offering most excellent fruites by Planting in Virginia*, by Robert Johnson, London 1609

Nova Britannia.
OFFERING MOST
Excellent fruites by Planting in
Virginia.
Exciting all such as be well affected
to further the same.

S 5 Tobacco exports from Virginia, 1616–1775 (in pounds)

Year	Tobacco exports
1616	2300
1617	20,000
1618	50,000
1622	60,000
1626	300,000
1639	1,500,000
1700	20,000,000
1775	100,000,000

S 8 Colonies in North America, 1750

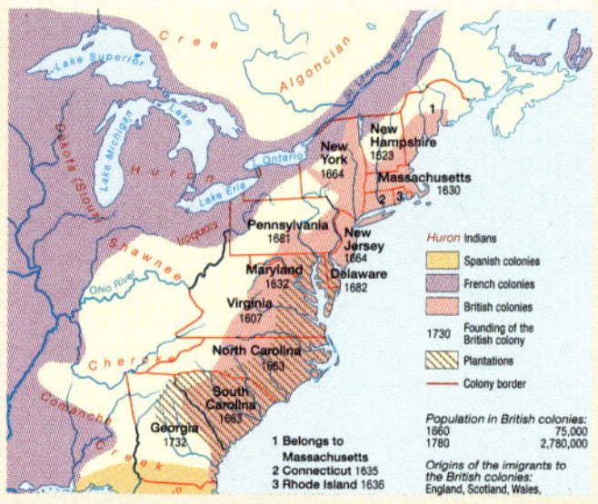

Study skills

Primary sources

1. Personal records[5] or documents: diaries, journals, letters, manuscripts, speeches
2. Autobiographies and memoirs[6]
3. Government documents and records, laws, census[7] statistics, treaties[8]
4. Court records
5. Business records and contracts[9]
6. Published materials: books, magazines, newspaper articles, reports written at the time
7. Novels, dramas written at the time
8. Visual materials: photographs, paintings, sculptures, films, video recordings, cartoons
9. Audio materials: radio broadcasts
10. Physical objects from that time: clothes, furniture, toys, buildings

Secondary sources

1. Articles and books on historical topics
2. Reference material such as encyclopaedias
3. Documentary films on historical topics
4. Biographies

1 primary source *Primärquelle*
2 fear *Angst*
3 secondary source *Sekundärquelle, Sekundärtext*
4 unification *Vereinigung*
5 record *Aufzeichnung*
6 memoir *Lebenserinnerung*
7 census *Volkszählung*
8 treaty *Vertrag zwischen Staaten*
9 contract *geschäftlicher Vertrag*

What can you learn from primary and secondary sources?

Many pupils expect to learn from their history textbook about the past "as it really happened". Historians writing textbooks today agree, however, that it is impossible to know what exactly happened in history, as nobody can say exactly what happened last week in their family, in their city, in their country, or anywhere in the world.

A history textbook is written by authors who have examined a subject, have studied primary and secondary sources, and have drawn certain conclusions. Of course, different authors draw different conclusions and interpret their sources differently.

Primary sources like letters, reports of an event, diaries, etc. also contain personal interpretations of what happened. Every document has a creator, and every creator has a point of view, blind spots[1] and biases[2]. Remember that just because something was published does not make it truthful, accurate or reliable[3].

S 7 Examples of primary and secondary sources

Primary source		Secondary source
Painting: Otto Dix, "Kriegskrüppel"	*p. 120*	Article in school textbook analysing the painting
Letter from a German emigrant to America	*p. 66*	Book about German emigration in the 19th century
Poem: Ernst Moritz Arndt, "The German Fatherland"	*p. 51*	Essay on poetry in the early 19th century
Statistics on the length of railway lines in European countries	*p. 71*	Article about the Industrial Revolution in an encyclopaedia
Cartoon of Bismarck in the London *Punch*	*p. 94*	Biography of Bismarck

S 13 **Johannes A. S. Oertel (1823–1909), New Yorkers pull down a statue of King George III on 9 July 1776, painting, c. 1859.** *The event took place after news of the Declaration of Independence.*

S 9 **The historian Alan Taylor writes about the white colonial population, 2003**

During the seventeenth century, New England (New Hampshire, Massachusetts, Connecticut, Rhode Island) received only 21,000 emigrants – very few compared to the 120,000 transported to the Chesapeake Bay area (Virginia, Maryland) or the 190,000 who colonized the West Indies (St. Kitts, Barbados, Bermuda, Nevis).

S 17 The US Constitution

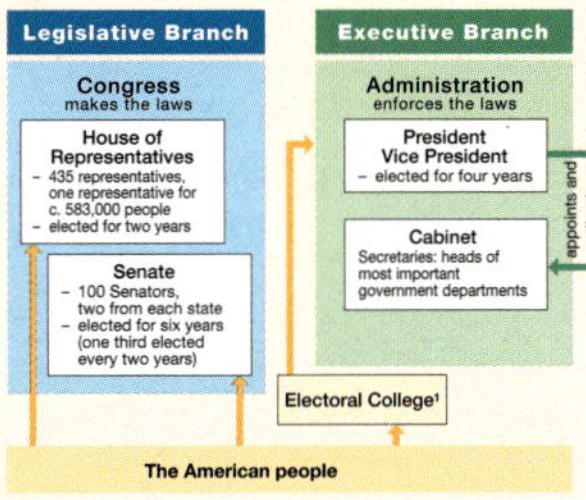

12 **a** Look at the primary sources listed in S 7: find out their dates of creation and put the primary sources in chronological order.
b Make a three-column chart like in S 7: fill in the primary sources used so far in Units 1.1 and 1.2. Then note down where these primary sources could be used (in which kind of secondary source).

13 Bias in primary sources: Many immigrants wrote letters to their families in Europe describing their new life in America. Are these letters good primary sources on life in America at a certain time? List the arguments for and against their use in a two-column chart.

14 **Extra research:** In class, choose an object (somebody's pencil case, mp3 player, maths exercise book, etc.). Imagine this object as a primary source in an exhibition[4] in 2100 about life in Germany at the beginning of the 21st century. Write a short text for the exhibition describing and explaining this object (its use, owner, design, etc.).

1 have blind spots *„auf einem Auge blind sein", bestimmte Dinge nicht wahrnehmen*
2 bias *Tendenz, Voreingenommenheit, Neigung*
3 reliable *verlässlich*
4 exhibition *Ausstellung*

1.3 The colonies

Who rules[1] in the colonies?

The royal government in London ruled its colonies through royal governors. But in North America, all free men had a say in government[2]. They elected representatives[3] to a parliament (assembly[4]) which had the right, for example, to vote on[5] taxes for their colony. Yet[6] free women had no right to vote.
The distance between England and its colonies made control of them difficult, and the colonies practically governed themselves.

S 8 Colonies in North America, 1750

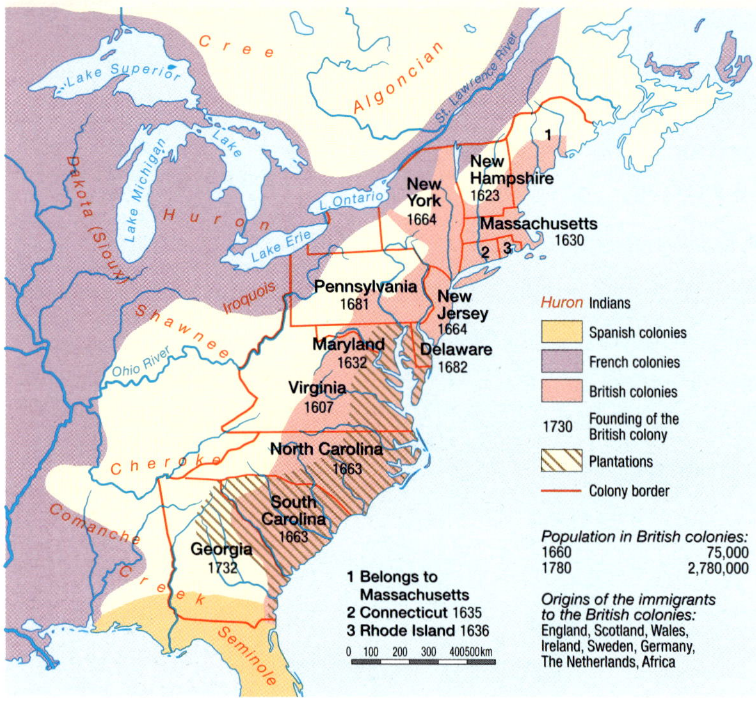

S 9 The historian Alan Taylor writes about the white colonial population, 2003

During the seventeenth century, New England (New Hampshire, Massachusetts, Connecticut, Rhode Island) received only 21,000 emigrants – very few compared to the 120,000 transported to the Chesapeake Bay area (Virginia, Maryland) or the 190,000 who colonized the West Indies (St. Kitts, Barbados, Bermuda, Nevis).
Yet in 1700 New England's population had grown to 91,000, while only 85,000 whites lived in the Chesapeake Bay area and 33,000 in the West Indies.

Alan Taylor, "The People of British America, 1700–1750" (2003), from: www.fpri.org/orbis/4702/taylor.peoplebritishamerica1700.html, 20 September 2005. Simplified by the author.

15 a Read the text and start an English-German vocabulary list "Political terms and phrases".
b "The political system of the colonies was democratic." Do you agree with this statement? Give reasons for your opinion (see **Activate your English**, p. 8).

16 Extra research: Photocopy the map in S 8. Compare it with a present-day map of the United States and label your copy with the most important cities in the former colonies.

17 a Compare the distances between the cities (see Task 16) with the distances between your hometown and some cities in Europe.
b Speculate on how the distances affected life in the colonies.

18 a Organize the information (given by Taylor) in S 9 in a table like the one below.
b Speculate about possible reasons for the differences. Vocabulary help: *White people might/could have ...*

Colonies	*Arrival of white emigrants during the 17th century*	*White population in 1700*
...	...	...

1 rule *herrschen*
2 have a say in government *ein Mitspracherecht in der Regierung haben*
3 representative *Abgeordneter*
4 assembly *Versammlung*
5 vote on sth. *über etwas abstimmen*
6 yet *jedoch, aber*

1.4 From resistance[1] to open rebellion (1763–1776)

1763: The turning point in American colonial history?

By the mid-1700s, Britain and France were bitter rivals for colonies in the Caribbean islands and on the North American continent. From 1756 to 1763 they fought the Seven Years War both in Europe and in America. At the end of the war, when the British army captured[2] Montreal and Quebec in "New France", the dream of a French empire[3] in North America was over. In 1763, the Peace Treaty of Paris gave all the lands between the Atlantic Ocean and the Mississippi River to the British.

The conflict between Britain and its American colonists began in 1763. In this year Parliament in London passed a law[4] to raise money[5] for its 10,000 troops in the colonies through a Stamp Tax. Colonists had to pay a tax on every piece of printed paper: ship's papers, legal documents, licenses, newspapers and even playing cards were taxed. A stamp on the pieces of paper showed that the tax had been paid. The colonists protested at once. Parliament had no right to tax them, they argued, since they elected no members of the Parliament in London.

The build-up[6] to revolution – A timeline

The following timeline shows how resistance* against the sugar tax in 1764 turned into an open rebellion against the British King in 1776:

1764 Sugar Act increases tax on all sugar; angry reactions, threat[7] of a boycott of English products.

1765 Stamp Act results in widespread opposition: meeting of delegates[8] from the different colonies in New York under the slogan "No taxation without representation"; protest meetings; attacks against stamp masters; boycott of British goods; riots[9].

1766 Stamp Act repealed[10].

1767 Townshend Duty Act imposes taxes[11] on paper, glass and tea imported from England. Boycott of British imports.

S 10 **British government stamp showing that a tax has been paid, 1765**

French text on the stamp: "Ho(n)ni soit qui mal y pense" (Ein Schuft, wer Böses dabei denkt).

1768 Customs officers[12] are attacked by a mob in Boston; rioting against British property[13]; British troops are stationed in Boston.

1770 Townshend Duty Act repealed (except tea).

1773 Tea Act excludes[14] colonial merchants and ship owners from the profitable tea trade[15]. Public anger[16] forces British ships full of tea to return to England. "Boston Tea Party": In December, colonists dressed as Indians throw tea into the water to protest against the tax on tea.

1774 Coercive Acts (called "Intolerable Acts" in America) close the port in Boston and give more power to the royal governors.

September/October: Representatives from all the colonies (except Georgia) attend the **First Continental Congress** and protest against the acts. The Congress votes to stop all trade with Great Britain until Parliament repeals the "Intolerable Acts".

1775 In New England men begin arming themselves.

April: The British commander in Boston sends soldiers to Concord (near Boston) to find illegal guns and munitions. At Lexington Green, the British are attacked by 70 armed Massachusetts militiamen[17] (Minutemen). The first shots kill eight and wound ten Americans.

August: King George III declares that the colonists stand in open rebellion to his authority and that the "rebels" in the colonies will be hung as traitors[18].

1 resistance *Widerstand*
2 capture sth. *etwas einnehmen*
3 empire *Reich*
4 pass a law *ein Gesetz verabschieden*
5 raise money *Gelder aufbringen*
6 build-up *Aufbau*
7 threat *Drohung*
8 delegate *Abgeordneter, Beauftragter*
9 riot *Aufruhr, Krawall*
10 repeal (a law) *(ein Gesetz) aufheben, abschaffen*
11 impose taxes *Steuern auferlegen*
12 customs officers *Zollbeamte*
13 property *Besitz*
14 exclude sb. *jdn. ausschließen*
15 trade *Handel*
16 anger *Wut, Zorn*
17 militia *Bürgerwehr, Miliz*
18 traitor *Verräter*

1776 January: Thomas Paine publishes bestselling pamphlet[1] *Common Sense* (120,000 copies are sold in three months). In it, he speaks openly of "independence" from Britain and of a government in which the people rule through their elected representatives.

4 July: Declaration of Independence[2]. Representatives of the thirteen colonies of North America, meeting for the Second Continental Congress since May 1775, declare their separation, freedom and independence from the United Kingdom of Great Britain.

1 pamphlet *Streitschrift*
2 Declaration of Independence *Unabhängigkeitserklärung*
3 disobedience *Ungehorsam*
4 injustice/unjust *Ungerechtigkeit/ungerecht* justice/just *Gerechtigkeit/gerecht*
5 refusal *Weigerung*
6 insurrection *Aufruhr, Aufstand, Erhebung*
7 suicide *Selbstmord*
8 aim *Ziel, Absicht*
9 dismissal *Entlassung*
10 abdication *Abdankung*
11 overthrow *Umsturz (einer Regierung)*
12 investigation *Untersuchung*
13 act *a law that has been passed by a parliament*
14 engraving *Stich, Druckgrafik*

Forms of resistance

When governments make unpopular laws or take actions which are highly unpopular, people openly show their resistance*. Protest, disobedience[3] or resistance can take many different forms:

- verbal protests (public debates, songs, etc.);
- written or printed protests to bring wider attention to the injustice[4] (political cartoons, pamphlets, etc.);
- refusal[5] to follow instructions or laws;
- economic protests (strikes, etc.);
- armed/violent resistance (mob riots, insurrections[6], civil war, etc.).

Other non-violent and violent examples of 21st-century resistance are: sit-ins, hunger strikes, street demonstrations, letters to the editor, kidnappings, suicide[7] bombings.

The aim[8] and result of resistance can be: the repeal of a law, reforms, the dismissal[9] of a minister, the abdication[10] of a monarch, the overthrow[11] of a government, independence.

Use the following questions to structure your investigation[12] of resistance down through history: What do people do to resist? What is the aim of the protest actions? What do people risk by resisting?

S 11 Daniel Chodowiecki (1726–1801), Resistance to the Stamp Act of 1765[13], engraving[14], Germany, 18th century

An angry Boston crowd burns a pile of stamps in resistance to the Stamp Act of 1765. Note that the artist included women and an African-American among the protesters.

S 12 Daniel Chodowiecki (1726–1801), The Boston Tea Party on 16 December 1773, engraving, Germany, 18th century

Colonists dressed as Indians throw tea into Boston Harbour to protest the tax on tea.

S 13 Johannes A. S. Oertel (1823–1909), New Yorkers pull down a statue of King George III on 9 July 1776, painting, c 1859

The event took place after the news of the Declaration of Independence had reached New York. Vocabulary help: a crowd of people – cheer sb. on – a rope is slung around – iron bars – wooden poles – smash to pieces – pedestal[1]

19 Read the text "Forms of resistance" on p. 14. Give a current example of an unpopular law or a government action and people's resistance to it.

20 Look at the timeline on pp. 13–14 and the visual sources S 11–S 13:

a Write down American colonists' demands in their protest meetings.

b Note down the causes of the colonist's protests.

c List the forms of the colonists' resistance to the laws of the British government and match them with those listed in the text "Forms of resistance".

d Place the forms of resistance in order from least violent to most violent.

e Describe how the British reacted to the complaints[2], demands and acts of violence.

f Discuss whether, in your opinion, the reactions were justified[3].

21 Copy the chart below and list people, objects and activities in S 13. For unknown terms and phrases, check the Glossary (pp. 124–127) or a German-English dictionary.

22 Write a newspaper article for the *London Illustrated News* about the events in New York on 9 July 1776. Speculate about people's motives.

people	*objects*	*activities*
...	...	...

1 pedestal *Sockel, Unterbau*

2 complaint *Beschwerde*

3 justify *rechtfertigen*

1.5 Winning independence

The American Revolutionary War (1775–1783)

The American Revolutionary War, also called the American War of Independence, lasted[1] from 1775 to 1783. It ended two centuries of British rule for most of the North American colonies and created the new United States of America.

The "shot heard round the world" fired at Lexington on 19 April 1775 (see timeline, pp. 13–14) began the war, and the Peace Treaty of Paris ended it eight and a half years later on 3 September 1783.

General George Washington (see Biography, p. 20) commanded the American army of 20,000 poorly paid and trained militiamen. 42,000 professional soldiers fought in the British army, along with 30,000 troops which the British government had bought from a number of German princes[2]. It seemed completely impossible that the "rebel army" could defeat the British. But General Washington proved to be a fine commander, and took advantage of the mistakes of the British generals. In 1778 Major General Baron von Steuben, who had been an officer in the Prussian[3] army, began training the American regiments. Slowly he turned them into a more powerful army.

Without French help, however, the colonists could not have defeated Britain's troops. France secretly gave supplies[4] and money to the colonies from 1776 to 1778. After declaring war on England in June 1778, the French government also sent soldiers and ships.

In the Treaty of Paris (1783), Great Britain formally recognized[5] the thirteen colonies as the United States of America.

Biography

Thomas Jefferson

Jefferson, a lawyer and wealthy plantation owner, was born in Virginia in 1743. The Declaration of Independence of 1776 (S 14) was written mostly by him. His ideas on self-government and the natural rights of the people greatly influenced the Declaration. In 1801, Jefferson became President of the United States and served until 1808. He died in 1826.

S 14 Extracts from the Declaration of Independence, 4 July 1776

English version	*German translation*
(1) When in the course of human events, it becomes necessary for one people to dissolve the political bands which have connected them with another [...], a decent respect to the opinions of mankind requires that they should declare the causes which impel them to the separation.	Wenn es im Laufe von geschichtlichen Ereignissen für ein Volk notwendig wird, die politischen Bande aufzulösen, die es bisher mit einem anderen vereinten [...], so erfordert die geziemende Achtung vor der Meinung der Welt, dass es die Gründe angibt, die es zur Trennung zwingen.
(2) We hold these truths to be self-evident, that all men are created equal; that they are endowed by their creator with certain unalienable rights, that among these are life, liberty and the pursuit of happiness; that to	Wir halten diese Wahrheiten für selbstverständlich, dass alle Menschen gleich geschaffen worden sind; dass sie von ihrem Schöpfer mit bestimmten unveräußerlichen Rechten ausgestattet sind, zu denen Leben,

1 last *dauern*
2 prince *Fürst*
3 Prussian/Prussia *preußisch/Preußen*
4 supply *here: munitions, arms, food, etc (Nachschub)*
5 recognize sth. *etwas anerkennen.*

secure these rights, governments are instituted among men, deriving their just powers from the consent of the governed; that whenever any form of government becomes destructive of these ends, it is the right of the people to alter or to abolish it, and to institute a new Government [...].

(3) The history of the present King of Great Britain [...] is a history [...] of an absolute tyranny[1] over these [colonies]. [He made it hard for parliaments to meet. He tried to abolish[2] parliaments. He kept armies in the country without the people's consent[3]. He introduced taxes without the people's consent. He began a war against Americans.] [...]

(4) We, therefore, the representatives of the United States of America [...] do, in the name [...] of the good people of these colonies, [...] declare, that these united colonies are [...] free and independent States [...], and that all political connection between them and the State of Great Britain, is [...] totally dissolved. [...]

Freiheit und Streben nach Glück gehören; dass zur Sicherung dieser Rechte Regierungen unter den Menschen eingesetzt sind, die ihre rechtmäßige Gewalt von der Zustimmung der Regierten herleiten; dass, wenn immer eine Regierungsform diesen Zielen schadet, es das Recht des Volkes ist, sie zu ändern oder abzuschaffen und eine neue Regierung einzusetzen [...].

English version: www.ushistory.org/declaration/document/index.htm, 20 December 2005. German translation: Wolfgang Lautemann et al. (ed.), Geschichte in Quellen, *vol. 4, BSV, München, 1981, p. 90.*

23 **a** Match the following summaries A–C to the first three extracts from the Declaration of Independence in S 14:

A *This part is a list of things the American colonists believed the King of England had done wrong, and which justified their fight for independence.*

B *This part explains the purpose[4] of the document.*

C *This part describes individual rights and the relation between people and their governments ("theory of good government").*

b Write down your own summary of the last extract in S 14.

24 Write down the text of parts 3 and 4 (S 14) in German. Do not try to translate word-for-word, but instead concentrate on the meaning.

25 In your own words:

a Explain what the purpose of the Declaration of Independence was.

b List the rights each person has by nature. Explain what the terms exactly mean.

c Describe the relation between people and government.

d Explain what a "good government" is (see Task 23).

e Discuss why, according to the explanation of what a good government is, the list of grievances[5] in part 3 of the Declaration justified the separation from Great Britain.

26 Identify the democratic principles named in the Declaration of Independence that all democratic governments are founded on.

27 Making connections: Explain France's possible motives for supporting the American "rebels".

28 **Extra research:** Give a presentation on Thomas Jefferson, the man who was mainly responsible for writing the Declaration of Independence.

1 tyranny *Tyrannei, Gewaltherrschaft*
2 abolish sth. *etwas abschaffen, beseitigen*
3 consent *Zustimmung*
4 purpose *Zweck*
5 list of grievances *Beschwerdeliste, Klageliste*

Analysing political cartoons

A political cartoon shows a cartoonist's point of view on a topic[1] or issue[2]. However, it is often not easy to identify his or her point of view, especially if the cartoon was produced many years ago. In order to "get it", you need background information from classroom discussion, a textbook or your own research. Once you have a general idea of the topic, you can start to decode[3] the message the cartoonist is trying to convey[4]. Just as writers use a language with 26 letters from A to Z, political cartoonists use their own language, i.e. cartoon techniques that convey their points of view, for example symbols and visual analogies[5]. Symbols, as used in cartoons, represent larger ideas or issues. In analogies two things are compared visually or in writing in order to stress their similarities.

Activate your English

Talking about cartoons

Context:

- *The cartoon was published in ... by ...*
- *The cartoon refers to ...*
- *The characters represent / stand for / symbolize ...*
- *The caption is ironic/humorous/... because ...*

Techniques and points of view:

- *The animal is drawn / presented in a realistic / an unrealistic way.*
- *Their sizes are exaggerated to suggest to / show the reader that ...*
- *The character is portrayed favourably / unfavourably / as being ...*
- *in the background / in the foreground*
- *on the left / in the middle / in the centre / on the right*
- *at the top / at the bottom*
- *in the top right-hand corner / in the bottom left-hand corner*

Target and message:

- *The cartoonist wants to show / criticizes / makes fun of / tries to convince[11] people that ...*

Study skills

Context: Identify the event the cartoon refers to. Look at the caption[6] to see where and when the cartoon was published and what type of magazine, newspaper or other publication it was in. Who was the intended audience for the cartoon?

Content: Describe the action taking place in the cartoon. Pay close attention to any captions, titles, labels[7], name tags, dialogue, or speech bubbles, as well as symbols used by the cartoonist to portray people, events and issues.

Target[8]: Who or what is being criticised? Is the cartoon criticising or sympathising with a person, group or country? On whose "side" is the cartoonist?

Technique: What techniques is the cartoonist using to express his or her view?

a Look for anything that seems exaggerated[9]. A cartoonist often exaggerates the characteristics of people's faces and clothes. Then, decide what point the cartoonist was trying to make through exaggeration.

b Look for symbols. Cartoonists use pictures as symbols for larger ideas, people, organizations, and so on.

c Look for analogies. Cartoonists describe a situation or event by comparing it to another historical, fictional or everyday situation or event. What two situations does the cartoon compare? What parallels does it draw?

Message: What is the cartoonist's message or comment? What is the cartoonist's position on the event? What is his or her point of view on the topic portrayed in the cartoon? Give examples to support your interpretation. What special groups would agree/disagree with the cartoon's messsage? Why? Do you agree with the cartoonist's message? Explain.

Evaluating[10] cartoons as historical sources: For historians, all sources are "windows to past events". What do we see and learn "through" the cartoon?

1 topic *Thema*
2 issue *Problem, Angelegenheit, Streitpunkt*
3 decode sth. *etwas entschlüsseln*
4 convey (a message) *(eine Botschaft) vermitteln*
5 analogy *comparison between things which have similar features (= vergleichbare Merkmale), often used to help explain a principle or idea*
6 caption *words printed below a picture or cartoon*
7 label *Beschriftung*
8 target *Ziel(-richtung)*
9 exaggerate *übertreiben*
10 evaluate sth. *etwas einschätzen, beurteilen*
11 convince *überzeugen*

S 15 **"The Horse 'America', Throwing His Master", artist unknown, British cartoon, 1 August 1779**

Describing the action

A well-fed horse called "America" is throwing the rider out of the saddle, while a soldier, who is carrying a flag with 13 stars, is running towards the rider. The rider is wearing fine clothes, a wig[1] and a sash[2]; a medal[3] is pinned on his chest[4]. He is about to lose control of the horse: he has already lost his reins[5], but he has not actually fallen off yet, and his foot is still loosely in the stirrup[6]. He is not looking at the horse or at the soldier, but upward into space. His riding stick[7] is a cruel[8] instrument with weapons attached, which he has used to discipline the horse.

29 Identify where and when the cartoon was published.

30 **a** Identify the figures in the cartoon.

b Identify who or what is being criticized. (Tip: Who was "master" of "America" at the time when the cartoon was published? See the timeline, pp. 13–14, and the text, p. 16.)

31 Identify the symbols and explain what they stand for.

32 Identify the two situations which are compared (visual analogies). Complete the sentences:

A *The cartoon compares riding "the horse America" to …*

B *The cartoon shows a rider who is "not in the saddle" anymore. This can be compared to …*

33 Identify the event which the cartoon refers to.

34 Discuss the cartoonist's message.

35 Write a complete and detailed analysis of the cartoon.

1 wig *Perücke*
2 sash *Schärpe*
3 medal *Orden, Ehrenzeichen*
4 chest *Brust(korb)*
5 reins *Zügel*
6 stirrup *Steigbügel*
7 riding stick *Reitgerte*
8 cruel *grausam*

1.6 "A more perfect union" – Constitution[1] and government

"We the people"

When the Revolutionary War was over and the United States of America was finally independent from Britain, Americans began to govern themselves. However, the form of government was still unclear.

In 1787, after much debate and compromise[2], the US Constitution* was adopted[3]. It begins with the words "We the people of the United States, in order to form a more perfect union, establish[4] ..." and has been in force[5] until today.

The document outlines[6] the relationships between the people and their governments. The Constitution of 1787

- makes the people, and not a king, sovereign[7];
- declares that governments must be elected by the majority of the people;
- separates the powers* of the government into three branches that check and balance* each other.

A constitution in process

The Bill of Rights[8]* (see S 19) were added to the Constitution in 1791. Yet, slave trade* and slavery* continued to exist, especially in the southern states where slaves worked on the tobacco, rice and cotton plantations of their white owners (see p. 9). Only at the end of the long Civil War between the northern and southern states (1861–1865) was slavery abolished[9] with the 13th Amendment (or addition).

Originally only white men with some property had the right to vote. Former male black slaves were given it in 1870 (15th Amendment); women did not win the right to vote until 1920 (19th Amendment).

S 16 **"Confidence in the constitution", US print, late 18th century**

Biography

George Washington was the first president of the United States. Born in Virginia in 1732, he was trained as a surveyor[10], fought in the French and Indian War (1756–1763) in the Virginia militia, managed his plantation, Mount Vernon, and was active in Virginia politics before he was appointed[11] to command the Continental Army against the British in 1775. In 1781 he led the Continental Army to victory against British troops near Yorktown. In 1787 he presided[12] over the Constitutional Convention in Philadelphia, Pennsylvania, where the US Constitution was written. He was elected President of the new republic in 1789 and again in1792. In 1799, Washington died in Mount Vernon, Virginia.

1 constitution *basic law of a country (Verfassung)*
2 compromise *Kompromiss (Übereinkunft durch gegenseitige Zugeständnisse)*
3 adopt (a constitution) *(eine Verfassung) annehmen, verabschieden*
4 establish *errichten, verordnen*
5 be in force *in Kraft sein*
6 outline *umreißen, grob beschreiben*
7 sovereign *a nation's ruler (Souverän)*
8 Bill of Rights *Grundrechtekatalog*
9 abolish *abschaffen*
10 surveyor *Landvermesser*
11 appoint sb. *jdn. ernennen*
12 preside *Vorsitz führen*

S 17 The US Constitution

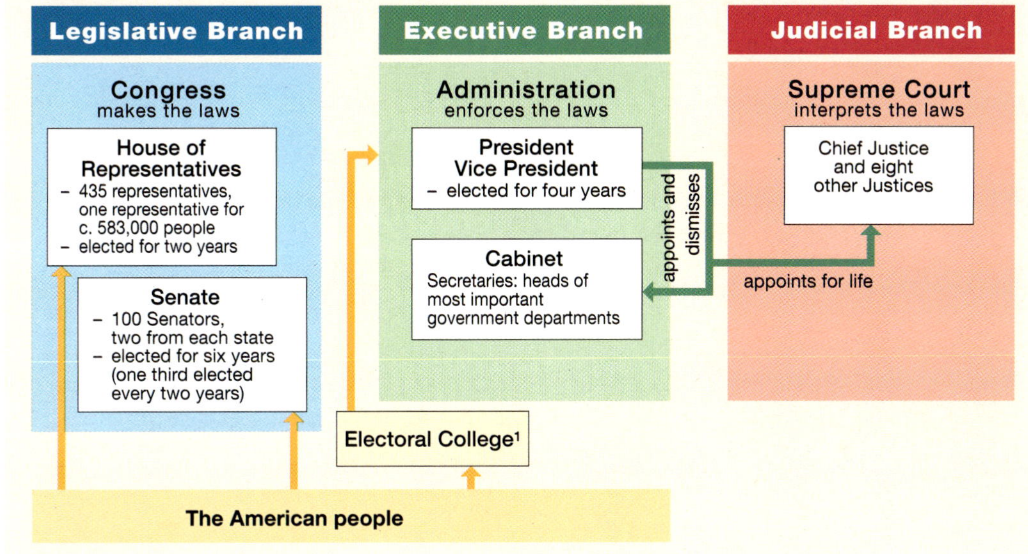

S 18 The system of "checks and balances" in the US Constitution

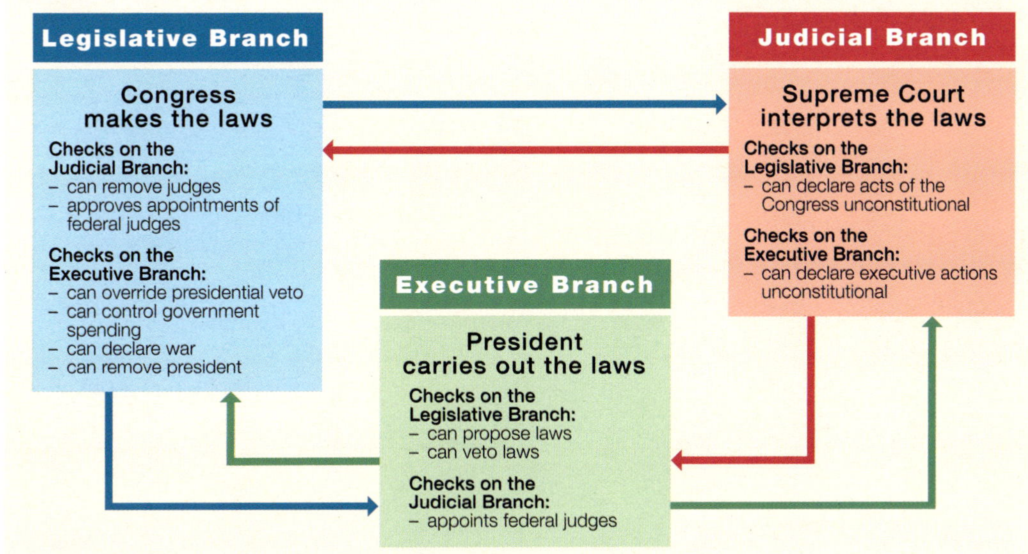

S 19 Guarantees of the US Bill of Rights, 1791

Freedom of religion	
Freedom of the press	
Freedom of speech	
Freedom of assembly[2]	gives citizens[3] the right to organize and to join any club, organization and party they wish; they are also free to hold public meetings.
Freedom and security of citizens	protects citizens against a search of their homes and arrest without a warrant[4].
Freedom of petition	gives citizens the right to contact their government representatives and ask them to work to pass a law or to change laws they do not like.
Right to a trial by jury[5]	is the right to a speedy and public trial[6] and a lawyer[7].

1 Electoral College *Wahlmänner*
2 freedom of assembly *Vereinigungsrecht*
3 citizen *inhabitant of a town, city or country (Bürger/Bürgerin)*
4 warrant *richterliche Anordnung, Haftbefehl*
5 trial by jury *Verhandlung vor einem Geschworenengericht*
6 trial *Prozess, Gerichtsverfahren*
7 lawyer *Rechtsanwalt*

36 **a** Read the text on p. 20 and create your own timeline titled "A constitution in progress". Write the dates below the line and the events, with explanations, above the line.
b Comment on your findings.

37 Give reasons why it is important to have a written constitution.

38 **Extra research:** Find a map of Washington, DC (guidebooks, internet) and locate the government buildings of the three branches of American government (S 17).

39 To explain the US system of "checks and balances", copy and fill in the following chart. For help and further information, see S 18.

Activate your English

Talking about a constitution

appoint sb. / appointment *jdn. ernennen / Ernennung*
dismiss sb. *jdn. entlassen*
remove (judges) *(Richter) abberufen*
approve sth. *etw. genehmigen, billigen*
declare (war) *(Krieg) erklären*
override (a veto) *(ein Veto) aufheben*
propose (laws) *(Gesetze) vorschlagen, einbringen*
veto sth. *Einspruch gegen etw. einlegen*
constitutional *verfassungsgemäß*
unconstitutional *verfassungswidrig*
government spending *(Regierungs-)Ausgaben*

*The **power** …*	*Which **branch** has the power?*	*Who **checks** the branch's power? (Can be more than one)*
1 to create and pass laws		
2 to veto laws		
3 to appoint federal judges		
4 to approve presidential appointments		
5 to declare laws unconstitutional		
6 to override presidential vetoes		
7 to remove the President		

40 The US Constitution is based on four principles:
1. *Popular sovereignty: the power of government is held by the people.*
2. *Limited government: the power of government is limited by law / by the Constitution.*
3. *Separation of powers: …*
4. *Checks and balances: …*

Copy the US constitutional principles and add the explanations where they are missing (for help see S 17, S 18).

41 After completing Task 40, split up into groups and create a poster for each of the four principles of the US Constitution. Each poster should include:
a the name of the principle, printed clearly;
b an explanation of what the principle means, including how it works in the government or how it is a part of the government;
c a drawing, picture or chart that reflects the idea of this principle.
Be prepared to explain your poster to the class.

42 Copy the first three rights of the Bill of Rights from S 19 and add the missing explanations.

43 Why did the US Congress add the Bill of Rights just four years after passing the Constitution? Tip: Compare and contrast the Declaration of Independence (see pp. 16–17, S 14) and the Constitution (S 17, S 18).

44 Discuss whether the government of the United States (S 17–S 19) is a "good government". For the idea of "good government", see the Declaration of Independence (see pp. 16–17, S 14, and Task 25 d).

Unit revision

The American Revolution

Key events

1607	First British colony in North America (Jamestown)
1756–1763	French and Indian War (= Seven Years' War)
1765	Stamp Act
1773	Boston Tea Party
1775–1783	War of Independence
1776	Declaration of Independence/ Bill of Rights
1783	Treaty of Paris

Key terms

Native Americans (= Indians), Pilgrim Fathers, Puritans, slave trade, colony, indentured servants, slavery, resistance, constitution, popular sovereignty, Bill of Rights, separation of powers, checks and balances

Key personalities

Thomas Jefferson
George Washington

History skills

Evaluating sources *(pp. 10–11)*
Analysing political cartoons *(pp. 18–19)*

Activate your English

Agreeing or disagreeing *(p. 8)*
Talking about statistics *(p. 9)*
Talking about cartoons *(p. 18)*
Talking about a constitution *(p. 22)*

S 20 **Donald Reilly, cartoon in *The New Yorker*, 2 January 1971,**
"We're here to escape religious persecution. What are you here for?"

1 Discuss if more key events and key terms are needed to describe "The winning of independence" and "Creating a democracy" in America.
2 With the help of key events, key terms and key personalities, prepare a three-minute talk on:
  a "The winning of independence" in America,
  b "Creating a democracy" in America.
3 List the words and phrases you would use to describe
  a the elements of a cartoon and the terms and phrases needed to analyse it;
  b how people "resist" and the effects of their resistance.
4 In groups of three or four, organize the new vocabulary in two mind maps (see Appendix). Explain the connection between the words in your mind map and the chapter topic.
5 Create a crossword puzzle with the new vocabulary. Use synonyms, sentences with a missing word, translations, etc. for the clues in your crossword. For example: *Inhabitant of a town, city or country = CITIZEN.*
6 1763: The turning point in American colonial history? Explain the answer to the person sitting next to you. Does the person agree with your interpretation?
7 a Split up into groups of three: Study the cartoon in S 20, identify the event the cartoon is referring to and explain the caption. Formulate the answer of the little boy with the feathers on his head.
  b Compare your results.

Alex Haley, Roots, 1977
The novel tells the story of the ancestors of African-American writer Alex Haley. The story goes back to the time of slavery in the southern United States and even to the West African roots of Haley's family in the 18th century.

Unit 2 19th-century Britain – A showcase[1] nation?

2.1 Great Britain – The first industrial society

S 1 Opening of the World Exhibition[2] in London by Queen Victoria, British engraving, 1851

On 1 May, 1851, Queen Victoria opened the "Great Exhibition of the Works of Industry of all Nations" at the Crystal Palace in London. There were over 100,000 exhibits. Most of them were from Great Britain, which wanted to show that it was the "Workshop of the World" – a country of mills[3] and factories, which produced more and cheaper goods than any other nation. In 1851, Britain was the most powerful industrial nation, producing more than half the world's iron, coal and cotton cloth[4].

The Industrial Revolution

A hundred years before the opening of the World Exhibition in London (S 1), Britain had been a totally different country. In the second half of the 18th century, most people worked as farmers and made most of their own clothing, furniture and tools. Local craftsmen[5] made the goods that people could not produce themselves, for example ploughs[6], in small workshops[7]* by hand or with simple tools or machines. Goods were transported either by canal boats or by horse-drawn cart[8] on roadways. Some textile mills used waterpower to drive the machinery. These were small factories* that employed only a handful of workers. With time, better machinery was developed and work was better organized. In the 1770s, a new source of power[9] was introduced to drive the cotton-spinning machinery. It was called the steam engine[10]*. This new technology marked the beginning of the Industrial Revolution*. It became possible to make large amounts of cloth in less time and for less money, and this resulted in extreme productivity growth[11]*. By the early 19th century, merchants were transporting mass-produced cloth to far-away customers by railway and steamship, and the prices of goods[12] fell dramatically.

As industries grew, so did the towns in the Midlands and North of England where they were based. Manchester (cotton), Leeds and Bradford (wool), Sheffield (iron, steel), and Birmingham all became industrial centres.

Biography

Queen Victoria

Victoria (1819–1901) was Queen of the United Kingdom of Great Britain and Ireland from 1837 and Empress[13] of India from 1877 until her death. She was the last British monarch of the House of Hanover. Her reign lasted longer than that of any other British monarch. Her lifetime became known as the Victorian Era, the era of the Industrial Revolution in Great Britain and of the expansion of the British Empire in Africa.

1 showcase *Modell*
2 exhibition/the exhibit *Ausstellung/Ausstellungsstück*
3 mill *Mühle, Fabrik*
4 cloth *Stoff*
5 craftsman *Handwerker (z. B. Schmiede, Maurer, Maler usw.)*
6 plough *Pflug*
7 workshop *Handwerksbetrieb*
8 cart *Karren*
9 source of power *Energiequelle*
10 steam engine *Dampfmaschine*
11 productivity growth *Produktivitätswachstum*
12 goods *Güter*
13 empire/emperor/empress *Kaiserreich/Kaiser/Kaiserin*

Changes in agriculture[1]

The changes in industry also led to changes in farming methods. Larger farms were developed so that larger areas of land could be cultivated. With the development of new farm machinery, intensive manuring[2] and crop rotation[3], farms were then able to produce much larger amounts of food to feed the growing urban[4] population.

Working in the factories

There were no laws regulating work in the factories. Dangerous machinery was used and workers were often seriously injured. To add to this, people had to work long hours, often through the night. Perhaps one of the worst aspects of factory work was child labour. Children were cheap, did not argue or complain[5], and were small enough to work in-between machines where adults could not fit. Young children worked extremely long hours under dangerous conditions[6], were beaten when they made mistakes and were paid very small wages[7].

People began to realize how bad these conditions were in many factories and started to campaign for improvements[8]. In 1833, the British government passed a Factory Act, which improved conditions for children working in textile factories.

S2 **A cotton spinner at work in her home, British drawing, 1810**

S3 **James Watt's condensing steam engine from 1769, drawing of a model, 2001**

S4 **A cotton mill, drawing from the book *The Progress of Cotton*, England, 1835**

The book was written to teach children in other countries about cotton manufacturing[9] in Britain. The drawing shows how belts transfer the energy from the steam engines to drive the spinning mules[10]. On the left a child is sweeping up[11] the cotton dust.

S5 **Cotton mill, drawing from the book *The White Slaves of England* by John Cobdon, England, 1860**

The book was part of the public campaign to improve conditions in the factories. The picture is an adaptation[12] of the drawing in S4.

1 agriculture *Landwirtschaft*
2 manuring *Düngen*
3 crop rotation *Fruchtfolge*
4 urban *städtisch*
5 complain *sich beschweren*
6 condition *Bedingung, Umstand*
7 wage *Lohn*
8 improvement *Verbesserung*
9 manufacturing *(verarbeitende) Industrie*
10 spinning mule *Spinnmaschine*
11 sweep sth. up *etwas auffegen*
12 adaptation *Bearbeitung, Anpassung*

Early trade[1] unions

Already in the 18th century, workers in different industries began to join[2] together. They formed local "friendly societies"[3] and "trade clubs"[4], where members could pay a little money and get insurance[5] against illness or unemployment. Some societies actively campaigned to raise wages, protect jobs and improve working conditions. British governments were strongly against these so-called trade unions*. The Combination Acts of 1799 and 1800 were laws that made it illegal for workers to join together and take action against their employers. Some trade unions continued secretly. After the government repealed the laws in 1825, new unions were founded, but employers reacted by locking out[6] union members and hiring[7] non-union members.
In the early 1860s, new national trade unions for skilled workers[8] successfully fought for higher wages, shorter working hours and better working conditions. However, the millions of unskilled workers in industry and servants in households (especially women) were not so lucky. Their wages and working conditions did not improve much until the 20th century.

S6 Certificate of trade union membership, 1851

In 1851, the "Amalgamated Society of Engineers, Machinists, Smiths, Millwrights and Patternmakers" was founded, a national union with 10,841 members. By 1861 the union had grown to over 33,000 members. Unions like this one gave their members certificates of membership, as shown here. Members proudly hung their framed[9] certificate in their best room at home. It showed that they were skilled workers and generally guaranteed them employment if they stayed healthy.

S7 Prices of British cotton yarn[10], 1786–1807 (in shillings/pence per lb)[11]

Year	Price
1786–1787	38 s
1800	10 s
1807	6 s 9 p

S8 Prices of a length[12] of British cotton cloth, 1770–1860 (in pounds/shillings)

Year	Price
1770	£ 29
1812	13 s
1860	5 s

S7, S8 from: Edgar Otten et al., Spotlight on History, Volume 1, *Cornelsen, 1995, p. 41.*

S9 Hand looms[13] and steam power looms in the British cotton industry, 1820–1860 (number of machines in millions)

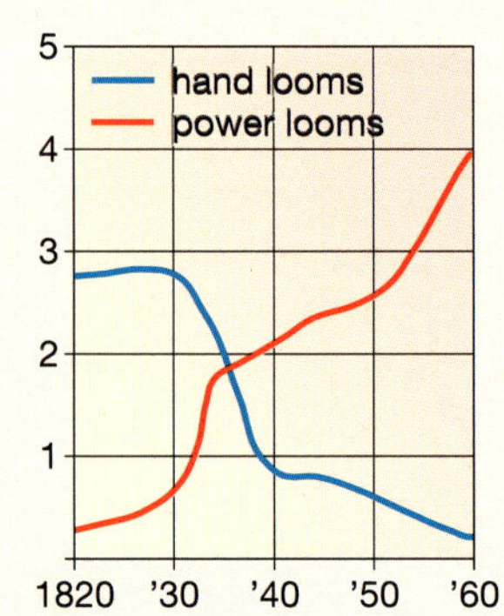

1 (trade) union *Gewerkschaft*
2 join *sich zusammenschließen*
3 society *(hier) Vereinigung*
4 trade *(hier) Gewerbe*
5 insurance *Versicherung*
6 lock sb. out *jdn. aussperren*
7 hire sb. *jdn. einstellen*
8 skilled/unskilled worker *Facharbeiter/Hilfs-, ungelernte Arbeiter*
9 frame sth. *etwas einrahmen*
10 yarn *Garn*
11 shillings/pence per lb *see Glossary "pound/shilling/pence"; lb. (abbr) = pound*
12 length *Stück*
13 loom *Webstuhl*

S 10 British imports of raw cotton, 1700–1900

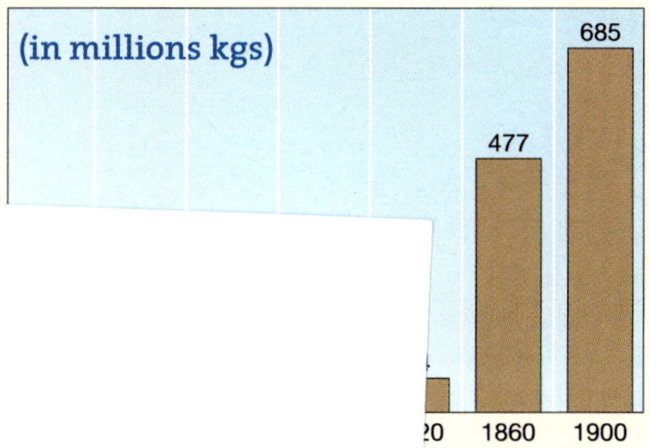

S 11 Exports of British cotton textiles, 1750–1830

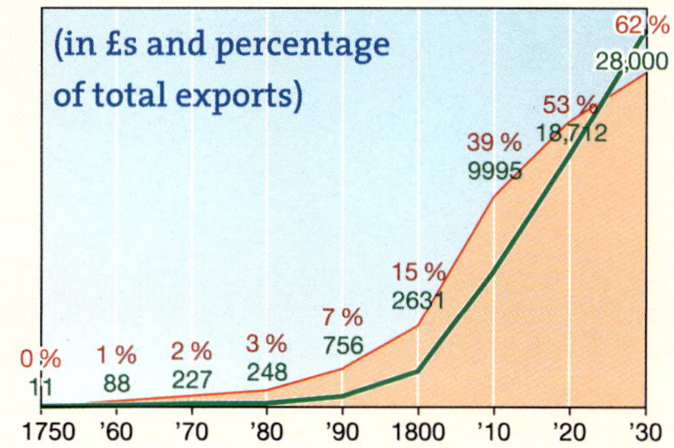

ake two English-German vocabulary lists titled "Words
ɔn" and "Working a job".
s:
shop C *productivity growth* D *trade union*
Copy and fill in the table below (see the text on

	How great was the change?	*What were the resulting working conditions?*
	…	…

iagram:

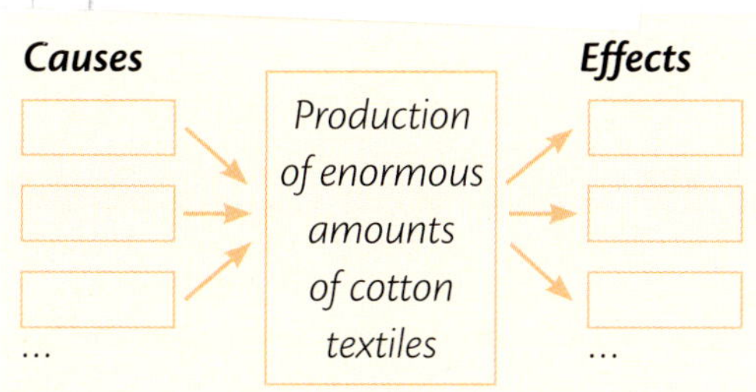

5 Cotton textiles were exported to other European countries. Discuss whether these exports were welcomed abroad.

6 a What arguments do you think employers[1] of young children used to defend themselves against criticism?

b How do you think parents reacted when child labour became illegal?

7 Visual sources are records of specific moments in time. However, like other primary sources (see pp. 10–11), a visual source's creator (artist, photographer, etc.) has a specific viewpoint and intention. Look at the two drawings in S 4 and S 5.

a Describe how each artist presents the work environment in the textile industry.

b Explain the two artists' points of view (see **Activate your English**).

Activate your English

Talking about points of view

There is a notable / striking contrast / not much of a contrast between …
In contrast to the drawing in S 4, the women in S 5 are …
The situation in … is noticeably different because …
… is standing with his/her back to …
The man … is about to …
The man/woman in the background seems to be …
… the factory looks/appears clean/tidy/ dark/depressing/spacious/cramped …
The artist/illustrator …
– has a positive/negative view of the textile industry because he shows …
– appears/seems to want to show (that/ how) …
– wants to convince the reader/viewer that … by showing …
The artist's/illustrator's intention is …

8 Write a caption for the picture in S 6 describing how the certificate shows the pride of a skilled worker. Vocabulary help: *A halo is a ring of light above the head of a holy*[2] *person in a religious painting.*

1 employer *Arbeitgeber*
2 holy *heilig*

2.2 Life in British towns

Population growth and urban growth

During the period of industrialization*, the population grew rapidly and towns and cities became bigger as people moved from the countryside. The wages in mills and factories were better than on the farms, and children could earn money in the mills. However, the housing situation for workers in the towns was bad. The houses stood in narrow streets without sewers[1], and many families lived in a single room.

Between 1848 and 1875, Parliament passed a series of laws called the Public Health Acts to improve health conditions in urban areas. The governement in London encouraged the towns to build sewers, improve the water supply[2], organize waste collection[3], inspect lodging houses[4] and check the quality of food for sale.

British society and industry around 1900

When Queen Victoria celebrated her Diamond Jubilee – 60 years as Queen – in 1897, Britain was the most urbanized* country in the world. Already in 1851, half the population lived in a town or city, and by 1901 the number had grown to three-quarters of the population.

By 1900, the USA had become the world's industrial powerhouse and Germany was also challenging[5] Britain's position (see Unit 6.3). But no country was as specialized as Britain in manufacturing: in 1901, less than ten per cent of its labour force[6] worked in agriculture. Over 75 per cent of its wheat[7] was imported (mostly from the USA and Russia). Food and industrial raw materials[8] from around the globe were paid for by exports of manufactured goods[9] and, increasingly, services[10] such as shipping, insurance and banking.

S 12 Housing and health

a *James Smith, who officially investigated health conditions in towns, wrote in a report in 1845 on conditions in Bradford:*
The chief[11] sewerage is open channels.

b *On Leeds, James Smith (see S 12 a) wrote:*
The streets of Leeds are very much as in all old towns. Fortunately for Leeds [...] there are many cheerful[12], open streets where the better classes reside[13]. The lower classes, here as elsewhere, inhabit the less healthy localities. By far the most unhealthy localities of Leeds are close squares of houses [which have been built for lower-class people]. [...] Some of these are airless from the enclosed structure, and are one mass of damp[14] and filth[15]. The ashes, garbage, and filth of all kinds are thrown from the doors and windows of the houses upon [...] the streets. The [toilets] are few in proportion to[16] the number of inhabitants. They are open to view [... and] in a filthy condition. [Many people are ill, that is why many drink and take drugs, which increases] poverty and [early] deaths.

c *Riddall Wood stated before Parliament in 1840:*
The poorer districts of Liverpool often have rough ground in which there are pits[17]. In autumn there is [...] water in them, in which there have been thrown dead dogs and cats and other [...] things. This water is used for cooking. I could not believe this. I thought it was only used for washing. Was that because there was no other water supply? There is good supply of water for the poor, if they had something to keep it in. The water is turned on for four hours a day. Each person fetches as much as they can in pans[18], but they have few of these and soon run out of water.

S 12 a–c from: Jon Cresswell / Peter Laurence, Expansion, Trade and Industry, *OUP, 1993, p. 42.*

1 sewerage/sewer *Kanalisation/ Abwasserkanal*
2 supply *Versorgung*
3 waste collection *Müllabfuhr*
4 lodging house *Wohnheim*
5 challenge *herausfordern*
6 labour force *Arbeitskräfte*
7 wheat *Weizen*
8 raw materials *Rohstoffe*
9 manufactured goods *Industriegüter*
10 sevice *here: Dienstleistung*
11 chief *Haupt-*
12 cheerful *freundlich, heiter*
13 reside *leben, wohnen*
14 damp *Feuchtigkeit*
15 filth *Schmutz*
16 in proportion to *im Verhältnis zu*
17 pit *Grube*
18 pan *Schüssel*

S 13 Urban growth – Excerpt from the British *Report of the Select Committee on the Health of Towns*, 1840

The increase of population in England and Wales in thirty years, 1801 to 1831, has been more than 47 %. The number of inhabitants of five of our most important towns has grown by more than double[1] that rate; being Manchester 109 %, Glasgow 108 %, Birmingham 73 %, Leeds 99 %, Liverpool 100 %, giving an average of almost 98 %.

From: Jon Cresswell and Peter Laurence, Expansion, Trade and Industry, *OUP, 1993, p. 39.*

S 14 William Heath, *"Monster Soup, commonly called Thames Water"*, British cartoon, c 1828

Heath called his cartoon "a correct representation of that precious stuff doled out[2] to us". It shows Heath's view of the life that a microscope would discover in London's drinking water.

9 In 1840, a parliamentary committee was set up to find out why health conditions were so bad among the poorer people in large towns. Look at sources S 12–S 15 and organize the the committee's findings in a table. Use the following headings:
Housing quality – Water quality – Sewage water disposal[3] – Air quality – Disease.

10 In 1842, the parliamentary committee (see Task 9) published its results in the *Report on the sanitary condition of the labouring population of Great Britain.* Explain why historians call the report one of the most influential[4] social documents of the 19th century.

S 15 Gustave Doré (1832–1883), Wentworth Street/Whitechapel, Illustration for the book *London: A Pilgrimage*, 1872

In his book, Doré wanted to offer a complete portrait of London. The book sold enormously well, but many critics felt that Doré concentrated too much on the poverty in London.

11 The conditions in slums in 19th-century industrial towns are well documented in paintings, drawings and photographs. Doré's illustration in S 15 is one example. But are these sources reliable evidence?

a Make a list of questions to be answered before you can decide if the sources are reliable. Look at the "Study skills" on p. 46 for ideas.

b Study Doré's illustration and answer your list of questions. Vocabulary help: *be surrounded by children – hold a baby – sit at sb.'s feet – play in the gutter[5] – look at the scene from a window.*

c In small groups, discuss whether the illustration is a reliable source of living conditions in 19th-century Britain.

12 Using the "Study skills" on p. 18, write an analysis of the cartoon in S 14.

13 **Extra research:** Cholera and typhus epidemics were frequent in 19th-century Britain. Give a PowerPoint presentation on these two diseases and explain the connection between the poor living conditions and the outbreak of the epidemics. These websites may be helpful:
www.jasa.net.au/london/sanitation.htm
www.eee.uci.edu/clients/bjbecker/PlaguesandPeople/week8e.html
www.makingthemodernworld.org.uk/stories/the_industrial_town/06.ST.02/?scene=6

1 double *verdoppeln*
2 dole sth. out to sb. *etwas an jemanden verteilen*
3 disposal *Entsorgung*
4 influential *einflussreich*
5 gutter *Gosse*

2.3 Struggle[1] for democracy

Political rights in 19th-century Britain

At the end of the 18th century, Britain was a parliamentary* but not a democratic* nation. Very few Englishmen could take part in elections. Only privileged property owners had the right to vote. Minority groups, especially Catholics, were discriminated against. Britain was also still involved[2] in the African-Atlantic slave trade.

Throughout the century, reformers – especially from the working class* – demanded that all men have the right to vote. In contrast to other European countries, Britain managed to expand voting rights without a violent revolution: after the three Parliamentary Reform Acts[3] in 1832, 1867 and 1884, the number of legal voters rose from about 500,000 in 1831 to over 5 million in 1885. However, this was only an increase from 4 to 14 per cent of the total population, because in the 19th century women and non-white citizens of the British Empire had no voting rights in parliamentary elections. The Catholic Emancipation Act[4] (1829) gave Catholics the right to hold public office. Then four years later, the Slavery Abolition Act[5] (1833) finally made slavery illegal and gave all slaves within the British Empire their freedom.

The fight for women's rights

In 1866, a group of women from the Kensington Society organized a petition with 1500 signatures that called for equal voting rights for men and women. The women took their petition to Henry Fawcett and John Stuart Mill, two MPs (members of parliament) who supported universal suffrage[6]*. In 1867, Mill added an amendment to the Parliamentary Reform Act that would give women the same political rights as men. The amendment was defeated[7] by 196 votes to 73. Local British women's societies continued to be active. In 1897, they united to form the National Union of Women's Suffrage Societies. The right to vote was not given to all British women until 1928.

Key terms

Suffrage

In most countries today, the right to vote is every person's birth right (universal suffrage). Up until the early 20th century, women were not allowed to vote because they were thought to be childlike and mentally inferior[8] to men. Until the end of the 19th century, only men with some property and income could vote (census suffrage) in most Western "democracies".

S 16 Detail from a poster[9] for a workers' demonstration in Birmingham, 1848

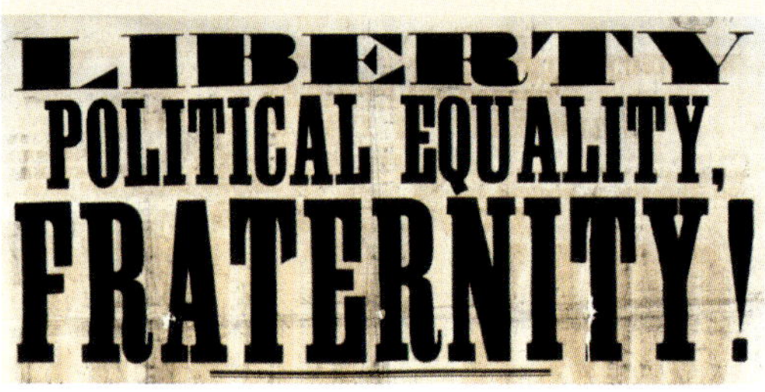

14 Go through the text and make an English-German vocabulary list titled "Terms and phrases of suffrage".

15 Discuss what exactly the workers were demanding in S 16.

16 The banner of the National Union of Women's Suffrage Societies states that the National Union is "Law-abiding"[10] and "No party". Discuss why the Union mentions this on its banner.

17 In 1832, the year of the first Parliamentary Reform Act, Mary Smith, a Yorkshire woman, demanded in a petition to Parliament that privileged women who qualified (i.e. who had enough property) should be able to vote. Look at the text as well as S 16 and list Mary's possible reasons why she wanted the right to vote.

18 **Extra research:** Give a presentation on the fight for women's rights in one of the following countries: A *Great Britain* B *Germany* C *United States*

1 struggle for sth. *Kampf um etwas*
2 involved in sth. *an etwas beteiligt*
3 Parliamentary Reform Acts *Wahlrechtsreformen*
4 Catholic Emancipation Act *Katholikenemanzipationsgesetz*
5 Slavery Abolition Act *Gesetz zur Abschaffung der Sklaverei*
6 suffrage/universal suffrage/census suffrage *Wahlrecht/allgemeines Wahlrecht/Zensuswahlrecht*
7 defeat sth. *here: etwas ablehnen*
8 mentally inferior *geistig unterlegen*
9 fraternity *Brüderlichkeit*
10 law-abiding *gesetzestreu*

Unit revision

19th-century Great Britain

Key events

1770s	Beginning of the Industrial Revolution in Britain
1832, 1867, 1884	Parliamentary Reform Acts
1829	Catholic Emancipation Act
1833	Factory Act Slavery Abolition Act
1837–1901	Reign of Queen Victoria
mid-19th century	Britain is the world's leading industrial power
1848	Revolutions in Europe, not in Britain
1848–1875	Public Health Acts
about 1900	USA becomes the world's leading industrial power

Key personalities

Queen Victoria

Key terms

Industrial Revolution, steam engine, industrialization, workshop, factory, urbanization, productivity growth, working class, trade unions, parliament, democracy, suffrage

History skills

Analysing visual sources *(p. 29, Task 11)*

Activate your English

Talking and writing about "industrialization" *(p. 27, Task 1)*
Talking and writing about "working a job" *(p. 27, Task 1)*
Talking and writing about "suffrage" *(p. 30, Task 14)*

S 17 **From the film *Oliver Twist* (2005), directed by Roman Polanski**

Oliver Twist (2005), directed by Roman Polanski.
Oliver, an orphan[1], meets a pickpocket[2] on the streets of London. From here, he joins a household of boys who are trained to steal for their master. The film is an adaptation of the classic British novel of the same name by Charles Dickens, which was first published in 1838. The story brought the social problems of 19th-century London to the public's attention.

1 orphan *Waisenkind*
2 pickpocket *Taschendieb*

1 Make vocabulary flash cards for the key events and key terms:

a On the front of each card, write one term or event to be learned. On the back, write the definition of the word and its translation. Examples:

Front:	*Slavery Abolition Act*	Back:	*British Act of Parliament which abolished slavery in 1833. (Gesetz zur Abschaffung der Sklaverei)*
Front:	*workshop*	Back:	*A small workplace where craftsmen make or repair things with tools and machines. (Handwerksbetrieb)*

b Work in pairs. Place all the cards on the desk in front of you with the terms facing upwards. One partner takes a card and reads the term. The other partner gives the definition without looking at the card. Take turns.

c Option: By making two sets of the cards, you can play a "memory game".

2 Between 1800 and 1900 Britain became a completely different country. Make a list of all the changes.

3 Britain has not had a violent political revolution since the civil wars of 1642–1651. Nearly every other state in Europe, however, experienced at least one violent overthrow of government in the 18th, 19th and 20th centuries. From what you know about Great Britain in the 19th century, how might this be explained?

4 Discuss in what way Great Britain could be called a showcase nation in the 19th century.

5 Start a list of English-German terms for the different groups and occupations in society. Example: *(un)skilled worker – (un)gelernter Arbeiter, Facharbeiter*

Unit 3 The French Revolution

3.1 France in crisis: French society before 1789

S1

Auguste Couder (1790-1873), Opening of the Estates-General[1] on 5 May 1789, French painting, c. 1840

A society divided in estates[3]

In the 18th century, the French king was an "absolute" monarch*. In the so-called *Ancien Régime** he was the supreme judge[4], he influenced all areas of government, and he declared war and peace. People believed that he "was appointed by God" and that he had the right to rule over everyone.

French society (like in the rest of Europe) was divided into three estates*.

The **First Estate** was the clergy[5], which numbered around 130,000, or 1 per cent of the population. They collected fees[6] and tithes[7] from the people. Bishops and other higher clergymen had enormous incomes; ordinary[8] priests, however, were overworked and earned very little. Most often the higher clergymen were sons of noble[9] families. The parents of ordinary priests, however, often belonged to the Third Estate (see below). About 15 per cent of the land in France belonged to the church – tax-free. Many people criticized the clergy for taking money from the poor.

The **Second Estate** was the nobility, about 350,000, or 2–3 per cent of the population. The nobles owned 40 per cent of the land. They held the top jobs in the army and in government and did not have to pay taxes. However, many of the 350,000 noblemen were not very rich and had to work on their land. They had debts[10], because their lifestyle was

Key terms

Estate
An estate was a very large group of people with certain rights and privileges. The First Estate was the clergy, the Second Estate was the nobility, and the Third Estate was everyone else. Your birth decided if you belonged to the Second or Third Estate.

1 Estates-General *Generalstände*
2 plumed hat *Federhut*
3 estates *Stände*
4 supreme judge *oberster Richter*
5 clergy/clergyman *Geistlichkeit/der Geistliche*
6 fee *Gebühr*
7 tithe *(Kirchen-)Zehnte*
8 ordinary *normal, gewöhnlich*
9 noble/nobility/the noble *adlig/der Adel/der Adlige*
10 debts *Schulden*

expensive. The noblemen were allowed to take dues[1] from the peasants. In the 1780s, they tried to raise the dues to be able to pay back their debts.

Key terms

Privilege
A privilege is an advantage that is enjoyed by a small, usually powerful group or class, especially to the disadvantage of others. For example, before 1789, nobles in France did not have to pay any taxes.

The Third Estate

Everybody else (25 million people, or 97 per cent of the population) belonged to the Third Estate: peasants, servants, skilled and unskilled workers, doctors, lawyers, teachers and shop owners. The average person of the Third Estate was a poor peasant (75–80 per cent of the population). The peasants owned 35–40 per cent of the land and paid almost all the taxes, which were taxes on land. They had very few rights. Because hunting was a privilege* of the nobility, peasants were not allowed to hunt the rabbits that ate the vegetables in their gardens or the pigeons[2] that ate their grain[3]. When the nobility went hunting, they often ruined the peasants' crops[4] and broke their fences[5], with no payment for these damages. It was a case of *"C'est la vie!"* – "That's life!".

During the 18th century, some members of the Third Estate became extremely rich as merchants, bankers, manufacturers[6] or ship owners. However, they were not allowed to take high positions in government. Especially university-educated people like lawyers and university teachers criticized the absolute power of the king and the privileges of the First and Second Estate. They wanted to change the political system, especially after the American Revolution in 1776 (see Unit 1.4).

The financial crisis and the calling of the Estates-General

By 1787, the French government was bankrupt[7] (see S2). King Louis XVI asked the nobility to help him reform the system of government and taxation. He wanted them to pay taxes, too, but they refused to do so. Instead, the nobility and clergy hoped to weaken the king's power so that they could have more influence on the government.

From 1787 to 1789, France was hit by terrible weather: heavy rain, hard winters and very hot summers. As a result, crops failed and farm animals became ill. Peasants had less income, and food prices in the cities went up sharply.

More and more families starved[8] because they could not buy enough food. Many people were so weak that they died of diseases. Throughout France, peasants and people in the towns rioted and attacked the castles of the nobility.

In August 1788, King Louis XVI decided to call an Estates-General* – a meeting of representatives from all three estates – for the next year. This had last happened in 1614.

S2 Income, spending and debt of the French government (in livres[9]), 1787

Income	503 million
Spending	630 million:
	50 %: interest on debts[10]
	26 %: army, wars
	6 %: the court[11]
	18 %: the rest
Total debt	4000 million

1 dues *Abgaben (in Form von Geld, Waren, Dienstleistungen)*
2 pigeon *Taube*
3 grain *Getreide*
4 crops *Ernte*
5 fence *Zaun*
6 manufacturer *Unternehmer*
7 bankrupt *bankrott*
8 starve *hungern*
9 livre *French currency (Währung) before 1789*
10 interest on debts *Kreditzinsen*
11 court *königlicher Hof*

S 3 Emmanuel-Josephe Abbé Siéyès on the situation of the Third Estate in a pamphlet, January 1789

What is the Third Estate?
We have three questions to ask ourselves:
What is the Third Estate? EVERYTHING.
What has it been in the political order until now? NOTHING.
What is it asking for? To become SOMETHING.

Who would dare to say that the Third Estate does not have in itself all that is needed to form a complete nation? It is a man who is strong and robust but still has one arm in chains[1]. Take away the privileged order[2], and the nation would not be less, but more.

Emmanuel-Josephe Sieyès, What is the Third Estate? (1789), ed. by S.E. Finer, London, Pall Mall Press, 1963, pp. 51–54. From: www.college.hmco.com/history/west/mosaic/chapter12/source50.html, 15 August 2005.

Biography

Abbé Siéyès

Emmanuel Joseph Abbé Siéyès (1748 to 1838) was a clergyman before the Revolution. His pamphlet *Qu'est-ce que le tiers état?* (S 3) was published in January 1789 and became enormously popular throughout France because it attacked the privileges of the First and Second Estates. Siéyès was elected representative to the Estates-General for the Third Estate in Paris.

S 4 Excerpts from the *Cahiers de doléances*, spring 1789

Each estate in every district in France wrote a list of grievances[3] for their representatives in the Estates-General in the spring of 1789.

4 a) District of Aix–en–Provence:

Gifts, pensions, and large profits reserved to nobles only take the spirit of competition away from both nobles and commoners[4]. [...] Competition is also taken away from the commoners because these people cannot aspire[5] to anything, and competition becomes useless to them.
To close off employment possibilities and respectable occupations[6] to the most numerous and useful class is like killing genius and talents. [...] The nobility enjoys and owns everything, and would like to free itself from everything.

4 b) District of Lignère la Doucelle:

For a long time now, the inhabitants have been crushed[7] beneath the excessive burden[8] of the many taxes that they have had to pay. [We demand] that all lords, country gentlemen, and others of the privileged class [...] pay the same taxes as the common people. That the lord's mills not be obligatory[9], allowing everyone to choose where he would like to mill his grain.

4 c) District of Belfort, Upper Alsace:

– Corvées[10]
  This lord requires[11] five days of work from [the peasants ...]. It is often the case that [they] are not able to fulfil their tasks in a day, whereupon[12] they [must] continue their work the next day, even though only one day of work is counted.
– Beating the Woods
  When it pleases [the noble], and it often pleases him, he [forces] them to beat the woods in order to satisfy his desire to hunt. [...] The farmer who is thus forced to wander through the woods for a whole day receives neither food, nor a bonus, nor payment.

S 4 a–c: English translation from: www.chnm.gmu.edu/revolution/d/368/, www.chnm.gmu.edu/revolution/d/558/ and www.chnm.gmu.edu/revolution/d/375/, 15 August 2005.

1 chain *Kette*
2 order *here:* estate
3 grievance *Beschwerde, Klage*
4 commoner *member of the Third Estate*
5 aspire to sth. *etwas anstreben*
6 occupation *Beschäftigung*
7 crush *zerdrücken*
8 burden *Last*
9 obligatory *verpflichtend*
10 corvées *Frondienste (von Bauern unentgeltlich zu erbringende Dienstleistungen)*
11 require *(er)fordern*
12 whereupon *woraufhin*

1 Work in pairs: Read the text on pp. 32–33 and organize the different groups of people in the three estates in a tree diagram titled "The Three Estates before 1789".

Tree diagram

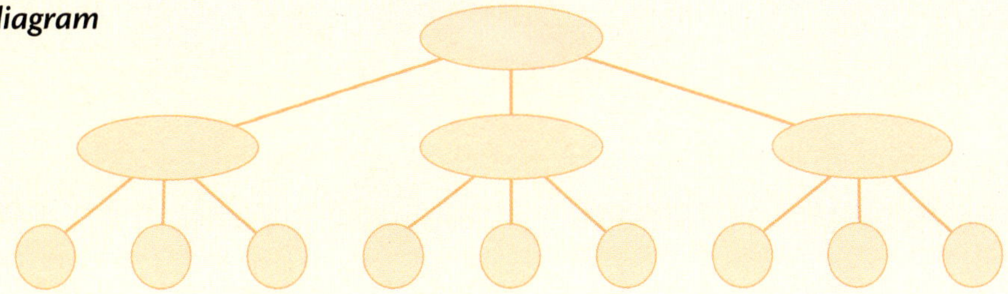

2 a Look at the table in S 2 and draw charts showing
- the French budget of 1787 (income and spending), so that it is clear how bankrupt the French government was;
- how the French government spent tax money.

b Making connections: From what you already know about France, give one reason for the government's financial problems.

3 a Look at the text on pp. 32–33 and fill in the cause-and-effect diagram below.

b Present and discuss your results in class. See **Activate your English** below.

Causes		***Effects***
Changes within the Third Estate (rich merchants, bankers etc.)	→	*Members of the Third Estate demand that …* the political system should be changed
Terrible weather, animal epidemics	→	*…* less income for peasants
… food prices went up sharply	→	*People cannot buy enough food.*
… families starved, died of diseases	→	*…* riots, castles attacked

4 Discuss the advantages and/or disadvantages of diagrams such as the cause-and-effect diagram. Vocabulary help:
One advantage of this type of diagram is that it clearly points to … / focuses on … / shows that … / gives a visual representation of …
A disadvantage is that it only shows / focuses on … / fails to show … / simplifies … too much.

Activate your English

Time expressions
first, then, finally
soon after, shortly after, after awhile
two days/weeks/months/years later
as soon as
in 1789, in July
in (the) spring/summer/autumn/winter
in the spring of 1789
on 14 July 1789
at the end of August / the 18th century
about / around 1800

Activate your English

Causes and effects I

Causes:
because of sth.
the reason why
the long-term[1] cause / short-term cause / trigger[2] was …
was caused by …
can be explained by …

Effects or consequences:
led to …
resulted in …
was followed by …
had the effect that …
as a result, …
the result/outcome was …
consequently, …
as a consequence, …
the consequence was …
brought about[3] …
triggered off[4] …
thus/therefore …

1 long-term/short-term *langfristig/kurzfristig*
2 trigger *Auslöser*
3 bring about sth. *etwas bewirken, zur Folge haben*
4 trigger off sth. *etwas auslösen, einleiten*

S 5 "We must hope that it will soon be over", anonymous French cartoon, June 1789

In 1789, this cartoon spread quickly through France. Vocabulary help: pigeons – carry sb. on your back – clergyman – field – First Estate – hoe – plumed hat – nobleman – peasant – rabbits – Second Estate – sword – Third Estate – wig – wooden clogs

5 a Organize the information on Siéyès in a mind map or a grid (see Biography, p. 34).
b Note down and explain Abbé Siéyès' complaint and demands in S 3.

6 Divide into groups of three or four. Divide the three letters in S 4 among the groups:
a Each group lists the complaints that are made in one of the letters.
b Discuss how you think representatives of the First and Second Estates might respond[1] to the complaints and demands.
c Present and explain your findings to the other groups.

7 Analyse the cartoon in S 5:
a Photocopy the cartoon and label it with all the necessary information.
b Write a short caption explaining the message of S 5. Remember the "History skills", pp. 18–19.

8 Write a lead article for the *London Illustrated News* for 4 May, 1789, the day before the first meeting of the Estates-General. Begin your article with the facts about the "sensational" meeting that will be taking place at Versailles (S 1). Then explain the Third Estate's hopes and expectations for the meeting (see pp. 32–33 and S 2–S 4). Use S 5 with your caption as an illustration for your article. See **Activate your English** (p. 35).

1 respond *reagieren*

3.2 Major events of the French Revolution

Timeline: 1789–1791

1789 Spring/summer: Louis XVI calls the Estates-General* to discuss tax reforms.

5 May: The Estates-General meets in Versailles with 291 representatives of the First Estate, 270 of the Second Estate and 578 of the Third Estate. At its last meeting 175 years before, the Third Estate had played no role. This time the situation is very different. There is disagreement on how to count the votes: By head or by estate? Should all representatives vote together as a single assembly, or – as the King wants – should each estate have just one vote?

17 June: The Third Estate rename themselves the **National Assembly***[1].

20 June: When the King tries to break up the meeting of the Third Estate, they swear an oath[2] (the **Tennis Court Oath**) to stay together until a constitution has been written and to resist pressures[3] from the outside to break up.

27 June: The King orders the First and Second Estates to join the Third: The Third Estate wins against the King.

S6 Storming of the Bastille, French watercolour, c 1789

The painting is based on information given by Lieutenant Claude Cholat, who took part in the storming of the Bastille.

14 July Fall of the Bastille: The Parisian masses storm and capture[4] the state prison. This event becomes the symbol of the revolution and the date of the French national holiday.

July: Beginning of the peasants' revolt. In the countryside, the people destroy hundreds of castles. They also destroy the records[5] which their lords use to demand dues from them.

4 August: A new law by the National Assembly at Versailles ends all privileges*, dues and tithes of the nobility and clergy. Members of the nobility begin to leave the country.

26 August: The National Assembly adopts the **Declaration of the Rights of Man and of the Citizen.**

5 October: The women's insurrection[6]. Women march from Paris to the King's palace at Versailles to complain about the lack[7] of bread. The next day they march back to Paris, forcing the King and Queen to go with them. The National Assembly soon follows them to Paris.

1791 June: Louis XVI tries to leave France but is stopped near the border and brought back to Paris. The people protest and call for a new head of government.

September: The National Assembly adopts the **French Constitution** of 1791. This gives the right to vote only to men with at least some income or property. Olympe de Gouges publishes her **Declaration of the Rights of Woman and the Female Citizen.**

1 National Assembly *Nationalversammlung*
2 swear an oath *einen Eid schwören*
3 resist pressures *dem Druck Widerstand leisten*
4 capture sth./sb. *etwas einnehmen, jdn. gefangen nehmen*
5 records *in Aufzeichnungen festgeschriebene Herrenrechte*
6 insurrection *Aufstand*
7 lack of *Mangel an*

Timeline: 1792–1804

1792 April: European monarchs fear the spread of the revolutionary ideas from France. They threaten to return the French King to power. To prevent[1] this, France declares war on Austria and its ally[2] Prussia. Fears of traitors within the country grow quickly.

July: Prussian troops begin their march toward Paris. Their commander, the Duke of Brunswick[3], demands that the French disarm[4] and threatens to destroy Paris if the citizens resist or harm[5] the royal family. This creates not only fear of the foreign army but also anger at the King. Parisians prepare to defend themselves and their city.

10 August: Parisians storm the Tuileries (the royal palace) and imprison the royal family.

21 September: The monarchy is abolished and the French Republic* is declared.

October 1792–January 1793: King Louis XVI is tried for treason[6], found guilty and sentenced[7] to death.

1793 21 January: Louis XVI is executed on the guillotine.

March–December: A counter-revolutionary[8] revolt is violently suppressed in the Vendée[9], where armed men and women tried to overthrow the republic and restore[10] the monarchy.

S7 **A revolutionary court, coloured etching, France, autumn 1794**

May/June: The beginning of the rule of the Jacobins*, the most radical political group in France. They believe that, politically and economically, the ordinary people (Sans-Culottes) have not profited enough from the revolution. They feel that harsh measures are needed to fight the enemies of the revolution inside France and to put an end to the terrible economic situation. Maximilien Robespierre, the leader of the Jacobins, begins the **Reign of Terror**[11] "to save the revolution". Tens of thousands of so-called "counter-revolutionaries" are arrested, tried before the revolutionary courts, and many are executed.

23 August: After the war against the European monarchs begins badly for France, the National Assembly creates the Committee for Public Safety[12], which declares on this day that all unmarried men between 18 and 25 have to do military service. Thus France's army grows to one million men, the largest in European history. This large army puts an end to the French defeats[13] and begins to attack.

1794 July: Robespierre is arrested and executed. The end of the Reign of Terror in France.

1797: Napoleon Bonaparte takes command of the French army against England.

1799: Napoleon makes himself First Consul.

1802: Slavery is re-introduced in the French colonies.

1804: Napoleon becomes Emperor.

1 prevent sth. *etwas verhindern*
2 ally/alliance *Verbündeter, Alliierter/Bündnis*
3 Brunswick *Braunschweig*
4 disarm *entwaffnen*
5 harm sb. *jdm. schaden, jdn. verletzen*
6 try sb. (in court) for treason *jdn. wegen Hochverrats vor Gericht stellen*
7 sentence sb. *jdn. verurteilen*
8 counter-revolutionary *gegenrevolutionär*
9 Vendée *region in the West of France*
10 restore *wiederherstellen*
11 Reign of Terror *Schreckensherrschaft*
12 Committee for Public Safety *Wohlfahrtsausschuss*
13 defeat *Niederlage*

Key terms

Republic
A republic is a form of government whose head of state is not a monarch but usually a president.

Key terms

Revolution
A revolution is a complete change of the social and political system of a country, especially when this takes place suddenly and with violence. The result is a fundamental change in overall living conditions.

Key terms

Reform
A reform is a step-by-step peaceful change of social and political conditions, for example by laws.

9 Look at the timeline on pp. 37–38. The French people fought against the old system (the *Ancien Régime*) with its inequality and its lack of political rights
A *at Versailles.*
B *in Paris.*
C *in the countryside.*
Make a table showing what happened, where and when. Comment on your findings. Discuss in class what kind of table works best for presenting this information.

10 The counting of votes in the Estates-General by head or by estate: Working in pairs, explain the difference to your partner.

11 **Extra research:** Give a presentation on the storming of the Bastille (S 6).
Tip: use your favourite search engine to find texts, images and a map of Paris (keywords: "The Storming of the Bastille").

12 Make your own timeline titled "King Louis XVI – From absolute monarch to political prisoner":
a List the major events in the King's life.
b Then create a line graph indicating the ups and downs in his life.
c Write the dates below the line and the events with explanations above the line.

13 **a** Organize the information on the Reign of Terror in an event map (see Appendix, pp. 142–143). One box of the event map should include the effects of the Reign of Terror. Discuss whether Robespierre's execution can be considered one of the effects. Compare your results in class.
b For a new online encyclopaedia for bilingual history classes in German-speaking countries, write a short paragraph about the positive and negative effects of the Reign of Terror titled "Did Robespierre save the Revolution?".

14 Describe the painting in S 7. Find out when it was made and explain whose point of view it shows.

15 Use a cause-and-effect diagram like the one here to show how the French Revolution led to war between France and its neighbours.

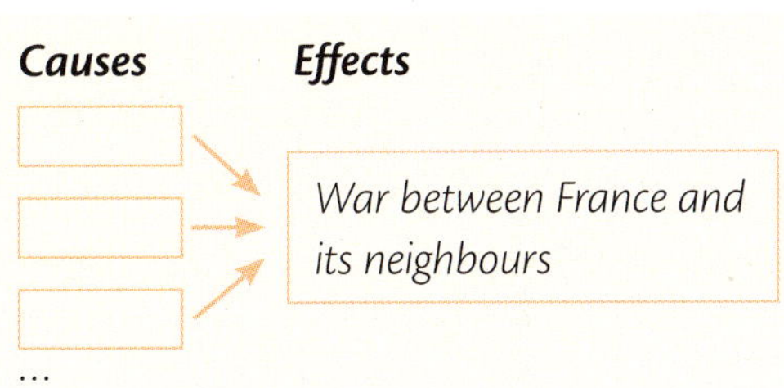

16 **a** Explain the difference between the terms "reform" and "revolution" (see "Key terms" above).
b Look at the results of Task 9. According to the definitions of "reform" and "revolution", do you think it is correct to call the period in France between 1789 and 1794 "The time of the French Revolution"? Give reasons (see **Activate your English**, p. 8).

17 **Extra research:** At the time of the French Revolution, women had no voting rights. Identify countries where women today still do not have the right to vote.

3.3 Declarations of human and civil rights*

Two documents which have shaped[1] our modern world

The French Declaration of the Rights of Man and of the Citizen (1789) was written by the Marquis de Lafayette (1757–1834) with help from his friend and neighbour, US minister to France, Thomas Jefferson (see p. 16). Lafayette had been a Major General in the North American colonies and had helped the colonials defeat the British during the American Revolutionary War (see p. 16). He had a deep respect for the man he called his "father", George Washington (see p. 20).

One hundred and fifty years later, in 1948, the 48 members of the United Nations proclaimed[2] The Universal Declaration of Human Rights, which is still recognized today.

S 8 **Oil painting by Jean Jacques Le Barbier, the elder (1738–1826) (Detail)**

S 9 The Declaration of the Rights of Man and of the Citizen, approved by the National Assembly of France, 26 August 1789

The 17 articles of the Declaration were added to the French Constitution of 1791. The following are abridged extracts:

I Men are born and remain free and equal in rights.

II These rights are liberty, property, security and resistance to oppression[3].

III No group or individual that is not elected by the people has the authority to make laws for the people. [...]

VI The law is the same for everyone.

VII No person shall be accused, arrested, or imprisoned except in the cases and according to the forms given by law. [...]

X All citizens have the right to practise their religion.

XI All citizens have the right to think, say and write what they like. [...]

XIII All citizens must pay taxes in proportion to their income. [...]

XVI A separation of powers [in which the legislative, executive and judiciary branches are independent of each other] is necessary for the proper functioning of society.

XVII No government has the right to take away a person's property.

From: Wolfgang Lautemann (ed.), Geschichte in Quellen, Volume 4, *BSV, München, 1981, pp. 199–201. Translated and simplified by the author.*

S 10 The Universal Declaration of Human Rights, 10 December 1948

The following extracts are from a simplified version prepared in 1978 for use in schools (for the original complete declaration, see: www.un.org/Overview/rights.html):

1 When children are born, they are free and each should be treated in the same way. They have reason[4] and conscience[5] and should act towards one another in a friendly way.

2 Everyone has the following rights, despite
- a different sex,
- a different skin colour,
- speaking a different language,
- thinking different things,
- believing in another religion,
- owning more or less,
- being born in another social group,
- coming from another country. [...]

1 shape sth. *etwas formen, prägen*
2 proclaim sth. *etwas verkünden, erklären*
3 oppression *Unterdrückung*
4 reason *Vernunft*
5 conscience *Gewissen*

3 You have the right to live, and to live in freedom and safety.

4 Nobody has the right to treat you as his or her slave and you should not make anyone your slave.

5 Nobody has the right to torture[1] you. [...]

7 The law is the same for everyone; [...]

9 Nobody has the right to put you in prison, to keep you there [...] without good reason.

10 If you go on trial[2] this should be done in public. [...]

13 You have the right to come and go as you wish within your country. You have the right to leave your country to go to another one; and you should be able to return to your country if you want. [...]

16 [Everybody] has the right to marry and have a family. [...] Men and women have the same rights when they are married and also when they are separated. Nobody should force a person to marry. [...]

17 You have the right to own things and nobody has the right to take these from you without a good reason.

18 You have the right to profess your religion[3] freely. [...]

19 You have the right to think what you want, to say what you like. [...]

20 You have the right to organize peaceful meetings or to take part in meetings in a peaceful way. [...]

23 You have the right to work, to be free to choose your work [...]. If a man and a woman do the same work, they should get the same pay.

From: www.un.org/cyberschoolbus/humanrights/resources/plain.asp, 15 August 2005.

18 **a** Photocopy the Declaration of 1789 (S 9) and mark
- in red the articles which outline citizens' freedoms,
- in yellow the articles which outline equality,
- in green the articles which limit[4] the governments' powers.

b Comment on your findings, including anything that surprises you.

19 Imagine it is 18th-century France and you are a

A *woman.* C *peasant.*
B *nobleman.* D *Parisian lawyer.*

Describe how the Declaration of 1789 (S 9) has or has not changed your life.

20 **a** Photocopy the Declaration of 1948 (S 10): Mark the articles in the same way you did for S 9. Comment on your findings (see Task 18).

b Use a Venn diagram like the one to the right to compare and contrast the Declaration of 1789 and the Declaration of 1948 (S 9, S 10; see **Activate your English**): List the similarities in the overlapping area of the circles and the differences in the non-overlapping areas under their correct headings.

21 Look at your Venn diagram (Task 19 b) and discuss in class which developments and advances[5] are most important and welcome for you as a

A *German* B *non-German* C *woman* D *teenager.*

Discuss also which of the articles are still violated[6] today.

Activate your English

Comparing Sources

The (articles in the) Declaration of ...
- *are/is more exact/precise*
- *give(s) more examples/details of*
- *are/is very general*
- *stress(es) that ...*
- *don't/doesn't exactly define ...*

The number of articles dealing with ... has grown ...

The two declarations differ / are different / are quite similar in the way they ...

... has developed most/significantly since ...

Venn diagram

Declaration 1789 *Human Rights 1948*

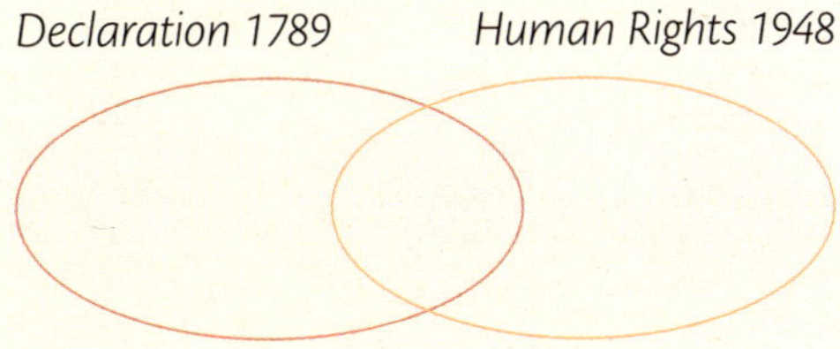

1 torture *foltern*
2 go on trial for sth. *einer Sache angeklagt sein*
3 profess your religion *sich zu einer Religion bekennen*
4 limit sth. *etwas begrenzen, beschränken*
5 advance *(hier) Fortschritt*
6 violate (a law) *(ein Gesetz) missachten, übertreten*

3.4 Women in the French Revolution

Liberty and equality – for all?

Many women greeted[1] the outbreak of the Revolution with hope and joy. Between 1789 and 1793, they founded political clubs and fought for equal rights. Marie Olympe de Gouges became a leading figure with the publication of her famous Declaration of the Rights of Woman and the Female Citizen in 1791. In the same year, French women won the right to divorce[2]. However, they still did not have the right to vote.

In October 1793, the National Assembly* dissolved[3] all women's political organizations. When a delegation of women appeared in the National Assembly a few days later to protest this decision, the Assembly refused to let them speak. Pierre-Gaspard Chaumette even attacked not only them personally, but also all political activity by women (S 12).

S 11 **Tricolour cockade[4], 1789**

Since 1789, the tricolour cockade has been a symbol of the French Revolution. Blue and red are the colours of the city of Paris, white the colour of King Louis XVI. In the inner circle: a rapier[5] is holding up a Liberty cap[6]. Its label reads: Egalité – Liberté *(equality, liberty). The cockade was usually pinned to a hat and showed that its wearer supported the Revolution.*

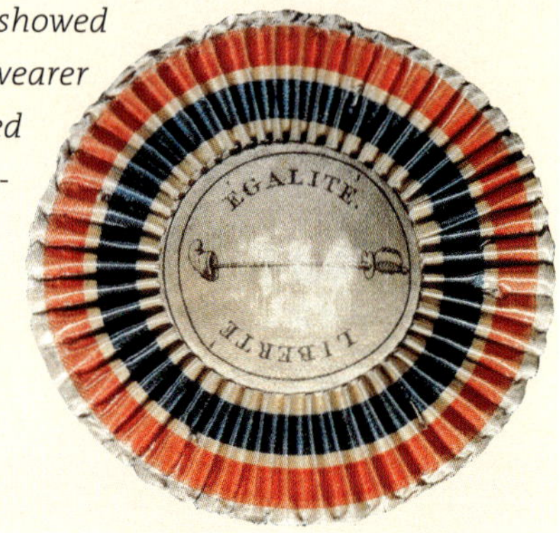

Biography

Olympe de Gouges

Marie Olympe de Gouges (1748–1793) was born in the south of France as the daughter of a butcher[7]. At the age of 20 – three years after marrying – she fled from her husband and went to Paris. Although she had little formal schooling, she began to write political articles, for example against slavery. She became a member of the *Cercle Social*, a group which began a campaign for women's rights in 1791. In the same year, Olympe de Gouges wrote her famous Declaration of the Rights of Woman and the Female Citizen, which did not win much support but made her notorious[8]. Like many other women who demanded equal rights, she was arrested, but punished much harder. She was executed on the guillotine on 3 November 1793.

Biography

Madame Roland

Jeanne Marie Roland de la Platière (1754–1793) was born as the daughter of a poor Paris craftsman. Her parents educated her so that she would have the "ability to think for herself". From early on, she read books by the most difficult thinkers. In 1779, she married Jean Marie Roland de la Platière. After the outbreak of the revolution, her home became a meeting place for revolutionary leaders such as Robespierre. However, when her husband (Minister of the Interior in 1792–1793) was accused[9] of sympathizing with the King, the couple became very unpopular. While her husband escaped, she was arrested, sentenced to death by a revolutionary court and executed on 8 November 1793. Before placing her head on the guillotine, she made her famous remark: "Oh Liberty, what crimes are committed[10] in your name!"

1 greet sth. *etwas begrüßen*
2 divorce *sich scheiden lassen*
3 dissolve *auflösen*
4 cockade *Abzeichen*
5 rapier *Degen*
6 Liberty/Phrygian cap *Freiheits-/Phrygische Mütze (französisches Nationalsymbol seit der Revolution)*
7 butcher *Schlachter*
8 notorious *berüchtigt*
9 accuse sb. *jdn. beschuldigen*
10 commit a crime *ein Verbrechen begehen*

S 12 Pierre-Gaspard Chaumette (1763–1794), Excerpts from a speech at City Hall on women's political activism, 17 November 1793

It is shocking; it is contrary to all the laws of nature for a woman to want to make herself a man. [...] Since when is it decent[1] to see women abandon[2] the pious[3] cares of their household, the cradle[4] of their children, to come into public places, to the galleries [of the National Assembly] to hear speeches [...]?

Remember that [...] wife of a foolish and treacherous[5] spouse[6], the Roland woman, who thought herself suited[7] to govern the republic and who raced to her death. Remember the shameless Olympe de Gouges, who was the first to set up women's clubs, who abandoned the cares of her household to involve herself in the republic, and whose head fell under the avenging blade[8] of the laws. Is it for[9] women to make motions[10]? Is it for women to put themselves at the head of our armies?

From: The French Revolution and Human Rights: A Brief Documentary History, *translated and edited by Lynn Hunt, Bedford/St. Martin's, Boston/New York, 1996, pp. 138–139, in: www./chnm.gmu.edu/revolution/d/489/, 15 August 2005.*

S 13 Guillotine, model, 20th century

The guillotine took its name from Josephe Guillotin, a French doctor and member of the National Assembly who introduced it in 1792 to carry out the death penalty. Historians estimate that during the "Reign of Terror" between 15,000 and 40,000 French citizens were guillotined.

S 14 *"Place de la Révolution"* in Paris, picture from the film *The French Revolution,* directed by Robert Enrico and Richard T. Heffron, 1989

22 Read the Biographies of Madame Roland and Olympe de Gouges (p. 42). Discuss whether a connection can be drawn between the deaths of the women and the development of the revolution (see the timelines, pp. 37–38). → radical phase, opposition suppressed, war!

23 Look at the Biography of Madame Roland. In class, discuss what she meant when she cried: "Oh Liberty, what crimes are committed in your name!"

24 **a** Read S 12 and answer these key questions for analysing a political speech: Who is the speaker? Where is he speaking? To whom? About what?

b Describe how Chaumette describes/attacks politically active women. Vocabulary help: *For Chaumette, these women are … / act … / behave … In his view, politically active women …*

c Describe Chaumette's idea of a woman's proper role[11]. Vocabulary help: *In his view, a proper woman … The role of a proper woman is as … / to …*

d Explain why Chaumette and other men, who had all demanded equal rights for themselves, attacked women who were demanding the same for women, especially the right to vote.

e Imagine being one of the women Chaumette attacked: How might she defend herself against these attacks? Which arguments might she use? Tip: Have a look at the Declaration of the Rights of Man (p. 40, S 9) and at the timelines for the French Revolution (pp. 37–38).

25 **Extra research:** Give a presentation on Marie Olympe de Gouges and her Declaration of the Rights of Woman. Tip: *www.chnm.gmu.edu/revolution* (search term: "de Gouges").

1 decent *anständig, annehmbar*
2 abandon sth. *etwas aufgeben*
3 pious *fromm*
4 cradle *Wiege*
5 treacherous *verräterisch*
6 spouse *Ehemann, Gemahl*
7 suited *geeignet*
8 under the avenging blade *(hier) unter der rächenden Klinge (der Guillotine)*
9 Is it for (women) *Gehört es sich für (Frauen)*
10 motion *Antrag in einer Sitzung*
11 proper role *eigentliche, schickliche, passende Rolle*

3.5 Napoleon – His rise and fall

A military career

Napoleon (1769–1821) was born the son of a Corsican nobleman. Already at the age of ten he began training to be an officer at a military academy. In 1796, the young man became commander of the French troops in Italy in the war against Austria. After defeating the Austrian army in 1797, he returned to France a hero. The government then wanted to send him off to invade[1] England. However, he convinced the government that the army was not ready for this. To weaken England, he argued, it would be better to take control of Egypt and this way damage[2] British trade with India, its most important colony. While Napoleon was in Egypt with his army, the English fleet, led by Admiral Nelson, defeated the French fleet at the Battle of Aboukir in 1798.

S 15

German translation of the Code Napoleon in an edition for the Grand Duchy Berg, 1810

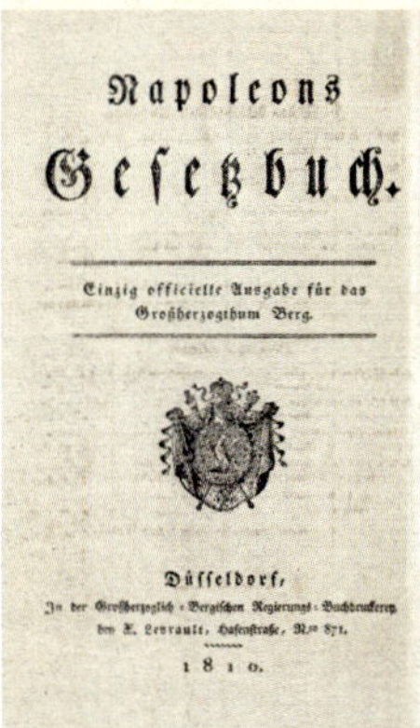
Napoleons Gesetzbuch.
Einzig officielle Ausgabe für das Großherzogthum Berg.
Düsseldorf,
1 8 1 0.

Consul, Emperor and the Civil Code

After the defeat at Aboukir, Napoleon left his soldiers secretly to return to France. In Paris he took part in a military *coup d'état*[3]* in 1799 that overthrew the government. The new government was called the Consulate*, and Napoleon was its First Consul. Only 30 years old at the time, he concentrated power in his own hands. In 1802, Napoleon made himself Consul for life. This was approved by a majority of the French people in a plebiscite*[4]. In 1804, the people voted to make him Emperor of the French. Napoleon then completely changed the legal system. This new system, called the Code Napoleon or Civil Code (S 16), guaranteed the rights of the citizens. Many states later adopted the Code either in total or in parts (e.g. in the German *Bürgerliches Gesetzbuch* of 1900).

Will Germany become French?

In the late 1780s, the map of Germany showed over 350 states and principalities[5]. After military victories in Italy and Spain, Napoleon began building a French empire in Europe. As part of this,

- he annexed[6] all German territories west of the Rhine[7] and turned them into a part of the French Republic in 1794; and
- he joined[8] together 17 of the states east of the Rhine in 1806 and formed the Confederation of the Rhine[9], which was under direct French control.

As a result, the Holy Roman Empire of German Nation[10] was dissolved on 6 August 1806 when the last Holy Roman Emperor Franz II resigned. All the people in the territories west of the Rhine became legally French (until Napoleon was finally defeated in 1815).

Napoleon in Europe: Resented[11] or welcomed?

Napoleon is mostly known as a military leader and as the master of Europe between 1807 and 1812, after his Grand Army had defeated the Prussian, Austrian and Russian armies. He then created a new European order. His "Grand Empire" consisted of three parts: the French Empire, dependent states and allied states. The only state which Napoleon was never able to invade because of its strong navy was Great Britain. In his empire, Napoleon tried to destroy the "old order" of the *Ancien Regime** and establish some of the principles of the revolution: legal equality, religious toleration and economic freedom. Many people in the conquered states at first welcomed these ideas and the French rule because many were extremely dissatisfied[12] with the rule of their own absolute monarchs*. However, in the German states, especially in Prussia, more and more people resented the French. Pride[13] in German culture and history slowly grew. Some Germans even dreamed of self-rule and a new unified and democratic Germany.

1 invade (a country) *(in ein Land) einmarschieren*
2 damage sth. *etwas schaden, Schaden zufügen*
3 coup d'état *Staatsstreich*
4 plebiscite *Plebiszit, Volksabstimmung*
5 pricipality/prince *Fürstentum/Fürst*
6 annex (a territory) *(ein Land) annektieren, gegen dessen Willen einverleiben*
7 territories west of the Rhine *linksrheinische Gebiete*
8 join sth. (together) *(hier) etwas verbinden, vereinigen*
9 Confederation of the Rhine *Rheinbund*
10 Holy Roman Empire of German Nation *Heiliges Römisches Reich Deutscher Nation*
11 resent *ablehnen*
12 dissatisfied with sth. *mit etwas unzufrieden*
13 pride in sth. *Stolz auf etwas*

The Fall of Napoleon

The turning point in Napoleon's career came in 1812 when his military campaign against Russia became a disaster. When his Grand Army reached Moscow in the middle of the harsh winter, they found it burning – set on fire by the Russians. Only 20,000 of his 600,000 soldiers survived. Russia and Prussia then began a War of Liberation[1].

The end came in 1813 when Napoleon lost the Battle of the Nations near Leipzig. The Treaty of Fontainebleau in April 1814 forced Napoleon to abdicate[2] and go into exile on the island of Elba. The final act took place in June 1815 when Napoleon, back from Elba, lost his last battle at Waterloo against Prussia and England (under Blücher and Wellington). Banned to the small island of Helena, Napoleon died from stomach cancer[3] in 1821.

S 16 Excerpts from the Code Napoleon, 1804 (in simplified form)

6. The law is the same everywhere in France.

8. Every Frenchman shall enjoy civil rights.

213. The husband must protect his wife; the wife must obey[4] her husband.

214. The wife cannot go to court without the authority[5] of her husband.

375–379. A father who is dissatisfied with his child's behaviour can have the child put in prison for up to one month.

1421. The husband alone administers[6] his and his wife's property.

From: www.historyguide.org/intellect/code_nap.html, 15 August 2005. Abridged and simplified by the author. For the original, see: www.napoleon-series.org

S 17 Jacques-Louis David (1748–1825), The Emperor Napoleon in his study at the Tuileries, painting, 204 x 125 cm, 1812

David, Napoleon's official painter, made the nearly life-size painting for the Marquess of Dougless, a Scottish lord who admired Napoleon. – For more information on the details of the painting go to: www.nga.gov/kids/napoleon/nap1.html – Vocabulary help: wall decorations (symbols from ancient Greece and Rome) – artist's signature and date – golden bees – burnt-down candles – Civil Code – clock is reading 4:13 – epaulets on the shoulders – lion (ancient Egyptian design) – (military) decoration is pinned to – Sunday uniform of foot soldiers – rapier – desk – vest – book: Plutarch's Lives.

26 **a** Read the information about Napoleon (pp. 44–45) and list the major events in his life.
b Then create a line graph indicating the ups and downs in his career. Write the dates below the line and the events with the explanations above the line. Identify the zenith[7] of his career.

27 Imagine you are an ordinary citizen voting on whether Napoleon should be emperor or not. How would you vote and why, after the French people have just established a republic?
I would (not) vote to make him emperor because ...   I would (not) / want ...

28 Use a Venn diagram (see p. 41) to compare and contrast the Declaration of the Rights of Man (S 9, p. 40) and the articles of the Code Napoleon (S 16).

29 Comment on the Code Napoleon from the perspective of a woman or a child.

30 **Extra research:** Borrow a historical atlas from the school library that has a map showing "Europe in the time of Napoleon":
a Look at S 15 and find out if the Grand Duchy Berg was a part of the French Empire or belonged to an allied or dependent state at that time.
b Make a list of all the countries that were occupied by or dependent states of France.

31 Make an English-German vocabulary list titled "Terms and phrases of international relations".

1 War of Liberation *Befreiungskrieg*
2 abdicate *abdanken*
3 cancer *Krebs*
4 obey sb. *jdm. gehorchen*
5 authority *(hier) Erlaubnis*
6 administer sth. *etwas verwalten*
7 zenith *Zenith, Höhepunkt*

Analysing a formal portrait

Study skills

1. Who, when, where?
Who painted the portrait?
When and **where** was it painted?
Was the painting commissioned[1]?

2. For whom?
Who was the intended **audience**[2] for the painting? Was it for the home or was it an official painting to be hung in an office or a formal setting[3] like a palace?

3. How?
Describing the scene: How is the sitter posed in each portrait? Describe the background and the clothes which the artist chose for the portrait. What objects does the artist use as "props"[4]? What is the light focussed on? Are the colours warm or cool? Dark or bright?

4. Purpose[5] and conclusions[6]
What was the **purpose** of the painting? In a commissioned painting, the painter almost always "celebrated" the sitter's[7] importance and made him or her look like a strong figure.
Does the sitter's pose and the perspective which the painter chose, succeed in making the sitter look grand, important and dignified[8]?
What does the pose say about the sitter's character or his or her (political) importance?
What do the clothes say about his or her personality or self-image or public role?
What does the setting say about his or her position in society, work or accomplishments[9]? How do the "props" help to do this?
Do any of the props have a symbolic meaning?
Is there a connection between the painted objects and his or her accomplishments?
What does the painter not show?
Drawing **conclusions:** For historians, all sources are "windows to past events or ideas and people's lives". What do we see and learn "through" the portrait?

Activate your English

Analysing portraits
The sitter:
The sitter looks friendly/tired/anxious/relaxed/serious/confident/elegant
The painter paints ... realistically ... him or her in profile / in full length
The painter makes the sitter look tall ...
The person is standing/sitting upright
... is wearing / is dressed as ...
his/her feet are both firmly on the ground
his/her arms/hands are ...
he/she seems to be looking at the viewer / into the distance ...
The scene:
The painter shows the person at home / at work in his office / in battle / riding on a horse / with the symbols of his power
The person is surrounded by ...
Conclusions and purpose:
The pose/setting[10] ...
The objects give information about ...
The sitter's level of importance is ...
The sitter stands for ... / symbolizes ...
The painter wants to make the viewer believe that ... / feel ... about ...
The person is presented as ...
The painter's purpose was
... to express the sitter's character by showing/placing/seating ...
... not to express the sitter's character but ...
The portrait makes the person look like ... / shows the person as ... / leaves the impression ... by presenting ...
The painter wanted to make the sitter look (like) ... The artist achieves this by/with ...

32 Photocopy the painting in S 17, p. 45, and label it with the vocabulary.
33 Analyse the portrait in S 17: See the "Study skills" above and **Activate your English**, p. 18 and above.
34 Discuss how much the portrait in S 17 reflects Napoleon's situation in 1812.
35 What image of yourself would you like others to see? Create your own portrait.

1 commission sth. *etwas bestellen*
2 audience *Adressaten*
3 setting *Umfeld, Umgebung, Rahmen*
4 props *Requisiten*
5 purpose *Zweck, Absicht*
6 conclusion *Schlussfolgerung*
7 sitter *Modell*
8 dignified *würdevoll, würdig*
9 accomplishment *Leistung*
10 setting *Umgebung, Bühnenbild*

The French Revolution

Key events

Abolition of the monarchy
Foundation of the Confederation of the Rhine
Fall of the Bastille
French National Assembly
Napoleon is crowned Emperor
End of the Holy Roman Empire of the German Nation
Adoption of the first French Constitution
Introduction of the Civil Code
Beginning of the Wars of Liberation
Execution of King Louis XVI
Napoleon's *coup d'état*
Reign of Terror
Beginning of the Revolutionary Wars
End of Napoleon's Reign
Declaration of the Rights of Man
Declaration of the French Republic

Key terms

Ancien Régime, privilege, absolute monarch, estate, Estates-General, revolution, reform, National Assembly, human and civil rights, republic, Jacobin, *coup d'état*, Consulate, plebiscite

Key personalities

Abbé Sieyès, Marie Olympe de Gouges, Madame Roland, Napoleon

History skills

Analysing a formal portrait *(p. 46)*

Activate your English

Time expressions *(p. 35)*
Causes and effects I *(p. 35)*
Comparing sources *(p. 41)*
Analysing portraits *(p. 46)*

1 Put the key events in the correct chronological order and add the date(s) for each.
2 Practise your vocabulary: Write a sentence about each key event. Example:
Abolition of the monarchy: The monarchy was abolished on 21 September 1792.
3 a Organize the causes that led to the French Revolution into a two- or three-column table.
b Explain them in a two-minute talk (see **Activate your English**, p. 35).
4 Identify the achievements[1] of the French Revolution. Organize your results in a tree diagram or a mind map. Rank them according to their importance. Compare and discuss in class.
5 Imagine you were a painter commissioned by the British navy to paint a portrait of Napoleon on his arrival on St. Helena. What setting and props would you use? Explain your choice.
6 Find out if, in the time of Napoleon, the city or federal state you live in
A *was a part of the French Empire,* B *belonged to an allied or dependent state.*
7 Fill in the biography organizer for Napoleon with information on the following:
Historical background: a brief description of the time when this person was active.
Influences: events and developments during this period that might have had an influence on his or her life and actions.
Actions and accomplishments: the most significant[2] things that he or she did.
Effects (immediate and long-term): the results of his or her actions and accomplishments.

1 achievement *Errungenschaft*
2 significant *bedeutend*

Unit 4 Germany and the rise of new political movements

4.1 Liberalism and nationalism

S1 **Illustration for Ernst Moritz Arndt's song *"Was ist des Deutschen Vaterland?"*, engraving, c 1815**

Vocabulary help: clearing[1] in a forest – soldier who fought in the War of Liberation – sword – farmer in his Sunday suit[2] – plough – kneel before sb./sth. – flag lying on the ground – Martin Luther (the Protestant reformer) with a bible in his hands – Johannes Gutenberg (the inventor of the printing press) – point a finger at sth. – Germania – laurel wreath[3] – halo – shield – German eagle[4] – German oak[5]

Two ideas born in France and exported to Germany

Two political movements – liberalism* and nationalism* – determined[6] European history in the 19th century. They were born in France during the French Revolution and were spread by revolutionary and Napoleonic armies to the rest of Europe (see Unit 3.5). Before the 19th century the nation-state* – a state in which people who share the same history, culture and language live – was nearly non-existent. People of different nationalities lived in one state or territory under one ruler. They thought of themselves as "people from Cologne", or "Catholics", but they were all loyal to "their" King or Duke or Count – no matter if their mother tongue was High German, Low German, Dutch, Danish, Czech or Polish. But they did not call themselves "German".

Key terms

Nationalism[7]

Nationalism arose[8] in Europe during the French Revolution. Nationalists felt
- that each nationality (group of people who speak the same language and have the same history or same culture) should form a state, its nation-state, and
- that this state should include all members of that nationality.

Nationalism is a strong feeling between people that unfortunately can also lead to the exclusion[9] of other people.

Key terms

Liberalism[10]

The ideas of liberalism spread in 19th-century Europe. Liberals demanded
- individual rights and freedom, legal equality, religious toleration and freedom of the press;
- to have a say[11] in government through institutions such as parliament and government ("government of the people, by the people, for the people", as US President Lincoln said in 1863);
- free trade (no taxes on the making of goods and no tariffs[12] on goods when they cross a nation's borders).

1 clearing *Waldlichtung*
2 Sunday suit *Sonntagskleidung*
3 laurel wreath *Lorbeerkranz*
4 German eagle *deutscher Reichsadler*
5 oak *Eiche*
6 determine sth. *etwas bestimmen*
7 nationalism/nationalists/nationalist/nationality/nation-state *Nationalismus/Nationalisten/nationalistisch/Nationalität/Nationalstaat*
8 arise *entstehen*
9 exclusion *Ausschluss*
10 liberalism/liberals *Liberalismus/Liberale*
11 have a say *Mitspracherechte haben*
12 tariff *Zoll*

S 2 **Lorenz Clasen (1812–1899), *"Germania auf der Wacht am Rhein"* (Germania's watch on the Rhine), oil painting, 1860**

Text on the shield: "Das deutsche Schwert beschützt den deutschen Rhein."

S 3 **Alexandre Colin (1798–1873), "The Republic", oil painting, 1848**

On the altar to the left are two stone tablets showing the constitution of the French Republic.

1 Read the text and explain why, before the 18th century, a Prussian did not call himself/herself "German".

2 **Extra research:** After nationalism was "born" about 1800, national symbols like flags, songs, etc. were created in every nation-state. Work in groups and list the modern-day national symbols of the following countries and explain their differences:
A *Federal Republic of Germany* B *United Kingdom* C *USA* D *another country*

3 The paintings S 2 and S 3 show two women who personify[1] Germany and France, together with carefully chosen "props" and settings:

a Divide into two groups, photocopy the painting S 2 or S 3 and label it with all the necessary information listed in **Activate your English** below. Present your results in class.

b Copies of these paintings sold enormously well at the time. Explain why. Consider the following: Why did the painter show the women in these settings with these props? Explain their significance for German and French history (see **Activate your English**).

wanted to become a nation-state ↳ were a nation-state

Activate your English

Describing paintings of 19th-century nationalism

shield
laurels, laurel wreaths (symbolizing immortality[2])
sword (symbolizing justice[3] and strength)
the Rhine (border between France and the German territories)
medieval[4] castles, German eagle
imperial crown (of the Holy Roman Empire)
imperial orb[5], imperial sceptre[6]
flag (French tricolour)
altar (with symbols from the ancient Roman Republic)
fruits (symbolizing affluence[7])
tablets with the constitution of the French Republic
Phrygian head (symbolizing the republic, liberty, but also unrest)
lion (symbolizing strength[8])
broken chain (symbolizing the end of oppression)

1 personify *personifizieren, vermenschlichen*
2 immortality *Unsterblichkeit*
3 justice *Gerechtigkeit*
4 medieval *mittelalterlich*
5 imperial orb *Reichsapfel (mit dem Kreuz – ein Sinnbild christlicher Herrschaft)*
6 sceptre *Szepter, Herrscherstab*
7 affluence *Wohlstand*
8 strength *Kraft*

Analysing written primary sources

Activate your English

Analysing written sources

The source:

was published in …
was written during the time of/when …
relates[4] *to the subject of …*

The author:

argues firstly …, secondly …, finally …
stresses that … not only … but also
points out … / demands … / asks the question …
is convinced that … / justifies … / accepts that … / welcomes that …
is hostile towards[5] *… / opposed to*[6] *… / is critical of … / criticizes … / rejects*[7] *… / resents …*
wants to persuade the audience that/ to …
wants to keep people from[8] *…*
wants us to think …
Referring to …, / Pointing to …, the author wants to …
stanza, verse[9]*, line*[10]

Study skills

Form/type of document:
What type of primary source is it? (See p. 10 for help.)
Author:
Who wrote it?
What do you know about the author?
What was the author's role in the events (e.g. participant, eyewitness, reporter, commentator, official, etc.)?
Date and setting:
When did the author write it?
Where did he or she write it?
Audience:
Who was it written for (e.g. a private person, the general public, the ruler of the country, etc.)?
What do you know about this audience?
Purpose:
What was the purpose or intention of the text (e.g. to inform or persuade others, to describe or demand something, to draw attention to something, to forbid something, to ban something)?
Understanding the source:
What are the key words in the source and what do they mean?
Summarize the main points, ideas, arguments. What point is the author trying to make?
What actions or outcomes[1] does the author expect[2]? From whom?
Evaluating written primary sources as historical sources:
What do we see and learn about the past "through" this source? What historical facts do you learn from it?
Reliability[3]:
Is the source a reliable "window to the past"? How accurate or reliable is … (for example, S 4) as a source of information on … (for example, nationalism in 19th-century Germany)?
What other information might you need for a complete picture? Remember, documents tell us only what the author *thought* happened, or perhaps only what the author *wants* us to think happened.
Bias:
Does the author have a one-sided view of people, ideas or events?
Does he or she leave out some facts?
Are these "blind spots" intentional or are some facts overlooked by mistake or because the person does not know better?

1 outcome *Ergebnis*
2 expect sth. *etwas erwarten*
3 reliability *Glaubwürdigkeit, Zuverlässigkeit*
4 relate (to a subject) *sich (auf ein Thema) beziehen*
5 be hostile towards sb./sth. *jdm./einer Sache feindselig gegenüberstehen*
6 oppose sth./sb. *sich wenden gegen/sich jdm. entgegenstellen*
7 reject sth. *etwas zurückweisen, ablehnen*
8 keep sb. from sth. *jdn. vor etwas bewahren*
9 stanza/verse *Strophe (eines Gedichtes/eines Liedes)*
10 line *Verszeile*

S 4 "Des Deutschen Vaterland", poem by Ernst Moritz Arndt, 1813 (excerpts)

In 1815, the composer Johannes Cotta set the poem to music. Listen to the melody of the song at: www.ingeb.org/Lieder/wasistde.mid

Original version

Was ist des Deutschen Vaterland?
Ist's Preußenland, ist's Schwabenland?
Ist's, wo am Rhein die Rebe blüht?

Ist's, wo am Belt die Möwe zieht?
O nein! nein! nein!
Sein Vaterland muss größer sein.
[...]

Was ist des Deutschen Vaterland?
So nenne mir das große Land!
So weit die deutsche Zunge klingt
Und Gott im Himmel Lieder singt,
Das soll es sein!
Das, wackrer Deutscher, nenne dein!
[...]

Das ist des Deutschen Vaterland,
Wo Zorn vertilgt den welschen Tand,
Wo jeder Franzmann heißet Feind,
Wo jeder Deutsche heißet Freund –
Das soll es sein!
Das ganze Deutschland soll es sein!

English translation

What is the fatherland of the German?
Is it Prussia? Is it Swabia?
Is it where the grapes grow on the Rhine?

Is it where the seagull flies across the Belt?
Ah, no, no, no!
His fatherland must be bigger.
[...]

What is the fatherland of the German?
Name me the great country!
Where the German tongue sounds
And sings songs in God's praise,
That's where it ought to be!
That, brave German, call it yours!
[...]

This is the fatherland of the German
Where anger destroys French nonsense,
Where every Frenchman is called enemy,
Where every German is called friend –
That's where it ought to be!
It ought to be the whole of Germany!

Original from: Heinrich Meisner (ed.), Gedichte von Ernst Moritz Arndt, *Volume 2, Karl Fr. Pfau, Leipzig, 1894, pp. 18–21. Quoted from: www.freiburger-anthologie.ub.uni-freiburg.de/fa/fa.pl, 3 January 2006. English translation simplified by the author.*

4 The poem/song by Ernst Moritz Arndt (S 4) is an example of how important it is to place a primary source in its historical context in order to fully understand it:
a Answer the questions in the "Study skills", p. 50. Help: For the historical context of S 4, see the "Key events", p. 57, and the text, p. 48. For a biography of Arndt, see the Appendix, p. 128. Keep in mind that not all the questions listed in the "Study skills" can be answered.
b Present your ideas on the message of the poem/song to the class.

5 There were a lot of non-German-speaking people in many German states (Polish speakers in Prussia, Czech speakers in Bohemia[1]): Discuss how this song must have made them feel.

6 Write an article about the song for a book on German songs of the 19th century. Describe the historical situation in 1813, the author's possible intention and why the song became a "hit". Do not forget to mention why this song also foreshadowed[2] the problems between the French and the Germans over the next 140 years. Vocabulary help: *At the time when … – In 1813, the situation was such that … – The author intended to / might have wanted to … – The song was popular and appealed to Germans because …*

7 **a** Describe the scene depicted[3] in S 1, p. 48.
b Explain why this illustration was printed together with Arndt's poem on pamphlets in 1815.

8 **a** Work in pairs: Design a poster titled "My Fatherland". Choose figures, props, settings, slogans.
b Compare the different posters with S 1: What has changed in the last two hundred years?

1 Bohemia *Böhmen*
2 foreshadow sth. *etwas vorausahnen lassen*
3 depict sth. *etwas darstellen, abbilden*

4.2 The political reorganization[1] of Germany, 1814–1815

The Congress of Vienna[2], 1814–1815

The Congress of Vienna was a conference of the representatives of the different European states. Their purpose was to reorganize Europe after the Napoleonic Wars. The men who redrew the map of Europe were: Emperor Franz I and Prince von Metternich of Austria, King Friedrich Wilhelm III and Prince von Hardenberg of Prussia, Tsar Alexander I of Russia, Viscount Castlereagh of England, Foreign Minister Talleyrand of France, and the representatives of the secondary[3] European states. All of them feared the principles and the ideas of the French Revolution and opposed the liberal* ideas of democratic government. After the many years of war since 1792 (see p. 38), Europe needed peace. To keep that peace for a long time, a balance of power* and a ring of strong states was created around the defeated France. These changes were quite successful, as they brought stability and peace to central Europe for the next fifty years.

S5 Central Europe after the Congress of Vienna, 1814–1815

Germany and the Congress of Vienna – disappointed hopes

Because the Congress was afraid that France would become dangerous again, it decided to make Prussia stronger and turned the Rhineland and Westphalia, a region soon to be the greatest industrial centre on the Continent, into Prussian provinces. Thus the kingdom of Prussia slowly became the most influential state in Germany.

The Congress did not create one unified Germany with one central government. What was created in 1815 at the Congress of Vienna was only a German Confederation[4]. This Confederation included 39 states: the two great powers, Austria and Prussia; the secondary kingdoms such as Bavaria, Wurtemberg, Saxony, and Hanover; smaller duchies[5], tiny[6] principalities and, finally, the free cities of Hamburg, Bremen, Lübeck, and Frankfurt-on-Main. The new borders in central Europe were a change from the mosaic of the Holy Roman Empire of the German Nation, with its over 300 sometimes very small independent states. However, there were still too many for the German nationalists. They wanted a unified Germany.

9 Read the text and create an event map (see Appendix, p. 142–143): Who did what, when, why, guided by which ideas at the Congress of Vienna?

10 Explain why the Congress believed it was necessary to "redraw the map of Europe" after the Napoleonic wars.

11 England and Russia agreed to make Prussia stronger, but they were against a unified Germany. Discuss their possible reasons.

12 Imagine you are a German nationalist and one of Arndt's friends (see S 4, p. 51). Write him a letter after hearing about the results of the Congress of Vienna. See **Activate your English,** p. 8.

1 reorganization *Umgestaltung*
2 Congress of Vienna *Wiener Kongress*
3 secondary *zweitrangig*
4 German Confederation *Deutscher Bund*
5 duchy *Herzogtum*
6 tiny *winzig*

4.3 The age of Metternich and the *Vormärz* epoch

The German Confederation – A police state?

The new organization of states in central Europe, the German Confederation, was a loose political union of 39 independent states. The union had no central government, only a Federal Diet[1]* that met in Frankfurt-on-Main to consider common laws[2]. They were ruled by absolute monarchs except for the kingdom of Wurtemberg, the duchy of Baden and the four self-governing cities (see S 5). Each state had its own laws, its own defences, and collected its own taxes.

The hopes of many people in 1815 for a unified and democratic Germany were not fulfilled[3]. The demands for unification and liberty were loudest among university students, who formed patriotic groups known as Universal Students' Unions[4]. In October 1817, at a festival at the Wartburg, a castle near Eisenach, they called for greater German unity and democratic reforms.

In March 1819, the student Karl Ludwig Sand assassinated[5] the conservative writer and diplomat August von Kotzebue. The leading government statesman in Vienna, Prince Klemens Metternich, then convinced the princes of the German Confederation that the political order was in extreme danger. The result was a package of measures[6] called the Carlsbad Decrees[7].

Biography

Prince Metternich

Prince Klemens Metternich (1773–1859) was an Austrian diplomat, politician and statesman. After Austria's defeat by Napoleon in 1809, he was made Austrian Foreign Minister. In 1821, he became Chancellor and dominated Austrian and European affairs until the 1840s. In his view, the monarchy* was the ideal political order, and the nobility played the most important role.

S 6 The Carlsbad Decrees, September 1819

University Law:

§ 2 The confederated governments mutually pledge themselves to remove from the universities or other public educational institutions all teachers who, [...] by [presenting] harmful [ideas] [...] subversive of existing governmental institutions, [...] have unmistakably proved their unfitness for the important [position] entrusted to them.

§ 3 Those laws which have for a long period been directed against secret and unauthorized societies in the universities shall be strictly enforced. These laws apply especially to [... the] Universal Students' Union [...].

Press Law:

§ 1 [...] No publication which appears in the form of daily issues, or as a serial not exceeding twenty sheets of printed matter, shall go to press in any state of the union without the [...] approval of the state officials.

Bundes-Universitätsgesetz:

§ 2 Die Bundesregierungen verpflichten sich gegeneinander, Universitäts- und andere öffentliche Lehrer, die [...] durch Verbreitung verderblicher, [...] die Grundlagen der bestehenden Staatseinrichtungen untergrabender Lehren, ihre Unfähigkeit [...] an den Tag gelegt haben, von den Universitäten und sonstigen Lehranstalten zu entfernen.

§ 3 Die seit langer Zeit bestehenden Gesetze gegen geheime oder nicht autorisierte Verbindungen auf den Universitäten sollen in ihrer ganzen Kraft und Strenge aufrechterhalten und [... auf die] Allgemeine Burschenschaft [...] ausgedehnt werden.

Bundes-Pressegesetz:

§ 1 [Es] dürfen Schriften, die in der Form täglicher Blätter oder heftweise erscheinen, desgleichen solche, die nicht über 20 Bogen im Druck stark sind, in keinem deutschen Bundesstaate ohne [...] Genehmhaltung der Landesbehörden [gedruckt] werden.

1 federal Diet *Bundestag*
2 (common) law *(gemeinsames) Gesetz*
3 fulfill sth. *etwas erfüllen*
4 Universal Students' Union *Burschenschaft*
5 assassinate sb. *ein Attentat auf jdn. verüben*
6 package of measures *Maßnahmenbündel*
7 Carlsbad Decrees *Karlsbader Beschlüsse*

Investigating Law:

§ 2 The object of the [established Investigating Committee at Mayence] shall be a [...] extensive investigation of the [...] revolutionary plots and demagogical[1] associations directed against the existing constitution and the internal peace both of the union and of the individual states.

Bundes-Untersuchungsgesetz:

§ 2 Der Zweck [der eingerichteten Zentraluntersuchungskommission in Mainz] ist [... die] umfassende Untersuchung [...] der gegen die bestehende Verfassung und innere Ruhe, sowohl des ganzen Bundes als einzelner Bundesstaaten, gerichteten revolutionären Umtriebe und demagogischen Verbindungen.

Original from: www.documentArchiv.de/nzjh/bduntsges.html, 4 January 2006.
English translation from: James H. Robinson (ed.), Readings in European History, *Volume 2, Ginn, Boston, 1906, pp. 547–550. Quoted from: http://history.hanover.edu/texts/carlsbad.htm, 4 January 2006.*

13 Write a short entry for a students' encyclopaedia about the German Confederation.

14 List the demands of the university students (see the text, p. 53). Explain why the princes of the German Confederation believed that these demands were a danger to the political order.

15 Analyse the Carlsbad Decrees (S 6) (see "Analysing written primary sources", p. 50). Before you start, read the questions on p. 50 and determine which have to be answered.

16 Identify the ideas which the governments had in mind when they spoke of "harmful ideas subversive of existing governmental institutions" (S 6).

17 Describe what happened to the professors who taught these ideas (S 6).

18 Copy and complete the flowchart using keywords. Then explain the chain of events with the help of the structures (1–5):

Congress of Vienna
– no national unity in Germany
– no democratic governments in the German states
Vocabulary: *fail to – (not) lead to*

1 →

German Confederation
– ...
– ...
Vocabulary: *establish – form – create*

2 ↙

University students
– ...
– ...
Vocabulary: *respond to – demand*

3 →

August von Kotzebue
– ...
Vocabulary: *assassinate*

4 ↙

Metternich and leaders of the Confederation
– ...
– ...
Vocabulary: *convince – argue – introduce – impose*

5 →

Carlsbad Decrees
– ... illegal for professors to ...
– ... illegal for students to ...
– ... illegal for everybody to ...
Vocabulary: *make it / be / become illegal to – not allowed to – allow to*

Vocabulary 1–5: outcome/result – cause – bring about – provoke – in connection with – lead to – trigger – cause – provoke – as a consequence – in reaction to – thus – therefore

19 The year is 1820 and a younger student asks you, a student in your third year at Humboldt University in Berlin, why he can't join one of the students' unions he has heard so much about. When you tell him, he is completely shocked. Write down your answer.

20 **Extra research:** Write a short biography of Metternich. Pay attention to his political ideas (see p. 53).

1 demagogical *demagogisch, hetzerisch*

4.4 The crisis of the 1840s

Build-up to a crisis

Until about 1850, Germany was still a country of villages and farms. Far more people worked on the land than in any other trade[1]. Non-agricultural products were usually produced in people's own homes or in small workshops. The number of factories with machinery driven by water or by steam engines was small and concentrated in Saxony and the Prussian part of the Rhineland. Because jobs outside agriculture were rare, there was not enough employment for the fast-growing population, especially in the rural areas. The import of cheaper British goods (see Unit 2.1) ruined many people working in the textile and clothing trades. As a result, wages and the standard of living for the majority of Germans declined until the 1840s.

S7 ***"Das Elend in Schlesien"*** **(Misery in Silesia), cartoon in *Fliegende Blätter*, Munich, 1848**

Revolt in Silesia

In 1844, in several towns in Silesia, 3000 frustrated handloom weavers[2] attacked bookkeepers[3] and destroyed the private homes of their employers. They accused them of exploitation[4] and of constantly cutting their wages. The Prussian government sent the military to crush[5] the protests, and the weavers were given long prison sentences[6].

The crop failures of 1845–1847 and mass poverty (pauperism*)

The harvests[7] of 1845–1846 were very poor in the German states. As a result, food prices rose dramatically. Especially in the spring of 1847, people in the towns and cities were starving[8]. Private organizations and the churches tried to help the starving population. The governments, however, did not help much and mostly very late – often only after violent food riots. In 1846 it was calculated that 50–60 per cent of the Prussian population lived on the edge of starvation[9]. In the country and the towns, among workers and peasants, there was growing unrest. The poor demanded social justice and a better life for themselves. However, the governments in the German states did very little for people who were out of work, hungry or homeless.

More power to the people?

In 1848, the majority of people in the German states were dissatisfied. The educated middle class[10] – lawyers, doctors, journalists, teachers, civil servants[11] – and wealthy businessmen, factory owners, bankers and merchants were not hungry or homeless, but were frustrated because of their lack of power and influence in politics. Liberal* and national* ideas became more and more attractive for them. Their calls for a voice in politics became louder despite censorship and controls. So-called Democrats even went so far to demand a republic where the head of the state was elected by the people. But only a minority believed that lower-class people[12] – peasants, craftsmen and industrial workers – should also have the right to vote.

1 trade *Gewerbe*
2 handloom weaver *Handweber*
3 bookkeeper *Buchhalter*
4 exploitation *Ausbeutung*
5 crush sth. *etwas niederschlagen*
6 prison sentence *Gefängnisstrafe*
7 harvest *Ernte*
8 starve *hungern, verhungern*
9 on the edge of starvation *am Rande des Hungertods*
10 middle class *Mittelschicht*
11 civil servant *Beamter*
12 lower-class people *Angehörige der Unterschicht*

S 8 Population in Germany, 1816–1910 (in millions)

	1816	1864	1910	Growth (index 1816 = 100)
Total	**24.8**	**39.4**	**64.9**	**262**
Berlin	0.2	0.6	2.0	1000
Pomerania	0.7	1.4	1.7	243
Silesia	1.9	3.5	5.2	274
Schleswig-Holstein	0.7	1.0	1.6	229
Rhineland	1.9	3.4	7.1	374
Bavaria	3.6	4.8	6.9	192
Hamburg	0.2	0.3	1.0	500

From: Hans D. Schmid (ed.), Fragen an die Geschichte, Volume 3, Cornelsen, Berlin, 1981, p. 201.

S 9 Birth rate* and death rate* in Germany, 1815–1969

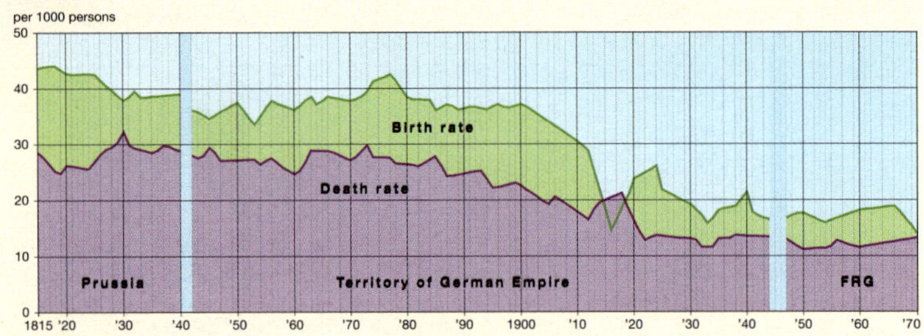

From: Herman Aubin/Wolfgang Zorn (ed.), Handbuch der deutschen Wirtschafts- und Sozialgeschichte, Volume 2, Klett Cotta, Stuttgart, 1976, p. 24.

S 10 The *Brockhaussche Enzyklopädie für die gebildeten Stände* on mass poverty, 1841

Pauperismus ist ein neu erfundener Ausdruck für eine höchst bedeutsame und unheilvolle Erscheinung[1], die man im Deutschen durch die Worte Massenarmut oder Armentum wiederzugeben versucht hat. Es handelt sich dabei nicht um die natürliche Armut, wie sie immerfort einige befallen mag, sondern der Pauperismus ist da vorhanden, wo eine zahlreiche Volksklasse sich durch die angestrengteste Arbeit[2] höchstens das notdürftigste Auskommen verdienen[3] kann, auch sich dessen nicht sicher ist, in der Regel von der Geburt an und auf Lebenszeit dieser Lage geopfert ist und keine Aussichten der Besserung hat.

From: Hans-Ulrich Wehler, Deutsche Gesellschaftsgeschichte 1815–1845, C.H. Beck, München, 1987, p. 283.

Activate your English

Talking about population statistics

birth/death rate
number of births/deaths per 1 000 inhabitants
rise/decline sharply/slightly by ... per cent
sudden population growth/decline
gap between ... and ...
surplus[4] of ...

21 **a** Working in pairs and using the skills from "Analysing statistics", p. 74, and **Activate your English** to the right, write a paragraph describing the statistical information in S 8 or S 9.
b Present your results in class.

22 **Extra research:** Make assumptions[5] to explain the trends in the statistics in S 9. It may help to first gather (online) reference material on population trends.

23 Imagine and discuss how the employers of handloom weavers in Silesia (see p. 55) defended themselves against the accusations of their workers.

24 Explain the cartoonist's point of view of the events in Silesia (S 7).

25 Look at the text and list how the governments of the German states reacted to the crises of the 1840s.

26 **a** Read source S 10: Is it a primary or secondary source? Give reasons.
b List the things you can learn from it.

27 The middle class, who demanded the right to vote, was unwilling to give the same right to lower-class people. Give possible reasons (see the text).

28 In the summer of 1847, a foreign correspondent of the *London Illustrated News* travels through the German states. Write his article called "Is there a cure for German gloom[6]?" Add appropriate[7] pictures (use your favorite search engine to find pictures).

1 Erscheinung *phenomenon*
2 angestrengteste Arbeit *efforts*
3 das notdürftigste Auskommen verdienen *earn a scanty living*
4 surplus *Überschuss*
5 make an assumption *eine Vermutung anstellen*
6 gloom *gedrückte Stimmung, Trübsinn*
7 appropriate *geeignet, passend*

Unit revision

Germany and the rise of new political movements

Key events

1813–1814 Wars of Liberation
1814–1815 Congress of Vienna
1815–1866 German Confederation
1817 Festival on the Wartburg
1819 Carlsbad Decrees
1844 Protests of Silesian Weavers [saɪˈliːziən]
1845–1847 Crop failures

Key terms

monarchical system / monarchy, liberalism, nationalism, nation-state, Federal Diet, balance of power, pauperism, birth rate, death rate

Key personalities

Prince Metternich

History skills

Analysing primary written sources (*pp. 50–51*)

Activate your English

Describing paintings of 19th-century nationalism (*p. 49*)
Analysing written sources (*p. 50*)
Talking about population statistics (*p. 56*)

S 11 ***"Der Denkerclub"*, German cartoon, unknown artist, c 1820**

to be muzzled = einen Maulkorb tragen

1 Use the key events and key terms to describe the situation in Germany, 1815–1848.
2 The painting *"Germania auf der Wacht am Rhein"* (S 2) was made about 40 years after Arndt wrote *"Was ist des Deutschen Vaterland?"* (S 4). Discuss whether German feelings towards the French changed in those years.
3 Add to your vocabulary file (see Unit 2, p. 31, Task 5) the terms in this unit for describing the different social groups in German society.
4 Now take the role of a textbook author: Which of the following sentences would you choose to explain the cartoon in S 11? Give reasons.
A *The message of the cartoon is "Silence is golden in 1820".*
B *The cartoonist shows his opposition to the removal of professors from the universities.*
C *As a liberal, the artist demands a free press.*
D *The cartoonist voices criticism of the Carlsbad Decrees.*
E *The cartoonist shows the consequences of Kotzebue's assassination.*
5 Look at pp. 55–56. Make a cause-and-effect diagram to explain mass poverty in Germany in the 1840s.
6 Using a two-column chart, list the political and economic reasons why different groups of people were dissatisfied during the *Vormärz* epoch in Germany.

Unit 5
The Revolution of 1848–1849 in Germany

5.1 Onto the barricades

S1 The revolution in print – Berlin in March 1848, lithograph by Gustav Kühn, Neuruppin, 1848

This lithograph is from the series "Das merkwürdige Jahr 1848. Europäische Freiheitskämpfe. Eine neue Bilderzeitung[1]". *Kühn, a successful businessman, made prints (lithographs) of the revolutionary events in Germany and other European countries within days after each event. They were printed with very little text on the most modern printing machines and sold cheaply by travelling salesmen all over Germany. These early "comics" gave information on world events to people who could not pay for books and newspapers or could not read at all.*

For unity and freedom

At the end of the 1840s, Germans tried to change their political system but failed[2]. The time seemed right, the people were ready and they knew what they wanted (see pp. 55–56) – so what went wrong?

The spark[3] for the revolution was the news of unrest in Paris, where the French King Louis Philippe was forced to abdicate on 24 February 1848. In contrast to the French Revolution the unrest quickly spread to Germany, not just because news now travelled fast by telegraph (invented in the 1830s), but because the time was ripe[4] for rebellion against the old order.

The first demonstrations took place in Mannheim on 27 February 1848 with thousands of people demanding political refoms. From there they spread to Heidelberg, Karlsruhe and Cologne, where one-third of the population was on public poor relief[5], and on to Frankfurt-on-Main and Munich on 4 March. On the same day, peasant unrest broke out in the Black Forest and spread along the Rhine into the Odenwald and the Taubergrund, into Franconia and to the area around Nuremberg. There, peasants burned castles, administration buildings and tax records. The violent unrest lasted into the autumn.

The surprisingly strong popular support for these movements forced rulers in the smaller German states to give in to[6] many of the so-called March Demands[7]. Liberal governments[8] (March Ministries) were installed in Saxony on 16 March and in Bavaria on 20 March.

1 Bilderzeitung *pictorial broadsheet*
2 fail *scheitern*
3 spark *Funke*
4 ripe *reif*
5 poor relief *Armenhilfe, Fürsorge*
6 give in to sth. *etwas nachgeben*
7 March Demands *Märzforderungen*
8 Liberal governments *Märzministerien*

What happened in Austria and Prussia?

The overall success of the revolution depended, however, on events in the two major German states, Austria and Prussia. In Vienna, violent demonstrators demanded the dismissal of the hated Chancellor Prince Metternich (see Biography, p. 53). When he offered his resignation[1] on 13 March, Ferdinand I (emperor, 1835–1848) accepted it at once. A new constitution was drawn up which guaranteed freedom of the press and basic civil rights. The revolutionaries seemed to have won. In Berlin, street fighting broke out on 18 March. After more than 200 people were killed, Friedrich Wilhelm IV (king, 1840–1858) ordered the withdrawal[2] of the 15,000 troops around the city. In his speech "To my dear Berliners" the next day, the king apologized[3] for the dead and placed himself under the protection of the citizens' militia. Later, he accepted practically all the demonstrators' demands: free parliamentary elections, a constitution and freedom of the press. He also promised that Prussia would lead the way to a united Germany. On the 23 March, Prussia placed its March Ministry under the rule of Rhineland bankers and businessmen Ludolf Camphausen and David Hansemann.

1 resignation *Rücktritt*
2 withdrawal *Rückzug*
3 apologize to sb. for sth. *sich bei jmd. für etwas entschuldigen*

S2 Gravestones in the cemetery[4] of Berlin-Friedrichshain, photographs, c. 2000

The civil victims of 18 March 1848 street fighting in Berlin were buried[5] four days later in a new cemetery in Friedrichshain. A crowd of 20,000, carrying the revolutionary flag of black, red and yellow, attended the burial.

S3 March Demands by 160 tenant farmers[6] to the Duke of Brunswick, 1848

A group of 160 tenant farmers called on the Duke of Brunswick to grant[7] them the following (published in the Osnabrücker Tageblatt, *16 April 1848):*

1. End of the head tax[8].
2. End of the practise of buying substitutes[9] for military service.
3. Representation in the state assembly and the village council[10].
4. Freedom from the school tax and other church taxes and improvements in the common schools.
5. End of all unpaid road work.
6. Enough land in the divided and undivided common lands[11] for free use.
7. Regulation of rental conditions[12]; no more unpaid service[13].
8. A public institution for the care of old and invalid tenant farmers.

From: Ohio Department of Education (ed.), Learning About Our World: Germany, *www-lib.iupui.edu/kade/unit19/apen19-k.html, 6 January 2006 (last update: 14 April 1997). Abridged by the author.*

4 cemetery *Friedhof*
5 bury sb. *jdn. beerdigen*
6 tenant farmer *Pachtbauer*
7 grant sth. *gestatten*
8 head tax *Personensteuer (im Gegensatz zur prozentualen Einkommenssteuer)*
9 substitute *Ersatz*
10 village council *Gemeinderat*
11 common lands *Allmende (Land, das allen zur Verfügung stand)*
12 rental condition *Pachtbedingungen*
13 unpaid services *unentgeltliche Dienstleistungen (für Adelige)*

S 4 March Demands by Dresden citizens to the Saxon government, flyer[1], 7 March 1848

German version

Wir (erwarten) von der sächsischen Staatsregierung: [...]

1. Freiheit der Presse. [...]
2. Freiheit des religiösen Bekenntnisses. [...]
3. Freiheit des Versammlungs- und Vereinsrechtes. [...]
4. Gesetzliche Sicherstellung der Person gegen willkürliche Verhaftung. [...]
5. Verbesserung des Wahlgesetzes [...] durch Herabsetzung des Zensus.
6. [...] Schwurgericht.
7. Vereidigung des Militärs auf die Verfassung.
8. Verminderung des stehenden Heeres. [...]
9. Vertretung der deutschen Völker bei dem Deutschen Bunde.
10. Lossagung [...] von den Karlsbader Beschlüssen. [...]

Wir zweifeln nicht an dem landesväterlichen Sinne des allverehrten, allgeliebten Königs. [...] Es lebe der König!

[Unterzeichnet wurden diese Forderungen von Handwerksmeistern, Rechtsanwälten, Ärzten und Fabrikanten.]

English translation

We (expect) the Saxon government to fulfil the following demands: [...]

1. Freedom of the press. [...]
2. Freedom of religious beliefs. [...]
3. Freedom of assembly. [...]
4. Laws against arbitrary arrests. [...]
5. Improvements of the electoral law [...] by lower property qualifications. [...]
6. [...] Trial by jury.
7. The army must be sworn in on the constitution
8. Reduction of the standing army. [...]
9. Representation of the German peoples in the German Confederation.
10. Breakaway from the Carlsbad Decrees. [...]

We have full confidence in the patriarchal spirit of our highly respected and beloved king. [...] Long live the king!

[These demands were signed by master craftsmen, lawyers, doctors and entrepreneurs[2].]

Original from: Karl Obermann, Flugblätter der Revolution 1848/49. Dokumente, *dtv, München, 1972, pp. 49–50. English translation by the author.*

S 5 March Demands by workers in Cologne to the City Council and the King of Prussia, pamphlet, 3 March 1848

1. Gesetzgebung und Verwaltung durch das Volk, da ein freies Volk [...] sich nicht mehr im Interesse einzelner ausbeuten lassen will [...], allgemeines Wahlrecht und allgemeine Wählbarkeit[3].
2. Unbedingte Freiheit der Rede und Presse.
3. Aufhebung des stehenden Heeres und Einführung einer allgemeinen Volksbewaffnung mit vom Volke gewählten Führern. [...]
4. Freies Vereinigungsrecht.
5. Schutz der Arbeit und Sicherstellung der menschlichen Bedürfnisse[4] für alle. [...] Nur die schlechte Verteilung[5] der Arbeit und ihre Ausbeutung im Interesse Einzelner verhindert es, dass genug hervorgebracht wird, um die Bedürfnisse aller Einzelnen zu befriedigen. Es ist daher Sache des Staates, die Produktion dem Interesse der Einzelnen zu entreißen und sie im Interesse aller zu leiten[6]. Jeder Mensch hat ein Recht auf Arbeit[7] sowie auf einen seinen Bedürfnissen angemessenen Lohn[8].
6. Vollständige Erziehung aller Kinder auf öffentliche Kosten.

From: Karl Obermann, Flugblätter der Revolution 1848/49. Dokumente, *dtv, München, 1972, pp. 47–48.*

1 flyer *Flugblatt*
2 entrepreneur *Unternehmer*
3 Wählbarkeit *eligibility*
4 Bedürfnisse sicherstellen *meet the needs*
5 Verteilung *distribution*
6 leiten *direct*
7 Recht auf Arbeit *right to work*
8 angemessener Lohn *adequate wages*

1 What happened in Germany in March 1848? Read the information on pp. 58–59 and look at the map in S 7, p. 63. Then organize the information in a chart, e.g. an event chain, a cause-and-effect diagram, or an event map (see Appendix, p. 142–143).

2 Define the terms "Liberal Government" and "March Demands".

3 Working in pairs, look at S 1 and make notes on the following questions (see **Activate your English**):

a Is the lithograph in S 1 a primary or a secondary source? Explain.

b What do you know about the artist? How was he involved in the events (e.g. as a participant, an eye-witness, a reporter, an official)?

c Identify the intended audience.

d Describe the scene (the setting, the people, their clothes and activities).

e What side do you think the artist is on – the street fighters' or the soldiers' side? Give reasons for your answer.

f How reliable is the lithograph as a source of information on what happened in Berlin on 18 March 1848?

Activate your English

Describing a street fighting scene

order sb. to fire *jdm. zu schießen befehlen*
shoot at the crowd *in die Menge schießen*
shoot sb. dead *jdn. erschießen*
hide sb. or sth. / hide from sb. *jdn. oder etwas verstecken / sich vor jdm. verstecken*
take away an injured / a wounded person *eine verletzte Person forttragen*
wave a flag *eine Flagge schwenken/hissen*
… is/are (dressed) in / wearing everyday clothes … *ist/sind in Alltagskleidung gekleidet*
… is/are (dressed) in uniform … *ist/sind in Uniform gekleidet*
paving stone *Pflasterstein*

4 **a** Photocopy S 3, S 4 and S 5, then mark in all three sources the economic demands in green and political demands in yellow.

b Comment on your findings: Are you surprised or did you expect these results?

c Use a Tri-Venn diagram (see illustration) to compare and contrast the three groups' demands. List the similarities in the area where the three circles overlap and the differences in each circle under their correct heading. How might similarities and differences be explained?

Tri-Venn diagram

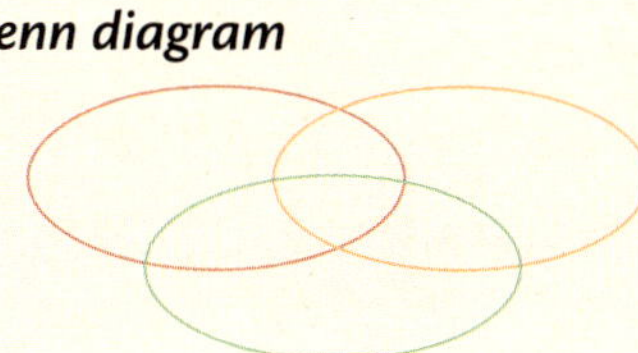

5 Write at least three conditional sentences based on the demands of the Cologne workers in S 5. For example: *If … had been abolished, then …*
If the workers had had the right to…, then they would have been able to … / could have …

6 Discuss which of the three groups' demands (S 3–S 5) are the most radical or extreme, i.e. which could change the society the most.

7 Working in pairs, imagine you are a textbook author:

a Study the gravestone inscriptions in S 2 and identify which social classes and/or groups the dead belonged to (check your own German-English vocabulary files). Which of the following sentences do you find most accurate and why?

A *Most of the Berlin revolutionaries in 1848 came from the city or the surroundings of Berlin.*
B *The Revolution in 1848 was a "peasant revolution".*
C *The Berlin victims of 18 March 1848 were mainly unskilled workers.*
D *Most of the revolutionaries in Germany had a university education.*
E *The Revolution in 1848 was a "skilled worker's revolution".*
F *On 18 March, Berlin women did not become active in the street fights.*

b Write a short paragraph about the different groups among the population that actively supported the protests. Explain their different actions (see pp. 58–59 and sources S 2–S 5).

5.2 The National Assembly and the failed Revolution

S6 Meeting of the National Assembly in St Paul's Church, engraving, 1848

Above the assembly is Philipp Veit's oil painting "Germania"; at the speaker's stand is the president of the National Assembly, Heinrich von Gagern.

The National Assembly meets in St Paul's Church[1]

Victory in the individual German states had been easy. But the revolutionaries had a more ambitious[2] aim: a unified Germany. To plan their strategy, 585 freely elected representatives from all the states (with voting rights for about 85 per cent of all men over 25 years, and no voting rights for farm and factory workers, nor for women), met in St Paul's Church in Frankfurt-on-Main. So many of the representatives were professors or had a university education that it was called a "parliament of professors"*. But there were no workers or peasants among them.

On 18 May 1848, this first German National Assembly began planning a unified and democratic Germany with a central government, a liberal constitution and a catalogue of civil rights.

Formulating the catalogue of basic civil rights was the most important task of the Assembly and discussions lasted until October. The catalogue was finally published in December 1848.

Setbacks[3]

While the representatives in St Paul's Church discussed the catalogue of civil rights, a provisional[4] central government was installed in Frankfurt. But this government had no territory, no civil servants, no police force, no military and no judiciary. The first unexpected shock for them came when other European countries and the governments in the 39 German states did not recognize the newly formed state.

Another setback was the problem of Schleswig-Holstein. Denmark wanted to annex these two territories, whose populations were mostly German. Prussia went to war to prevent this but soon agreed to an armistice[5] after Russia, Sweden and England put pressure on Prussia to withdraw its troops. It seemed as if these German-speaking provinces would then become Danish. The National Assembly, whose aim was to create a state which included all Germans, voted against accepting the peace treaty on 5 September 1848. But because it had no influence and

1 St Paul's Church *Frankfurter Paulskirche*
2 ambitious *ehrgeizig*
3 (suffer a) setback *(einen) Rückschlag (erleiden)*
4 provisional *provisorisch, vorläufig*
5 armistice *Waffenstillstand*

S7 Unrest in Europe in 1848

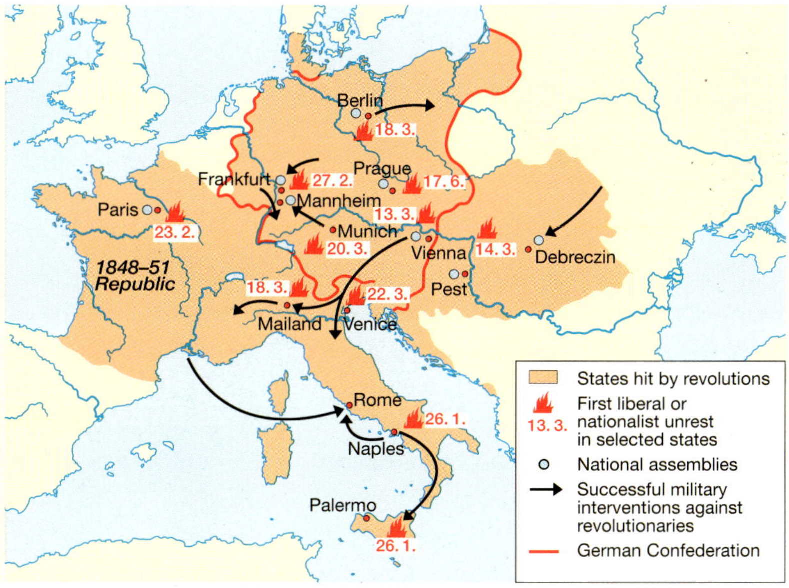

could not change Prussia's mind, the National Assembly changed its vote[1] on 16 September, and Schleswig-Holstein was lost to Denmark. This hurt the National Assembly's reputation[2] with the German public.

A third setback came the next day, when radicals violently tried to break up the National Assembly, install a more radical one and declare a republic. Because the National Assembly had no police force and no military, it had to ask for protection by troops of the rulers whose powers it had tried to limit.

S8 Present-day photograph of St Paul's Church

Discussions on the future German constitution

Discussions on the constitution started in the National Assembly in the autumn of 1848:

- Should the new Germany be a hereditary monarchy[3], have an elected monarch, or even become a republic?
- Should it include Austria to create a "Greater Germany"[4]*, or exclude Austria in a "Little Germany"[5]*, with Prussia as the leading state?
- Should it be a federation* of independent states or have a strong central government?

The Revolution fails

While the Assembly in Frankfurt-on-Main was still discussing the problem of "Greater Germany" or "Little Germany", the Prussian king and the Austrian emperor showed what they had learned from the events in Frankfurt in September.

In October 1848, imperial[6] Austrian troops bombarded Vienna and defeated the radicals in the city. Two thousand people lost their lives and many were arrested and imprisoned. All the democratic and liberal achievements were undone[7] by the emperor.

On 10 November 1848, General von Wrangel, acting on the orders of the Prussian King Friedrich Wilhelm IV, entered Berlin with 13,000 troops and met no resistance. The elected Prussian state parliament was dissolved on 12 December.

Although Prussia, Austria and many other German states completely undid all the achievements of the March Revolution, the discussions in Frankfurt-on-Main continued, more and more out of touch with reality. On 28 March 1849, the draft[8] of the constitution was passed by the National Assembly. The new Germany would be a constitutional monarchy*, and the King of Prussia the hereditary head of state (*Kaiser* = Emperor).

1 vote *(hier) Abstimmungsergebnis*
2 reputation *Ruf*
3 hereditary monarchy *Erbmonarchie*
4 Greater Germany *Großdeutschland*
5 Little Germany *Kleindeutschland*
6 imperial *kaiserlich*
7 undo an achievement *eine Leistung, ein Erfolg zunichte machen*
8 draft *Entwurf*

On 2 April 1849, a delegation of the National Assembly met with the Prussian King Friedrich Wilhelm IV in Berlin and offered him the crown of the Emperor of the new Little Germany under the new constitution. Friedrich Wilhelm politely told the delegation that he felt honoured. But he was King of Prussia "by the grace of God", and so he did not accept the idea that his legal government needed the "consent of the governed"[1]. Later, in a letter, he wrote what he really thought of the crown that had been offered to him: that he felt deeply insulted by a crown "from the gutter"[2] and "disgraced[3] by the stink of revolution, baked of dirt and mud". The German revolutionaries had failed, and the National Assembly slowly dissolved.

S9 Front page of the German magazine *Der Spiegel*, 1998

Wilhelm IV imposes a constitution on Prussia

In 1850, King Wilhelm IV imposed[4] the first constitution on Prussia – a constitution which was undemocratic but granted civil rights and remained unchanged until 1918. Three classes of voters elected about 430 representatives to the Prussian parliament. Prussia's Three-Class Election System* *(Dreiklassenwahlrecht)* reserved one third of the seats in parliament for the top tax-paying group of voters, one third for the middle group and one third for the poor, with the result that the few big land and factory owners were overrepresented.

8 In 1848–1849, the National Assembly tried to create a unified and democratic Germany. This was pioneer work and an extremely difficult task. Using different charts (see Appendix, pp. 142–143), gather and organize the information from the previous pages on:
a the things which had to be created to achieve this aim
b the problems/setbacks the National Assembly ran into
c the causes and effects of the setbacks.

9 **a** In a two-column chart, compare and contrast what happened in the National Assembly in St Paul's Church and what happened "outside".

Events/developments in the German territories	***Events/developments in the National Assembly***
…	…

b Discuss in class what went wrong.

10 List the achievements of the March Revolution which were later undone by the governments of the German territories (see p. 62).

11 Make a radio broadcast titled "This day in history: 2 April 1849":
Explain to your listeners what happened and the reasons why the Prussian King Friedrich Wilhelm IV did not accept the crown offered to him by the National Assembly to become the Emperor (i.e. head of state) of a unified and democratic Germany.

12 Questioning[5] secondary sources: Look at the cover page of *Der Spiegel* (S9). Discuss in class what the magazine means by *"Die halbe Revolution"*. Do you agree with this interpretation of what happened in 1848? (see **Activate your English**, p. 8)

1 consent of the governed *Zustimmung der Regierten*
2 gutter *Gosse, Rinnstein*
3 disgrace sb./sth. *jdn./etwas entehren*
4 impose sth. *etwas auferlegen*
5 question sth. *etwas hinterfragen, prüfen*

5.3 Emigration[1] to America

Mass emigration

Many Germans who had hoped for the success of the revolution were unwilling to return to life in an unchanged Germany, and so they emigrated*. Some left for a new life in Brazil, Argentina or Chile, but most of them went to the United States. Coming mainly from Westphalia and the Rhineland as well as from Mecklenburg and Eastern Prussia, they settled in the Midwestern states of Illinois, Indiana, Michigan, Ohio and Wisconsin. This was a region where they could buy farm land at acceptable prices and where German-language churches and some German schools already existed.

1 emigration *Auswanderung, Emigration*
2 flee *flüchten*
3 secretary of the interior *Innenminister*
4 pauper labor *Billigarbeiter*
5 hold office *politisches Amt einnehmen*

Biography

Carl Schurz

Carl Schurz was born in Cologne in 1829. As a student at the University of Bonn, he became involved in radical politics and took part in the 1848 German Revolution. He was forced to flee[2] and went to Switzerland, France and then England before emigrating to the United States in 1852. Only 16 years later, Schurz became a US senator for Missouri. He then served as secretary of the interior[3] from 1877 to 1881. He died in New York City in 1906.

S 10 Emigrants on a ship to America, engraving from *Harper's Weekly*, USA, 1878

S 11 Advertisement for the short-lived newspaper *American Patriot*, Boston, 1852

The newspaper favoured, among other things, "The protection of American mechanics against foreign pauper labor"[4] and was opposed to "foreigners holding office"[5]. One of the slogans on the banners of the people coming off the ships says "Fradom of Spache and Action!".

S 12 German Emigration, 1820–1859

Years	Number of emigrants	Emigrants to the USA (in % of all German emigrants)
1820–1824	9800	19.4
1825–1829	12,700	29.9
1830–1834	51,100	76.9
1835–1839	94,000	91.0
1840–1844	110,600	90.9
1845–1849	308,200	92.4
1850–1854	728,300	89.8
1855–1859	372,000	86.5

From: Peter Marschalck, Deutsche Überseewanderung im 19. Jahrhundert, *Klett, Stuttgart, 1973, p. 48.*

S 13 Immigration to the USA, 1820–1899

	in millions	in %
Great Britain	3.0	16.1
Ireland	3.8	20.5
Italy	0.9	5.0
Germany	5.0	26.7
Scandinavia	1.4	7.5
Other countries	4.6	24.2
Total	18.7	100.0

From: US Census Bureau (ed.), Historical Statistics of the United States – Colonial Times to 1957, *Washington, D.C., 1960, pp. 56–60.*

S 14 The German emigrant John Kerler (1800–1885) wrote in a letter after settling in Wisconsin in 1849:

I would prefer the civilized, cultured Germany to America if it were still in its former orderly condition, but as it has turned out recently, and with the threatening prospect for the future of religion and politics, I prefer America. Here I can live a more quiet and undisturbed life. One lives in such safety here in the country that you seldom lock your door at night, leaving cattle[1], wagons, ploughs[2], everything, out in the open without having to fear thievery.

From: www.spartacus.schoolnet.co.uk/USAEgermany.htm, 20 September 2005.

13 Write a paragraph describing and explaining the statistical information in S 12 and S 13 (see **Activate your English**, pp. 9 and 56).

14 Review the reasons why Germans were dissatisfied during the *Vormärz* epoch (p. 61, Task 6). Then read the information on "Mass emigration" on p. 65 and John Kerler's letter in S 14. Make a two-column chart showing what the emigrants were searching for and what they were escaping from (the "pull and push" factors of German mass emigration in the 1850s).

15 Evaluate John Kerler's letter (S 14) as a source on German emigration to the USA in 1849. For help with evaluating sources, see "History skills", pp. 10 and 50.

16 **a** Imagine being a reporter for the US magazine *Harper's Weekly* on board the *Star of the West*, 6 July 1850, sailing from Bremen to Boston with hundreds of emigrants from German-speaking territories. Write an interview with one of them (S 10).

b Look at S 11. Discuss the possible difficulties this emigrant has to expect. Pay attention to the slogan "Fradom of Spache and Action!"

c Evaluate S 11 as a "window to the past". What do you learn through this source? How accurate or reliable is S 11 as a source of information?

17 **Extra research:** Choose one of the following:

a Collect information on Carl Schurz and present your findings under the heading "Carl Schurz – a German-American: From political refugee to Minister of the Interior".
Tip: *www.spartacus.schoolnet.co.uk/USAEgermany.htm*

b "From Hamburg and Bremen to America". Collect information on travelling "steerage"[3]: ships, routes, lengths of voyages, conditions on board, etc.
Tip: *fhh1.hamburg.de/fhh/internetausstellungen/emigration/englisch/emigration_index.htm*
www.deutsche-auswanderer-datenbank.de/History.47.0.html

1 cattle *Vieh, Rinder*
2 plough *Pflug*
3 steerage *Zwischendeck (Dritte-Klasse-Ticket)*

Unit revision

The German Revolution of 1848–1849

Key events

1840–1861	Friedrich Wilhelm IV, King of Prussia
March 1848	March Demands March Ministries
May 1848–1849	National Assembly in St Paul's Church, Frankfurt-on-Main
Oct–Dec 1848	Catalogue of civil liberties
March 1849	Constitution

Key terms

Greater Germany / Little Germany, constitutional monarchy, federation, Three-Class Election System, parliament of professors, emigration

Key personalities

Carl Schurz

Activate your English

Describing a street-fighting scene *(p. 61)*

S 15 Saxonian revolutionaries are shot, German painting, unknown artist, 1849

1 Add appropriate verbs or nouns to make sentences from the Key events. Examples:
1840–1861 Friedrich Wilhelm IV, King of Prussia, ruled from …
The Reign of Friedrich Wilhelm IV lasted from … until …

2 Find new terms from this chapter to add to your German-English vocabulary files:
a different social classes and groups (Unit 2, p. 31, Task 5; Unit 4, p. 57, Task 3)
b how people "resist" and the effects of their resistance (Unit 1, p. 23, Task 3 b)
c suffrage (Unit 2, p. 30, Task 14)
d political terms and phrases (Unit 1, p. 12, Task 15 a).

3 The Revolution of 1848 was the first attempt to establish a democratic system in Germany. Gather words and phrases having to do with a democratic system of government into a mind map (e.g. institutions and offices, bill of rights, etc.).

4 Practising vocabulary: make crossword puzzles (see p. 23, Task 5) and vocabulary flash cards (see p. 31, Task 1) for the Key events and Key terms.

5 Translate the following expressions, then use each to formulate a complete sentence:
A … *wollten nicht länger ausgebeutet werden …*
B … *wurden ermutigt durch …*
C … *wurden niedergebrannt durch …*
D … *wurden annektiert …*
E … *mussten durch … gerettet werden*
F … *wurde die Krone angeboten*
G … *wurde durch die Entscheidung/Ablehnung der Krone schwer enttäuscht*
H … *wurden zunichte gemacht durch …*
I … *wurde nach Hause geschickt*
J … *wurde bombardiert*

6 **a** Organize the causes that led to the 1848 Revolution in Germany into a three-column table showing the long- and short-term causes and the triggers. Discuss your conclusions in class.
b Read the information on the course of the Revolution again and note the date when it was clear that the Revolution had failed. Identify possible causes for the failure of the Revolution.

Unit 6 Germany on its way to an industrial society

6.1 The *Zollverein* – A successful economic union?

S1

"Gränzverlegenheit", **German cartoon, artist unknown, published in *Fliegende Blätter*, first half of the 19th century**

„Sie sehen, Herr Gränzwächter, daß ich nix zu verzolle hab', denn was hinte auf'm Wagen ist, hat die Lippi'sche Gränz noch nit überschritten, in der Mitt' ist nix, und was vorn drauf is, ist schon wieder über der Lippischen Gränze drüben."

The *Zollverein* (Customs Union)

After the Congress of Vienna (1814–1815) Germany was split into 39 states (see the map, p. 52). Merchants who travelled, for example, 50 kilometres sometimes had to cross several state borders and pass through several customs[1]. In addition, there were different currencies[2], different weights and measures as well as different laws in every state.

In 1819, Prussia began making treaties with other German states to form a customs union to promote[3] trade. The *Zollverein*, or Customs Union*, came into existence in 1834. All tariffs between the states were abolished and weights and measures were standardized. All the states in the German Confederation joined except the *Hanse* port cities and Austria. The Austrian Empire refused because this would have divided it into two parts: one part belonging to the German Confederation as well as to the Customs Union, and the non-German part not belonging to the German Customs Union. In addition, Austria had a large home market of its own. For 25 million Germans, however, the *Zollverein* meant economic unification – without the help of political unification.

1 customs *Zoll*
2 currency *Währung*
3 promote sth. *etwas fördern, vorantreiben*
4 petition *Bittschrift*
5 submit sth. *etwas einreichen*
6 spokesman *Sprecher*
7 Zoll- und Mautlinien *borders where customs duties have to be paid*
8 jdn./etwas lähmen *paralyze sb./sth.*
9 Durchgangszoll *tariff*

S2 **Merchants and factory owners on their situation in the German Confederation, 1819**

Excerpt from a petition[4] to the federal Diet of the German Confederation submitted[5] by Friedrich List, the spokesman[6] for the German "Handels- und Gewerbverein" on 20 April 1819:

Achtunddreißig Zoll- und Mautlinien[7] in Deutschland lähmen[8] den Verkehr im Inneren. Um von Hamburg nach Österreich, von Berlin in die Schweiz zu handeln, hat man zehn Staaten zu durchschneiden, zehn Zoll- und Mautordnungen zu studieren, zehnmal Durchgangszoll[9] zu bezahlen. Wer aber das Unglück hat, auf einer Grenze

zu wohnen, wo drei oder vier Staaten zusammenstoßen, der verlebt sein ganzes Leben mitten unter feindlich gesinnten Zöllnern und Mautnern[1], der hat kein Vaterland.
Trostlos[2] ist dieser Zustand für Männer, welche wirken und handeln[3] möchten; mit neidischen[4] Blicken sehen sie hinüber über den Rhein, wo ein großes Volk vom Kanal bis an das Mittelländische Meer, vom Rhein bis an die Pyrenäen, von der Grenze Hollands bis Italien auf freien Flüssen und offenen Landstraßen Handel treibt, ohne einem Mautner zu begegnen.

From: Friedrich List, Schriften, Reden, Briefe, *Volume 1, ed. by Karl Goeser/Wilhelm von Sonntag, (1933), Scientia Verlag, Aalen, 1971, p. 491.*

S 3 **Economic unification in Germany, 1828–1867**

1 **a** Read S 2 and list the reasons for the dissatisfaction of German merchants and factory owners.
b Discuss what List, the author of the petition in S 2, may have suggested to overcome the difficulties[5] of trade in the German Confederation.

2 Keeping the difficulties of trade in mind, decide if the following goods were exported or not exported in 1819. List the goods in a chart (see below) and note down the reasons for your choice:
- *luxury products (e.g. silk textiles, jewellery)*
- *agricultural tools (e.g. hoes)*
- *fruit and vegetables*
- *industrial products (e.g. cotton textiles)*
- *ordinary pottery*[6]

Exported goods	*Non-exported goods*	*Reasons*
…		…

3 Describe what happened to the price of the exported goods on their way from producer to consumer.

4 **a** Identify who benefited[7] from the many customs barriers that existed in Germany before 1834. Consumers? Small local workshops? Bigger industrial enterprises[8]? Governments? Give reasons for your conclusions.
b Discuss whether German economic unification was welcomed by everyone.

5 Look at the cartoon in S 1: Identify and discuss the cartoonist's view of the situation of trade in the German territories.

6 You are the owner of a small but growing textile company in Ratingen near Düsseldorf. You produce cotton cloth with the newest water-driven machines. Write a letter to Friedrich List with your reasons why the customs barriers in the German Confederation must fall.

7 Make an event map (see Appendix, pp. 142–143) of the founding of the Customs Union in Germany (see the text, p. 68, and S 2, S 3).

1 Zöllner und Mautner *customs officer*
2 trostlos *desperate*
3 wirken und handeln *be active and trade*
4 neidisch *envious*
5 overcome difficulties *Schwierigkeiten überwinden*
6 ordinary pottery *gewöhnliches Geschirr aus Ton*
7 benefit *profitieren, Nutzen ziehen*
8 industrial enterprise *Industrieunternehmen*

6.2 The "first" Industrial Revolution* in Germany

The building of railways

In 1835, the first railway in Germany ran the six kilometres between Nuremberg and Fürth. In the 1840s, German governments began promoting the construction of more railways. The net grew rapidly together with the demand[1] for steel and coal. Historians call the construction of railways the "locomotive" of the "first" Industrial Revolution* in Germany (beginning in the 1840s) because it played a major role in the development of the German coal, iron and steel industries. Since states had to cooperate to build railway lines running across borders, the railways also helped to unify Germany. When people travelled across Germany, they began to see it more as one country and not as different states anymore.

Industrialized regions in Germany

Yet, until the mid-19th century, the number of industrial enterprises was small and concentrated in a handful of towns and regions of the German Confederation: Hamburg and Bremen, as industrial ports; Bohemia, a province of the Austrian Habsburg Empire, as a producer of iron ore; Saxony as an area of small cotton textile mills; and Silesia with its coal mines.

There were also coal mines in the Prussian part of the Rhineland, and the Ruhr Valley became famous for its high-quality coal. As industrialization increased after 1850, Rhineland-Westphalia, Saxony and Silesia became the most heavily industrialized regions in continental Europe.

Industrialization brought great opportunities for entrepreneurs. But for millions of others, wages and standards of living declined, especially in the textile and clothing trades, where workers were driven into ruin as a result of early industrialization (see Unit 4.4).

1 demand *Nachfrage*

S4 **Paul Friedrich Meyerheim (1842–1915), *"Post und Eisenbahn"*, oil painting, 1875**

Meyerheim painted S4 for the castle-like home of Albert Borsig, the owner of the second largest locomotive-building company in the world.

It took Berliners who travelled by horse-drawn coach at least 64 hours in 1848 to attend the National Assembly meetings at St. Paul's Church in Frankfurt-on-Main. Ten years later, the same trip took only 13 hours by train. Today Berlin–Frankfurt is four hours by high-speed train and one hour by plane.

In 1923, a bus replaced the last stagecoach running in Hanover.

Activate your English

Transport

The train/ship/coach takes … (hours, minutes) to go from … to …

It took emigrants at least 43 days by sailing ship to go from Bremen to New York in 1850.

Eisenbahn

railway (BE) = (AE) railroad *Eisenbahn*
wagon, car, coach *Waggon*
steam locomotive *Dampflok*
tracks, rails *Gleis, Schienen*
railway bridge *Eisenbahnbrücke*
railway net *Eisenbahnliniennetz*
train journey *Eisenbahnreise*
passenger *Fahrgast, Reisender*

Kutsche

horse-drawn coach/carriage *Pferdekutsche*
stagecoach *Postkutsche*
(have a) ride in a coach/carriage *in einer Kutsche fahren*
driver *Kutscher*
gallop / ride at a gallop *im Galopp fahren*

Schiff

go by sailing ship / steamship / ship *mit dem Segel- / Dampf- / Schiff fahren*
shipping on the Rhine *Schiffahrt auf dem Rhein*

8 In the painting in S 4, the artist Meyerheim contrasts transport by stagecoach with transport by train. Discuss whether the painter wanted to

A *celebrate "the good old times".*
B *make fun of travelling by coach.*
C *show how modern transportation triumphs over the old.*
D *show how enjoyable travelling by coach is in contrast to …*

The words and phrases in **Activate your English** (see above) may help you.

Spread of railways in five selected countries, 1840–1900 (length of line open, in km)

	1840	1860	1880	1900
Great Britain	2390	14,603	25,060	30,079
France	496	9167	23,089	38,109
Germany	469	11,089	33,838	51,678
Austria-Hungary	144	4543	18,507	36,330
Russia	27	1626	22,865	53,234

From: Internet Modern History Sourcebook, *www.fordham.edu/halsall/mod/indrev6.html, 9 March 2006.*

S 6 Output of pig iron[1] in five selected countries (in thousand metric tons; annual averages)

	Great Britain	France	Germany	Austria-Hungary	Russia
1781–1790	69	141	–	–	–
1825–1829	669	212	90	85	164
1855–1859	3583	900	422	306	254
1875–1879	6484	1462	1770	418	424
1900–1914	8778	2665	7925	1425	2773

From: Internet Modern History Sourcebook, *www.fordham.edu/halsall/mod/indrevtabs1.html, 9 March 2006.*

S 7 Economic effects of railway building in the 19th century

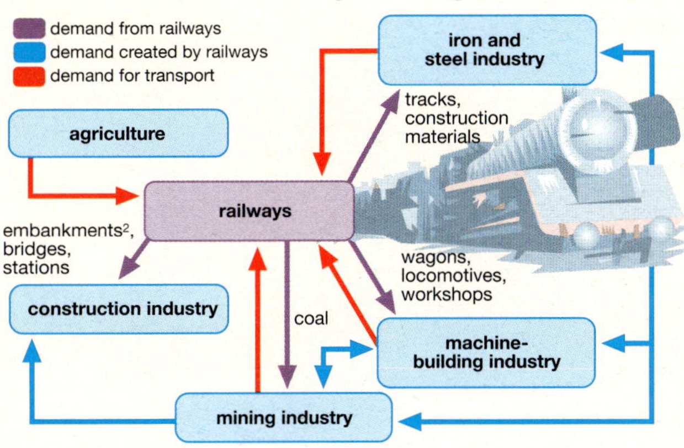

S 8 Employment structure in the United Kingdom, 1700–2000

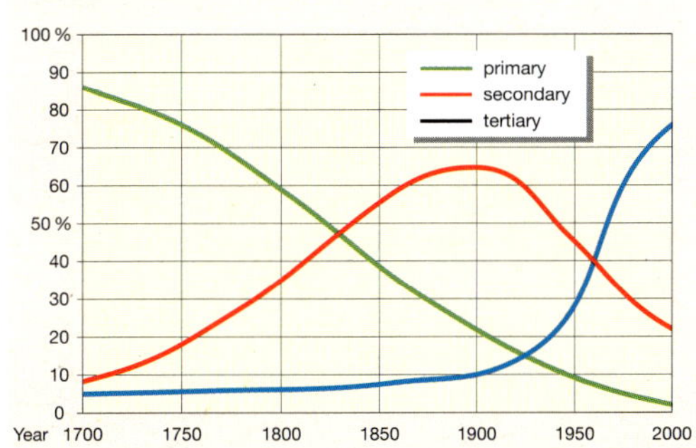

From: www.bbc.co.uk/schools/gcsebitesize/geography/economic/industryrev5.shtml, 5 Mai 2006.

1 pig iron *Roheisen*
2 embankment *Bahndamm*

9 **Extra Research:** Follow these links to study the map showing the development of the German railway net: *www.ieg-maps.uni-mainz.de / Serie AK: Animierte Karten / railways.*

a Find out in what year the owner of the textile company from Ratingen (see p. 69, Task 6) could send his cotton cloth from Düsseldorf to Königsberg in East Prussia by train.

b Describe how his company benefited from the transportation by train.

c Discuss to what extent the people in Königsberg also benefited from the mass transportation of industrial goods by train.

10 Railways helped the secondary sector (see **Activate your English** below) in Germany to grow enormously:

a The chart in S 7 shows the sectors and branches of industry that were affected by 19th-century railway building. List them and their products for railway building. For example: *The* ***construction industry*** *produces/provides*[1]*/delivers*[2] ...

b Add more economic sectors or industries which may have grown as a result of railway building.

c Imagine you are a textbook author: Write a paragraph about the connection between the construction of the railways and the growth of the iron and steel industries in Germany (S 7).

11 Historians argue that industrial mass production* would have been impossible without the spread of railways (and canals). Write a short article titled "Mass production without railways – Is that possible?" The words and phrases in **Activate your English** (below) may help you.

Activate your English

Economic sectors

People are usually employed[3] *in one of three economic sectors*[4]*:*
primary sector, secondary sector, tertiary sector

The primary sector

... wins/extracts the raw materials.

The secondary or manufacturing sector

... processes[5] *the raw materials from the primary sector and makes them into finished*[6]*/manufactured/processed goods.*
- *food processing (making wheat into bread)*
- *heavy and light manufacturing (e.g. steel, cars, pharmaceuticals, petrol)*
- *building*

The tertiary or service sector

... provides services:
- *banking*
- *insurance*[7]
- *transportation*
- *retail*[8]
- *health services*
- *education*
- *police*
- *information and communication*

Activate your English

Causes and effects II

Causes

have its origin in sth. *seinen Ursprung in etwas haben*
give rise to sth. *zu etwas führen, Anlass geben zu etwas*
have its roots in sth. *seine Wurzeln in etwas haben*

Positive and negative effects

initiate sth. *etwas einleiten*
provoke sth. *etwas hervorrufen, provozieren*
have effects on sth. *Auswirkungen auf etwas haben*
profit from sb./sth. *von jdm./etwas profitieren*
catch up with sb. *jdn. einholen*
benefit from sth. *Nutzen ziehen aus etwas*
unable to compete *unfähig am Wettbewerb teilzunehmen / zu konkurrieren*
go into (economic/political) decline *sich im (wirtschaftlichen/politischen) Niedergang befinden*
fall behind *zurückfallen*
be ruined *ruiniert sein*
drive sb./sth. into ruin *jdn./etwas in den Ruin treiben*

1 provide sth. *etwas anbieten, bereitstellen*
2 deliver sth. *etwas liefern*
3 employ sb. *jdn. beschäftigen*
4 economic sector *Wirtschaftssektor*
5 process sth. *etwas weiterverarbeiten*
6 finished goods *Fertigwaren*
7 insurance *Versicherung*
8 retail *Einzelhandel*

Presenting statistics

Statistics can be presented in tables or in graphs:
Line graphs show trends and changes over time. They have an x-axis (horizontal) and a y-axis (vertical). Usually, the x-axis has numbers for the time period, and the y-axis has numbers for what is being measured.
Bar charts are often used for comparing sizes, amounts and quantities.
Pie charts usually present percentages.
Information is generally easier to understand when it is presented in a graph. But pay attention to *how* it is presented. For example, if you change the scale[1] on the axis of a line graph, a "slight rise" in railway building can become a "sharp rise" (which can be interpreted as a rapid change in transport history).

S9

9 a) Line graph

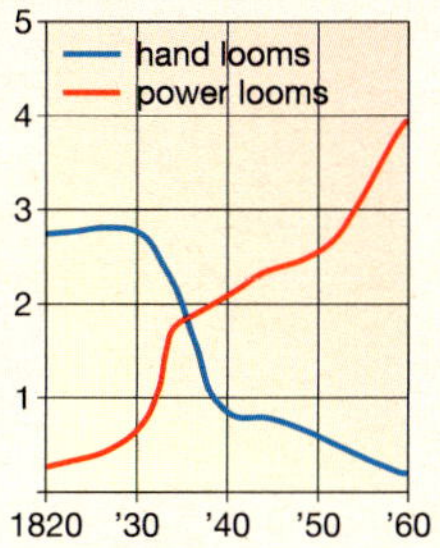

9 b) Bar chart

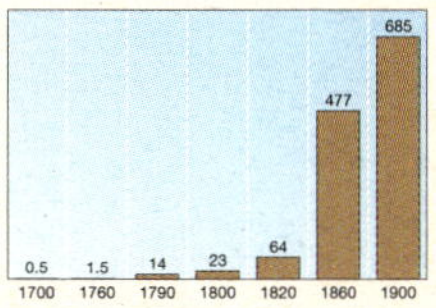

9 c) Pie chart

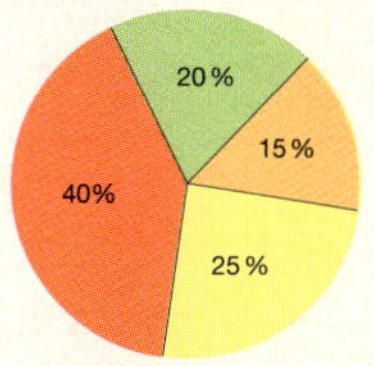

12 Use graphs or charts to display
a the German output of pig iron (S 6) and
b the spread of the German railway network (S 5).
In each case create two different graphs or charts (by hand or with a computer program).

13 Read the "Study skills" on p. 74 and, working in pairs, analyse the statistics in S 5:
a Answer the basic questions in steps 1 to 6. Make notes.
b Imagine you are a textbook author. Write a paragraph describing and explaining the statistical information on the spread of the German railway net (S 5) and German output of pig iron (S 6).
c Draw conclusions about what the statistics mean.

14 **a** Look at the line graph in S 9 a: Which of the following statements do you agree with? Give reasons for your answer.
A *The line graph S 9 a indicates that the number of hand looms in Britain dropped sharply and the number of power looms rose dramatically between 1820 and 1860.*
B *The line graph S 9 a indicates that the number of hand looms in Britain dropped slightly and the number of power looms rose gradually between 1820 and 1860.*
b Make the same line graph with the same scale on the y-axis but *multiply the distances between the numbers on the x-axis (1820, 1830, etc.) by four!* Then look again at statements A and B above: Which of them do you agree with now?

15 Making connections: S 8 shows employment trends in the United Kingdom.
a Compare the dates of industrialization in the United Kingdom (Unit 2.1) with the information on industrialization in Germany.
b Discuss which changes would have to be made in the employment statistics in S 8 to show the German employment trends in the 19th century.

16 **Extra research:** Find out the structure of employment in Germany today from the *Statistisches Bundesamt* (Federal Statistical Office): *www.destatis.de/basis/e/erwerb/erwerbtab6.htm.*

17 Who's working where? Copy the chart below and fill in these jobs:
nurse – construction worker – bank clerk – motor mechanic – carpenter – plumber – insurance agent – call centre agent – lawyer – information technology specialist – teacher – lorry driver – hairdresser – salesperson – chemist – auto worker
Use your dictionary for help with unknown jobs.

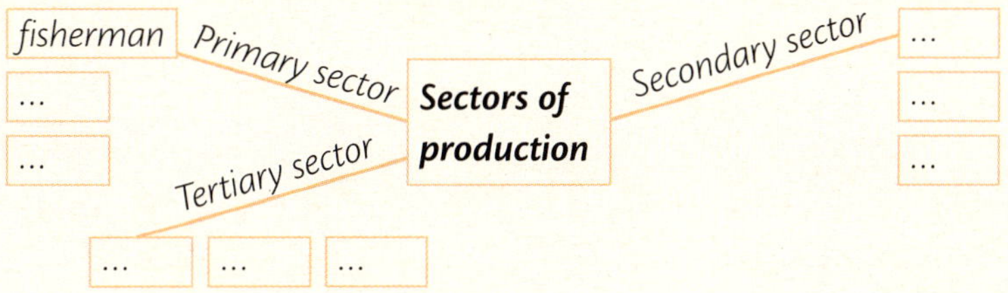

1 scale *Maßeinheit*

Analysing statistics

In Unit 1.2, p. 9, you began using statistics. In this Unit, you will learn how to analyse statistics more systematically. Official government statistics are as old as recorded history. At first they were population statistics, but slowly other branches of statistics were added, such as agricultural statistics, statistics on local government finances, and poor relief statistics. Most of the national statistical offices were founded during the 19th century. Today German statistics are compiled by the *Statistisches Bundesamt* (Federal Statistical Office). For more information on the history of statistics see: *www.destatis.de/basis/e/erwerb/erwerbtab6.htm.*

Study skills

Basic questions

Step 1: Determine how the statistical data are presented: *table – line graph – bar chart – pie chart – other*

Step 2: Study the elements of the presentation:
- *the title*
- *the headings on columns or rows*
- *the labels on the axes of a graph*
- *What is being measured?*
- *In what units is it being measured?*

Step 3: Statistics describe events which happened in a particular place and time:
- *What geographic area is being described?*
- *What time period does it cover?*

Step 4: Find out how this information was compiled[1]:
- *What is the source of the information?*
- *How reliable is it?*

Analysis questions

Step 5: What is taking place?
- *How do the numbers change over time?*
- *Do the numbers increase or decrease?*
- *Is the increase or decrease steady, sharp, cyclical[2] or inconsistent[3]?*
- *Does the distribution become more equal or more unequal?*
- *Do you see patterns in your data?*

Step 6: What is the reason for it? If you do not know, speculate.

Pay close attention to when changes take place in the patterns you described in step 5. Think about what was happening politically, economically or socially at this time.

Summary and conclusions

Step7: Write a paragraph describing and explaining the statistical information. Draw conclusions about what the statistics mean.

Activate your English

Describing and explaining statistics

Describing statistics

Figures increased / rose / went up ...
There was an increase / a rise in ... / from ... to ...
Figures decreased/dropped/fell ...
There was a decrease/drop/fall in ... / from ... to ...
... rose sharply/dramatically/slightly/ gradually
... rose by ... per cent / at a rate of ... per cent / by 100,000 / by ... times
... reached a peak of ... / fell to a low of ...
... doubled/tripled/quadrupled
a twofold/threefold increase/decrease in ... / from ... to ...
a significant/sharp/rapid/steep increase/ decrease in ... / from ... to ...
a gradual/slow increase/decrease in ... / from ... to ...
... remained (fairly) constant/steady / stayed (virtually) the same
around/about/circa/approximately
over a span of ... years
the proportion of ... on the total

Explaining statistics

The graph shows / indicates / deals with ...
Compared with/to ...
The cause for the increase was ...
The increase can be explained by ...
This/These statistic(s) demonstrate(s) ...
What we learn from this/these statistic(s) is that ...

1 compile statistics *Statistiken erstellen*
2 cyclical *zyklisch, periodisch*
3 inconsistent *unbeständig*

6.3 The "second" Industrial Revolution* in Germany

New "Sunrise industries"[1]

In the last decade of the 19th century, the German economy began to boom after a long economic crisis from 1873 to 1895. The new so-called "Sunrise industries"* – the electrical industry, telecommunications (telegraphy, telephone), machine-building, car and chemical industries – had turned Germany into an industrial power and the "world champion of exports". And finally, workers' wages began to increase slowly.

S 10 **Postcard *"Elektrotechnische Ausstellung 1891"*, Frankfurt-on-Main, 1891**

Electricity, with a shining bulb in her right hand, triumphs over the "traditional" types of lighting: candle, kerosene, gas and oil lamp. About 1.4 million people from every industrialized country visited the international exhibition – a showcase of the most advanced technology of its time. The first long-distance transmission of alternating current[2] (AC) in Europe took place after a 175-kilometre-long power line had been installed between Lauffen at the Neckar and Frankfurt. Together with new types of AC motors, this made the electrification of households and industries possible.

S 11 **Dolivo-Dobrowolsky's AC motor, photograph, 1889**

The chief engineer of AEG (Allgemeine Elektrizitäts-Gesellschaft), *Michael von Dolivo-Dobrowolsky (1862–1919), constructed an AC motor so small that it could power individual machines. Up until then electricity had only been used for indoor lighting. Now factories could use electric motors instead of steam engines to drive machines. With the AC motor it was also possible to make household devices[3] driven by electricity.*

S 12 **Mass production of small electric motors at AEG, Berlin, photograph, c 1900**

In the yearly company report of 1898–1899, AEG management was very satisfied with the new methods of production. Production had gone up without increasing the number of workers.

1 Sunrise industries *Zukunftsindustrien*
2 alternating current (AC) *Wechselstrom*
3 device *Gerät*

S 13 Excerpt from a book by Earl Dean Howard on German industries, 1907

Howard (1907–1941), Professor of Sociology and Economics at Northwestern University, Evanston, Illinois, USA, attended the University of Berlin in 1904–1905, where he wrote his thesis[1] The Cause and Extent[2] of the Recent Industrial Progress of Germany *(1907):*

In 1850, Germany exported foodstuffs and raw materials, and imported manufactured goods; now her principal[3] exports are manufactured goods, and her imports are raw materials and foodstuffs. In this period she has changed from an agricultural to a manufacturing and commercial[4] nation. [...] As in the case of Britain, the industrial strength of modern Germany is based on her iron and steel manufactures. [...] The rapid increase since 1888 has been due in large part to the development of the electrical industry. [...] It is in the electrical industry that Germany has made her greatest progress, one of the direct results, no doubt, of her excellent technical schools. In 1880 electricity was commercially employed only in telegraphy, and in 1882 the total number of persons employed in the industry was too small to be separately enumerated [...], the number at the present time is estimated at 50,000. [...] This tremendous and rapid growth [...] has placed Germany second only to the United States in the industry. [...] In the chemical industry Germany is easily the first nation of the world. [...] This splendid industry is the direct produce of German technical education. [... The country's] technical schools and university laboratories may be regarded as the corner-stone of the nation's industrial greatness [...]. The most interesting branch of the chemical industry is the manufacture of dye-stuffs[5] from coal-tar[6]. [...] In 1860, all the dyes used were organic, and Germany was almost entirely dependent on foreign countries for her supply. [... Today] four-fifths of all the world's products of dye-stuffs as well as a large proportion of the medical preparations derived from coal tar, are made in Germany. [...] This is but one instance of the advantage Germany has derived from the labors of her army of scientifically trained chemists. [...] In studying the educational methods and systems of Germany [...] we are dealing with one of the most fundamental causes of her recent industrial progress. [...] The technical [universities ...] are the institutions which have enabled Germany to take a place in the front rank of industrial nations.

From: Earl Dean Howard, The Cause and Extent of the Recent Industrial Progress of Germany, *Houghton & Mifflin, Boston, 1907. Quoted from: web.jjay.cuny.edu/~jobrien/reference/ob49.html, 7 August 2005.*

S 14 Distribution of the world's manufacturing production, 1870–1913 (percentage of world total)

	1870	1913
USA	23.3	35.8
Germany	13.2	15.7
United Kingdom	31.8	14.0
France	10.3	6.4
Russia	3.7	5.5
Italy	2.4	2.7
Canada	1.0	2.3
Belgium	2.9	2.1
Sweden	0.4	1.0
Japan	–	1.2
India	11.0	1.1
Other Countries	–	12.2

From: Internet Modern History Sourcebook, *www.fordham.edu/halsall/mod/indrevtabs1.html, 9 March* 2006.

1 thesis *Doktorarbeit*
2 extent *Ausmaß*
3 principal *Haupt-, hauptsächlich*
4 commercial *Handels-, kommerziell, gewerblich*
5 dye-stuff *Farben*
6 coal-tar *(Steinkohlen-) Teer*

Healing social wrongs[1]

Low wages for long workdays, child labour, extreme poverty, unsafe working conditions in the factories, overcrowded flats and unhygienic cities made life very hard for the growing number of workers in the factories. This misery of the working class led to social reform movements that worked for a solution to the *Soziale Frage** (social question).

Some factory owners began building new homes for their workers with gardens and small stables for chickens and pigs. In the Catholic and Protestant churches, men like Adolph Kolping (1813–1865), Friedrich von Bodelschwingh (1831–1910) or Wilhelm Emmanuel von Ketteler (1811–1877) tried to help orphans and homeless and ill people, and to improve the education of working-class people.

The workers themselves formed trade unions and went on strike for better wages, shorter working hours, safer working conditions and better education. They also founded workers' parties which demanded fundamental changes in society. Their aim was to end the capitalist system (capitalism*) with its class-rule of the bourgeoisie[2]* and the nobility. In 1875, the two German workers' parties – one under the leadership of Ferdinand Lassalle (1825–1865), the other under August Bebel (1840–1913) and Wilhelm Liebknecht (1826–1900) – united in the *Sozialistische Arbeiter Partei* (Socialist Workers' Party) in 1875. However, the question of *how* to change society had not been answered: Was it possible to win enough voters who wanted to change society by slow reforms made in parliament? Or was a change only possible by revolution?

The government also became active in trying to "heal the social wrongs" and to "advance[3] the well-being of the workers", as it claimed. The chancellor of the German Empire, Otto von Bismarck, introduced the most modern social security system[4]* in the world: a health and accident insurance as well as an invalidity[5] and old age pension (1883–1889). This gave an insured person a small pension at the age of seventy. Life expectancy[6] in Germany around 1890 was 50 years.

1 heal a social wrong *soziale Unrecht wiedergutmachen*
2 bourgeoisie *das Bürgertum*
3 advance sth. *etwas (be)fördern, voranbringen*
4 social security system *Sozialversicherungssystem*
5 invalidity *Berufsunfähigkeit*
6 life expectancy *Lebenserwartung*
7 means of production *Produktionsmittel*
8 exploit sb. *jdn. ausbeuten*

S 15
Working-class families in rented flats, Germany, photograph, c 1900

S 16
Family home of the factory owner von Bohlen und Halbach in Badenweiler, Germany, photograph, 1880s

Biography

Karl Marx

"Working men of all countries, unite!" Marx (1818–1883) wrote these famous words in the *Communist Manifesto*, published together with Friedrich Engels (1820–1895) in February 1848. Nobody at that time would have thought that the *Manifesto* would become the most widely read document in the world in the 1860s. Marx was born into a wealthy lawyer family in Trier and studied in Bonn and Berlin. In 1842, he became the editor of the *Rheinische Zeitung*, a revolutionary Cologne newspaper, which was closed down by the Prussian censors in 1843. He moved to Paris, where he met Engels, the son of a German factory owner. In 1848, he went back to Cologne, but was banished from Prussia in 1849. He then moved to London and lived there until his death. In the *Communist Manifesto* Marx and Engels demanded that the land, factories and their machines (the means of production[7]) belonged to everybody. Why? If the means of production were in the hands of a few factory owners, they argued, the workers would always be exploited[8]. For this reason workers had to unite and win political power. Then they could turn the land, factories and machines into the property of all to stop exploitation and social misery.

S 17 **Real wages and cost of living in Germany, 1871–1913**

	wages	cost of living
1871	70	106
1875	98	113
1880	82	104
1885	87	99
1890	98	102
1895	100	100
1900	118	106
1905	128	112
1910	147	124
1913	163	130

From: Ashok V. Desai, Real Wages in Germany 1871–1913*, OUP, Oxford, 1968, p. 36.*

S 18 **Chemical factory in Oppau after an explosion, Germany, photograph, 1921**

18 Evaluate S 13 as a "window to past events":

a Photocopy S 13 and mark the different industries and their products.

b What historical facts do you learn from this source? Mark the things the author said that you think are important.

c Discuss to what extent S 13 is a reliable "window to the past". How accurate is it as a source of information on …?

d Discuss who might have been interested in reading Howard's analysis of the German economy at the beginning of the 20th century. Discuss why.

A *The high command of the British Army*
B *The US chemical industry*
C *The British Secretary of Education*
D *The British Secretary of State for Trade and Industry*
E *Anybody else*

19 Write a short paragraph on the German industry's position in world manufacturing at the beginning of the 20th century (see the text, p. 75, and S 10–S 14).

20 **Extra research:** Collect information on the history of a German company (e.g. AEG). Present your results on the wall in the form of a newspaper page.

21 **a** Note down what Marx saw as the key social and economic "wrong" (see Biography, p. 78).

b Discuss whether Marx would have been satisfied with Bismarck's social security system (see the text, p. 77).

22 **Extra research:** Your class has been asked to design the showroom for "Technological progress in Germany in the 'second' Industrial Revolution", which will be part of Germany's new technology museum (S 10–S 18). The activities below will help you.

a Split up into groups of four. Decide as a group what exhibition piece you want to present.

b Collect information and organize your notes in the graphic organizer below.

c Write a short informative text on your object for the museum showroom.

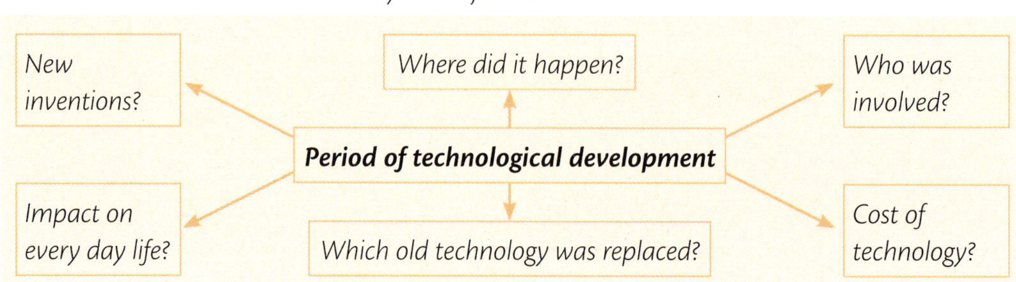

Germany on its way to an industrial society

Key events

1834	*Zollverein* (Customs Union)
1835	Railway line between Nuremberg and Fürth
1848	*Communist Manifesto*
1875	*Sozialistische Arbeiter Partei* (Socialist Workers' Party)
1883–1889	Social Security Laws

Key terms

"first" Industrial Revolution,
"second" Industrial Revolution
Customs Union, Sunrise industries,
capitalism, mass production,
bourgeosie, social security system,
Soziale Frage (social question)

Key personalities

Karl Marx

History skills

Displaying statistics *(p. 73)*
Analysing statistics *(p. 74)*

Activate your English

Transport *(p. 71)*
Economic sectors *(p. 72)*
Causes and effects II *(p. 72)*
Describing and explaining statistics *(p. 74)*

S 19 Mass production of small electric motors at AEG, Berlin, photograph, c 1900

1 Add the relevant new terms to your German-English vocabulary files "Industrialization" and "Working a job" (see Unit 2.1, p. 27, Task 1)

2 List the factors which contributed[1] to the economic modernization of Germany and their specific contributions in a two-column chart.

Factors	*Contributions*
technological progress (steam engine)	...

3 a Identify the achievements of industrialization and the changes which resulted from it.
b Discuss to what extent industrialization improved people's lives (S 15–S 18).

4 Look at S 19. Imagine you are a graphic novel[2] writer:
a Photocopy the photograph in S 19, add thought bubbles and write what the three men might be thinking.
b Draw and write the next scene based on the following information:
Person A: *age 40, member of the Social Democratic Party and active in his trade union, offered to become a foreman*[3]
Person B: *age 20, extremely happy, first employment in a big company*
Person C: *age 67, has terrible pains in his legs and his back because he has been standing for the last 9 hours*

1 contribute sth. *etwas beitragen*
2 graphic novel *Comicroman*
3 foreman *Vorarbeiter*

Unit 7 German unification – Unification "by blood and iron"?

7.1 Prussia grows in strength

S1 Anton von Werner (1843–1915), King Wilhelm I of Prussia is proclaimed[1] German Emperor in the Hall of Mirrors at Versailles on 18 January, 1871, oil painting, 170 x 200 cm, Germany, 1885

The Crown Prince Friedrich Wilhelm invited the painter von Werner to the proclamation ceremony at Versailles in January 1871. The painting S1 is the third version of the event. Emperor Wilhelm I gave it to Bismarck for his 70th birthday. The painting shows the moment in which the battle flags and standards of the regiments are lifted. The officers and princes raise their helmets and sabres as they answer the call of the Grand Duke of Baden for three cheers for the new German Emperor.

Germany after the failed revolution

The disaster of the failed revolution of 1848 (see Unit 5.2) did not mean that the idea of German unification* was forgotten in the German states. But it remained a dream until the Prussian King Wilhelm I (1858–1888) appointed Otto von Bismarck Prime Minister *(Ministerpräsident)* in 1862. In only nine years after his appointment and thirteen years after the failed revolution, he strengthened Prussia, ended Austrias influence over German affairs and unified Germany.

1864 – Prussia and Austria together against Denmark (German-Danish War)

The duchies of Schleswig and Holstein were largely settled by Germans and were part of the German Confederation, though they had been ruled since the Middle Ages[2] by the King of Denmark as duke. When he tried to annex the two duchies and turn them into a part of Denmark, Bismarck saw his first chance to act. He provoked Austria to declare war on the militarily weak Denmark and to take control of the two territories. After a short war fought with a combined Prussian and Austrian army, Prussia occupied Schleswig and Austria took over Holstein.

1 proclaim sb./sth. *jdn./etwas ausrufen, verkünden*

2 Middle Ages *Mittelalter (Epoche zwischen ca. 500 und 1500)*

1866 – Prussia and Austria fight against each other (Austro-Prussian War)

Prussia and Austria could not agree on the administration of Schleswig-Holstein and in June 1866, Austria declared war on Prussia. Austria was no match[1] for the Prussian army, which also used telegraph and railways in its mobilization of 250,000 soldiers. Prussia overran Austria and its six German allies (Bavaria, Nassau, Saxony, Hanover, Hesse-Kassel, and Frankfurt-on-Main) in only seven weeks of fighting.

The battle on 3 July 1866 for the former Austrian city of Königgrätz – now called Hradec Králové and located in the Czech Republic – was the largest of its time, with nearly 500,000 troops involved. It was also the first battle where the outcome was a direct result of the use of new technologies, including the railway, telegraph, cast steel rifled cannon[2] and breech-loading needle rifle[3]. The losses in the battle were immense on both sides.

The Treaty of Prague of August 1866 officially ended the war and changed the map of Germany enormously. Prussia managed to:

- dissolve the German Confederation of 1815;
- take control of both Schleswig and Holstein;
- take control of and annex, against all international law, the German states north of the Main, which had fought on the Austrian side;
- form the North German Confederation[4] under Prussian control – and without Austria.

The founding of the North German Confederation marked the end of Austrian influence in Germany. Bismarck's aim had been achieved. Only the German states in the south such as Bavaria, Baden, Wurtemberg and Hesse-Darmstadt remained independent. Although the south German states feared further "Prussianization" in Germany, they also feared France. So they were militarily allied with the new North German Confederation and joined the Prussian-dominated *Zollverein* (see Unit 6.1).

S2 **"Now you're big enough. You mustn't get any bigger. I'm telling you this for your own health." French cartoon, 1867**

Vocabulary help: tape measure[5] – measure sb.[6]

1 be a match for sb. *jdm. ebenbürtig sein*

2 cast steel rifled cannon *Gussstahlkanone*

3 breech-loading needle rifle *Zündnadelgewehr*

4 North German Confederation *Norddeutscher Bund*

5 tape measure *Metermaß*

6 measure sb. *jdn. messen*

Biography

Otto von Bismarck (1815–1898)
An opinion poll[1] published by the *Berlin Illustrated News* in 1899 declared Bismarck the greatest statesman of the century – a cosmopolitan, a "man of the world", who spoke several languages and had a clear understanding of European life.
Bismarck was born in Schönhausen (now in Saxony-Anhalt) as the son of a noble Prussian landowning family (*Junker**). When he was seven, he was sent to a boarding school in Berlin. At the age of seventeen he began to study law in Göttingen. After passing his exams, he served as a Prussian civil servant, but he became bored and resigned after a short time. He fell desperately in love with an English girl, Isabella Loraine-Smith, and followed her around Germany. After his mother's death in 1839, Bismarck returned to his family estates[2] and read and travelled widely. In 1847, he married Johanna von Puttkammer.
Like most Prussian *Junker*-families in north-east Germany, Bismarck had little respect for parliamentary democracy and believed that the monarchy was the best form of government. When Bismarck was chosen as a representative to the newly created Prussian State Assembly (*Landtag*) in 1847, he became known as a monarchist. He openly expressed the idea that the monarch had a divine right[3] to rule and was responsible only to God. During the Revolution of 1848–1849 he defended the "old order" in the National Assembly in Frankfurt-on-Main and, later, in the Diet of the German Confederation. He served as Prussian ambassador[4] in Paris and St Petersburg. When the Prussian *Landtag* refused to pass the state budget[5] which would give the government money to strengthen the army, the Prussian King appointed Bismarck Prime Minister in 1862. It was in this year that he made his famous remark: "Not through speeches and majority decisions[6] are the great questions of the day decided – that was the great mistake of 1848 and 1849 – but by blood and iron".
In 1871, Wilhelm I, Emperor of the newly founded German Empire, made him Chancellor ("Iron Chancellor"). But when the crown went to the new Emperor Willhelm II in 1888, Bismarck was forced to resign. He died in 1898.

1 Read Otto von Bismarcks biography. Then copy the chart below and list the important dates in his life, giving information on what happened, and match them with developments and events from German and/or European history.

Dates	***Bismarck***	***What happened in German or European history***
1815	*born in Schönhausen in Prussia*	*Waterloo, Congress of Vienna*

2 **a** Explain in your own words the phrase "unification by blood and iron" (see Biography).
b Discuss whether the war of 1866 can be called a German civil war (see the text, pp. 80–81).

3 Count Eckstadt was the Saxon ambassador in London. Eckstadt wrote in his diary in 1862 what the Prime Minister Bismarck had said to a British politician in a personal conversation: "My first care will be to organize the army, with or without the help of the Prussian State Assembly." Discuss what historians can learn from this source about Bismarck's political views.

4 Working in pairs, look at the cartoon in S 2 and
a describe the action taking place in the cartoon.
b identify the French cartoonist's point of view on Prussia (see "History skills", p. 18).
c Do you agree with the view?

1 opinion poll *Meinungsumfrage*
2 estates *(hier) Ländereien*
3 divine right *(hier) Recht von Gottes Gnaden*
4 ambassador *Botschafter*
5 pass the state budget *Staatshaushalt verabschieden*
6 majority decisions *Mehrheitsbeschlüsse*

7.2 The Franco-Prussian War and the proclamation of the German Empire, 1870–1871

S3 **"Die wilde Jagd" (The Wild Hunt), cartoon published in the Austrian newspaper *Der Floh*, December 1870**

The cartoon shows the Prussian King, Wilhelm I, as triumphant winner in his war chariot[1]. The driver Bismarck is holding the reins in one hand and a flag in the other which reads: "Force before law". The two figures on his right and left symbolize death.

Causes and key events

France was opposed to a unified Germany because it feared a strong neighbour on its eastern border. For Bismarck it was clear that as long as France was in a position to do something against it, Germany could not be unified. Luckily, the Spanish government gave him the chance to act again.

At the end of the 1860s, the Spanish government offered a Hohenzollern prince – a relative[2] of the Prussian Hohenzollern King Wilhelm I (1858–1888) – the Spanish throne. Bismarck encouraged the prince to accept the offer to become King of Spain. However, a Hohenzollern prince on the Spanish throne was unacceptable to France because it feared being surrounded by Hohenzollern kings. King Wilhelm did not want to start trouble with France, so the prince turned down the Spanish offer.

But this was not enough for France. The French government asked Wilhelm to guarantee that the prince would *never* try to become King of Spain. The demand was presented to King Wilhelm I by the French ambassador[3] in the spa town[4] of Bad Ems. Wilhelm refused to promise, but in a friendly way. He sent Bismarck a telegram (the so-called Ems telegram* = *Emser Depesche*) describing in polite, diplomatic words why he had refused the French ambassador's new demand. Bismarck carefully cut and rearranged the King's words to create the impression that Wilhelm I had openly insulted[5] and humiliated[6] France.

1 war chariot *(antiker) Kriegswagen*
2 relative *Verwandter*
3 ambassador *Botschafter*
4 spa town *Kurort*
5 insult sb. *jdn. beleidigen*
6 humiliate sb. *jdn. demütigen, erniedrigen*

S4 **Deaths in the German wars of unification, 1864–1871**

German-Danish War, 1864		Austro-Prussian War, 1866		Franco-Prussian War, 1870–1871	
Deaths	*4500*	*Deaths*	*36,100*	*Deaths*	*187,500*
– Prussia	1000	– Prussia	10,000		
– Austria	500	– Austria	20,000		
– Denmark	3000	– Italy	4000		
		– Saxony	600		
		– Bavaria	500		
		– Hanover	500		

From: www.regis-net.de/krieg/preudan64.html; mypage.bluewin.ch/pickelhaube/prkk66.html; www.regis-net.de/krieg/kriegframe.html, 20 September 2005.

War and peace settlement[1]

When Bismarck's version of the King's telegram was published in the press, France felt openly provoked and declared war on Prussia on 19 July 1870. Fearing a French attack, the south German states joined the North German Confederation, fulfilling[2] Bismarck's dreams.

After only two months, France was totally defeated by the Prussian and other German forces. On 18 January 1871, in the Palace of Versailles in France, Wilhelm I was proclaimed Emperor *(Kaiser)* of the new German Empire. Germany now had a population of 39 million people (compared with Great Britain's 26 million and France's 36 million people).

The peace settlement of Frankfurt-on-Main (May 1871) humiliated France and laid the ground for future conflict. In the settlement, the German Empire

- demanded reparations* of five billion francs;
- annexed the territories of mostly German-speaking Alsace and coal-producing Lorraine[3];
- stationed an army in France for four years until the reparations were paid.

Germany was now "satiated[4] and ready for peace", Bismarck said after the war. Germany had no wish to gain[5] any further territory. But German unification* completely changed the balance of power in Europe: Bismarck's Germany had become the most powerful country in continental Europe and a rival in industrial output and military power for all other countries (see Unit 6.3).

S5 **"The accursed year" *(Das verfluchte Jahr)*, cartoon published in an illustrated newspaper, 1 January 1872**

Vocabulary help: hearse[11].

S6 **In 1988, the historian Paul Kennedy wrote about the reasons for Germany's victory in the Franco-Prussian War**

The triumph of Prussian-Germany was, quite clearly, a triumph of its military systems: but [...] behind the sweeping advances[6] of the German columns[7] [...] there lay a nation much better equipped and prepared for modern warfare than any other in Europe. In 1870 the German states [...] already possessed a larger population than France, and only disunity had disguised[8] the fact: Germany had more miles of railway lines, better arranged for military purposes. Its gross national product[9] and its iron and steel production were 2 1/2 times as great, and its consumption from modern energy was 50 % larger [...]. The army's short-service system[10] [...] mobilised the manpower of the nation for warlike purposes more effectively than [the systems in the western and eastern states in Europe].

Paul Kennedy, The Rise and Fall of the Great Powers *(1988). Quoted in: Clive Lodge,* From Confederation to Empire – Germany 1848–1914, *Hodder and Stoughton, London, 1997, p. 48.*

1 peace settlement *Friedensvereinbarung*
2 fulfill sth. *etwas erfüllen*
3 Alsace, Lorraine *Elsass, Lothringen*
4 satiated *gesättigt*
5 gain sth *etwas bekommen, gewinnen*
6 sweeping advance *überwältigender Vormarsch*
7 column *(hier) (Heeres-)Kolonne*
8 disguise sth. *etwas verdecken*
9 gross national product *Bruttosozialprodukt*
10 short-service system *kurzer Wehrdienst*
11 hearse *Leichenwagen*

S 7 German unification, 1871: A British, a German and an American point of view

7 a) The British authors of Chronicle of Britain *(1992) describe the view from Great Britain on 26 February 1871:*

With a peace treaty signed today at Versailles [...], the old European order is [...] cracked, with a newly powerful Germany poised[1] to send troops into Paris and demonstrate its mastery. An era of armed peace appears to have begun and the British government – long absorbed by home affairs and the empire – is starting to wake up to the existence of a German menace[2].

From: Henrietta Heald, ed., Chronicle of Britain, *Chronicle Communications, Farnborough, 1992, p. 943.*

7 b) The German Baroness Hildegard von Spitzemberg (1843–1914), who lived in Berlin, wrote in her diary on 3 March 1871:

Und was für ein Friede für uns Deutsche! [...] Vereint zu einem Reiche, dem größten, mächtigsten, gefürchtetsten in Europa, groß durch seine physische Macht nicht allein, größer noch durch seine Bildung und den Geist[3], der das Volk durchdringt[4]! [...] Möge Gott den Geist meines Volkes so lenken, dass seine Entwicklung eine friedliche und zivilisatorische[5] bleibe, sein Reich ein Reich des Lichts, der Freiheit, der wahren, christlichen Gesinnung[6] sei!

From: Wolfgang Lautemann et al., ed., Geschichte in Quellen, *Vol. 5, bsv, München, 1980, p. 370.*

7 c) The author of a book review summarized what Henry Adams (1838–1918), an American historian and grandson of the US president, wrote about Germany:

Germany, wrote Henry Adams in 1901, is "the great disturbing element in the world". He compared it to a great "powder magazine[7]" which "sooner or later" must explode, and went on to predict[8] that there would be no equilibrium[9], either political or economic, until its "explosive force" had been exhausted[10].

From: Geoffrey Barraclough, "The Great Disturbing Element", in: The New York Review of Books, *24 October 1968. Quoted from: www.nybooks.com/articles/article-preview?article_id=11523, 28 March 2006.*

5 Working in pairs, look at the texts of Units 7.1 and 7.2 and make a flow chart or an event chain of the German Wars of Unification. Before you start, discuss which information your chart should include. Make a difference between the triggers and long term causes.

6 **a** Analyse the cartoon in S 5 (for help, see "Study skills", p. 18).
b Discuss in class whether the cartoon appeared in a German or a French newspaper.

7 Look at the painting in S 1, p. 80:
a Identify Bismarck, the Grand Duke of Baden and King Wilhelm in the painting.
b Identify other groups of people and the "props".
c Discuss the purpose of the painting (for help, see "Study skills", p. 46).
d The Germans chose the Palace of Versailles for the proclamation ceremony. Discuss the message that this choice sent to the French and to the Germans.
e Speculate on the effect of this choice of location on the French-German relationship in the decades that followed.

8 Study and read S 3 and S 7 a–c: Which is a primary source and which is a secondary source? Explain your answer.

9 Group work: Every group chooses one of the sources (S 3, S 7 a–c) and makes notes on the author's point of view on German unification in 1871. Then each group presents their results in class. Finally, summarize the results in a four-column chart.

10 **a** The historian Kennedy (S 6) regards a country's military superiority as the result of economic strength, technological progress and the availability[11] of modern energy and communication lines. Explain in detail how this relates to Germany in the 1860s.
b Today the USA is the militarily superior country. Apply Kennedy's ideas to explain this.

1 poised *bereit*
2 menace *Bedrohung*
3 Geist *spirit*
4 jdn./etwas durchdringen *(here) fill sb./sth.*
5 zivilisatorisch *civilizing*
6 Gesinnung *(here) character*
7 powder magazine *(hier) Pulverfass*
8 predict sth. *etw. vorhersagen*
9 equilibrum *Gleichgewicht*
10 exhaust *erschöpfen*
11 availability *Verfügbarkeit*

7.3 Germany in the era of Bismarck

The German Empire – A democratic state?

In an opinion poll carried out in 1899, most Germans considered[1] the time of Bismarck to be the happiest period in the century. But were all Germans really happy with politics and everyday life? Bismarck wanted to turn Germany into a strong European power. To reach this goal, national unity was extremely important. In order to "unite" Germans, Bismarck attacked a number of so-called "enemies of the state". Between 1872 and 1878 he attacked the Catholic Church in Germany (at the time, 36 % of the population was Catholic, 62 % Protestant and 1 % Jewish). The so-called *Kulturkampf*[2] led to a series of laws that discriminated[3] against Catholics: Some priests had to leave Germany; the Catholic Church did not get any money from the government; and all Church schools as well as all wedding ceremonies were now state controlled.

Bismarck also attacked the socialists. The Anti-Socialist Law *(Sozialistengesetz)* was passed in 1878, outlawing[4] all activities of trade unions and of the *Sozialistische Arbeiter Partei* (organizations, newspapers and meetings were forbidden). But voters were still allowed to vote for its candidates at national elections for the the *Reichstag**, the German national parliament. The law failed to weaken the party. Instead, the number of socialist members of parliament grew from 12 in 1877 to 35 in 1890 when the law was finally abolished.

The so-called "enemies" also included minority groups such as Poles and Jews.

Key terms

Anti-Semitism

Semitic is a term for the family of languages spoken across much of the Middle East and North and East Africa which includes Hebrew[5] and Arabic.

The term "anti-Semitism" was first used in 1879 by the German journalist Wilhelm Marr. It means hatred[6] of Jewish people as a religious, social or ethnic group that is considered to be morally and physically inferior to other groups and races.

The German constitution of 1871 gave full civil rights to all Jews. However, strong anti-Semitism began to spread throughout the German Empire, especially after 1873 as a result of the economic crisis.

S 8 **Postcard from Frankfurt-on-Main, 1897**

"Geehrter Herr Pfarrer! Da ich mich aus dem Judengewimmel in der Stadt in obiges Lokal geflüchtet habe, um in Ruhe ein Pilsner zu schlürfen, gedenke ich Ihrer und sende die besten Grüße." (Dear Pastor, I'm thinking of you, drinking a beer in the pub which you see on the postcard, undisturbed after fleeing the bustle of Jews in town, with kind regards.)

1 consider sth. *etwas betrachten*
2 Kulturkampf *struggle for culture*
3 discriminate against sb. *gegen jdn. diskriminieren, jdn. benachteiligen*
4 outlaw sth. *etwas verbieten*
5 Hebrew *hebräisch*
6 hatred *Hass*

S9 The constitution of the German Empire

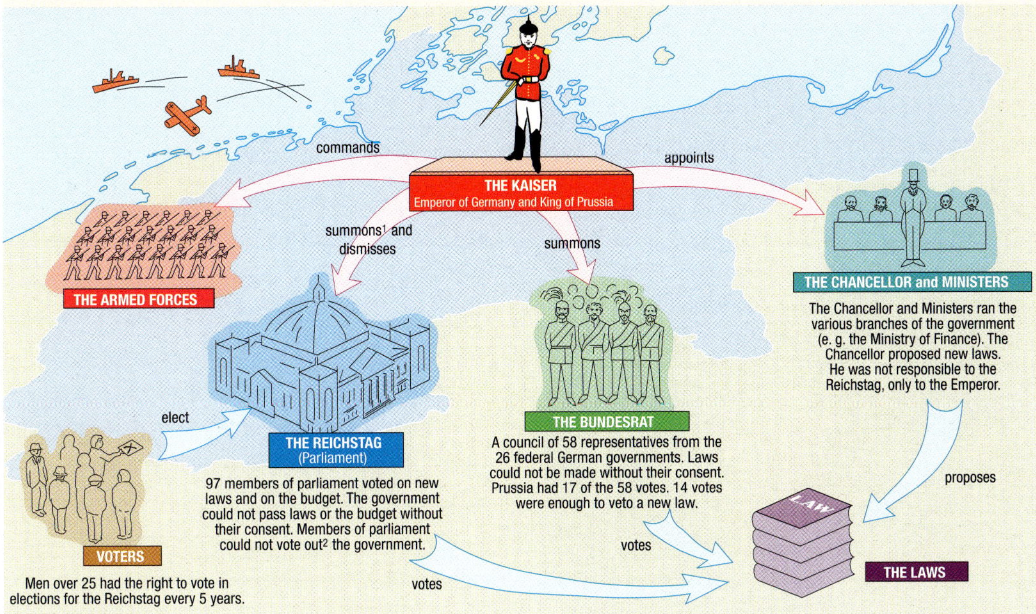

1 summon *einberufen*
2 vote out (the government) *(die Regierung) abwählen*
3 fuss about *Getue um*
4 commercial code *Handelsgesetz*

S 10 Was everybody in the German Empire happy with unification and the new order?

The following are six typical contemporary viewpoints on unification and everyday life:

A A law professor from Hesse

Lots of things have gone totally wrong. We wanted a unified Germany, but without the princes, kings and emperors. It's sad that the people still don't have much say in politics. Where has freedom gone?

B A worker from Northern Germany

Bismarck has made everybody blind to the facts with his fuss about[3] the new emperor. I'm out of work. I can't openly say what I think. Bismarck saw to that with his new laws against the socialists. There are spies everywhere. I'm leaving. I bought my ticket last week for the ship to New York. There are five million Germans in the US already. And there … I'll be free.

C A Prussian peasant

I'm proud. My king is now German Emperor. All the other Europeans will finally take us seriously.

D A post-office clerk from Bavaria

I can't accept that my cousins in Austria are not German anymore. And why was the Prussian king chosen to become German emperor? … On the other hand, it's nice that most Germans live in one state now.

E A Polish farm worker from East Prussia

Germany just for Germans? That's a joke. There are Polish and Danish in the Empire and now even French in Alsace province.

F A factory owner from the Rhineland

A dream has come true: the many small states are a thing of the past. They made trade difficult. Now we have one currency, one central bank and one commercial code[4]. Politically, Germany is now a major power just like Great Britain and Russia. And economically the future is "Made in Germany".

S 11 **Grammar school[1] pupils from Hamburg celebrate Sedan Day, photograph, 1891**

The day on which the German army's victory over the French at Sedan on 2 September 1870, was celebrated, became a nationwide but "unofficial" holiday in the German Empire. Elementary school[2] (for children aged 6 to 14) was free in the German Empire. However, schools offering higher education had to be paid for. Moreover, German girls could not do the Abitur *until 1907.*

S 12 **Excerpt from a speech by Wilhelm II, German Emperor 1888–1918, to German teachers, 1890**

Wir müssen als Grundlage[3] für das Gymnasium das Deutsche[4] nehmen; wir sollen[5] nationale junge Deutsche erziehen und nicht junge Griechen und Römer. [...] Ebenso möchte ich das Nationale bei uns weiter gefördert sehen in Fragen der Geschichte, Geografie und Sage[6]. [...] Bedenken Sie, was uns für ein Nachwuchs[7] für die Landesverteidigung erwächst[8]. Ich suche nach Soldaten, wir wollen eine kräftige Generation haben, die auch als geistige Führer und Beamte dem Vaterland dienen.[9]

From: Wilhelm II., „Ansprache zur Eröffnung der Schulkonferenz in Berlin" (1890) in: Kaiserreden. Ein Charakterbild des deutschen Kaisers, *Weber, Leipzig, 1902, pp. 283–285.*

11 Was the German Empire a democratic state? Read the text on p. 86 and study S 9. List the "democratic" and "non-democratic" aspects of the German Empire in a two-column chart. Do not forget to include the democratic rights which were abolished by the Anti-Socialist Law. Then discuss your results.

12 Read the comments on German unification and the German Empire in S 10:

a List what the people agreed or disagreed with. Place the arguments in order so that the one you find most convincing is at the top and the one you like least is at the bottom.

b Compare and discuss your results in class.

13 In this Unit and Units 4–6 you have learned about:

A *monarchists* B *democrats* C *liberals* D *socialists*
E *nationalists (for Greater Germany or Little Germany)*

Working in pairs or groups, look at S 10 and match the above terms with the people to show their political attitudes. Give reasons for your choices.

14 One photograph – three captions: write a possible caption for the photograph in S 11 for a German, British and French newspaper. Write in English and keep in mind the audience you are writing for.

15 Imagine you are a reporter for the *London Illustrated News*. Write an article on Wilhelm II's speech to German teachers (see S 12). In the first paragraph, describe the circumstances (who, to whom, where, why), then paraphrase[10] what he said and, in your last paragraph, comment on it. You can use either direct or indirect speech to report what the Emperor said. If you use indirect speech remember the "backshift of tenses" (see **Activate your English**).

Activate your English

From direct to indirect speech

simple present → simple past
we must → they had to

simple past → past perfect
we believed → they had believed

present progressive → past progressive
I am looking for → he or she was looking for

present perfect → past perfect
I have always wanted → he or she had always wanted

1 grammar school *Gymnasium*
2 elementary school *Volksschule*
3 Grundlage *basis*
4 das Deutsche/Nationale *German/national ideas*
5 sollen *(here) be expected to*
6 Sage *legend*
7 Nachwuchs *new generation*
8 erwachsen *grow up*
9 dem Vaterland dienen *serve the fatherland*
10 paraphrase sth. *etwas umschreiben*

Project work – Investigating monuments to Bismarck

S 13 Bismarck memorial[1] in Hamburg, photograph, c 2002

S 14 The Bismarck memorial in Hamburg: a profile (see S 13)

Features[2]	Notes	From notes to spoken text
Location	*located in Hamburg, next to the Michaeliskirche; the figure is looking out at the harbour*	*Let me start/ begin by saying that ...* *To start/begin with, the memorial ...*
Client[3]	*the mayor[4] of Hamburg*	*The memorial was commissioned by ...*
Date of construction	*1903–1906*	*It was constructed/built between ... and ...* *The building/construction began in ... and ended in ...* *The construction was completed in ...*
Opening	*2 June 1906*	*The opening took place on ...*
Measurements	*total height: 34 meters* *height of the pedestal: 19 meters* *height of the figure: 15 meters* *height of the head: 1.83 meters* *length of the sword: 8 meters*	*The ... is ... meters* *The monument/pedestal/... is ... meters high* *The ... alone measures ...* *The ... is ... meters long*
Material	*granite rock[5]*	*The monument is made of ...* *... was used (in the construction)*
Appearance	*full medieval armour[6] (sword, coat) = a "Roland", the symbol of the free cities*	*The figure is presented in ...* *It looks like ...* *All in all, the figure is/looks/appears ...*
Reactions at the time	*bourgeoisie: welcomed the memorial* *working class: were against the memorial*	*There were mixed reactions to the monument ...* *The monument received mixed reactions ...* *While/Although the bourgeoisie ..., the working class ...*

1 memorial *Denkmal*
2 feature *Merkmal*
3 client *(hier) Auftraggeber*
4 mayor *Bürgermeister*
5 granite rock *Granitstein*
6 medieval armour *mittelalterliche Rüstung*

S 15 Bismarck tower in Bochum, opened in 1910, photograph, c 2002

Bismarck towers were built on four continents – in Europe, Australia, South America and Africa. The first tower was opened in 1895. Of the 240 Bismarck towers, 172 still remain.

16 **a** Use the notes in the profile of the Bismarck memorial (S 14) to describe the memorial (S 13).

b What do you learn "through" the memorial?

17 **Project work: Presenting a Bismarck tower**

a Divide into groups of not more than four.

b Find the location of a Bismarck tower in your hometown or area and gather information on its history.
Tip: *www.bismarcktuerme.de*

c Present the memorial to the class as suggested in the "Study skills" below. Make sure to use the language suggestions in S 14.

18 **Project work: Drawing a model**

Plan, draw or create a model for a monument or memorial that commemorates the German soldiers who lost their lives in the Wars of Unification. When you present it, explain your point of view, values and beliefs which you express in the memorial. For help, see the "Study skills" below.

Study skills

1 Planning the project

a Brainstorm ideas about what you want to do.
b What kinds of materials do you need? Where and how can you get them?
c Draw up a plan for the project work period and divide the work among the members of your group.
d Decide what form the end product will take, e.g. a poster, tourist information brochure or website, newspaper article, radio or TV feature ("This day in history"), etc.

2 Collecting material

Find reference material in the Internet, in libraries, museums, city or church archives, etc.

3 Drafting[1] (parts of) your presentation

Discuss your drafts and suggest changes. Check the language for spelling mistakes, grammar mistakes (e.g. tenses, word order), missing punctuation (e.g. quotation marks) and incomplete sentences.

4 Writing the final version of your presentation

5 Evaluating the projects

When you are finished, evaluate the sources of information, the material and the final product. Did everything run smoothly? What could have been improved?

1 draft sth. *etwas entwerfen*

Unit revision

German unification

Key events

1862–1890	Bismarck serves as Minister President of Prussia
1864	German-Danish War
1866	Austro-Prussian War North German Confederation
1870–1871	Franco-Prussian War
1871–1918	German Empire
1871–1888	Reign of Emperor Wilhelm I
1871–1890	Bismarck serves as Chancellor of the German Empire
1872–1878	*Kulturkampf*
1878–1890	Anti-Socialist Law

Key personalities

Otto von Bismarck

Key terms

Junker, Ems Telegram, unification, anti-Semitism, reparations, *Bundesrat* (federal council of the German states), *Reichstag* (German national parliament)

History skills

Monuments to Bismarck (*pp. 89–90*)

Activate your English

From direct to indirect speech (*p. 88*)

Theodor Fontane, Effie Briest, 1895
Set in Bismarck's Germany, Effi Briest, a naïve girl of seventeen, marries a noble diplomat much older than herself. While living with him in a far-away Baltic port, she drifts into a short affair with another man. The full effects are felt only six years later ...

1 Photocopy the three maps which show the different stages of German unification and label them with the necessary information.

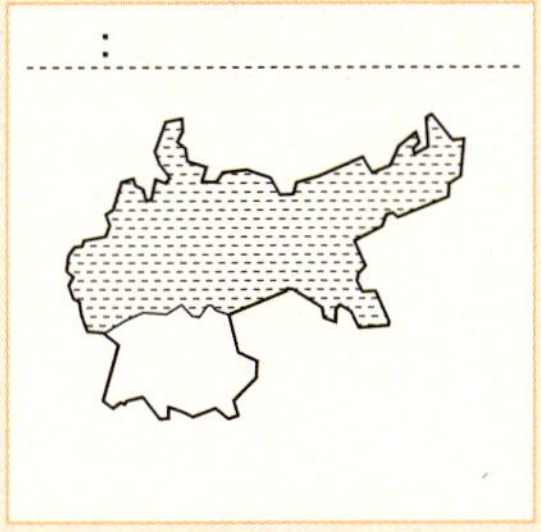

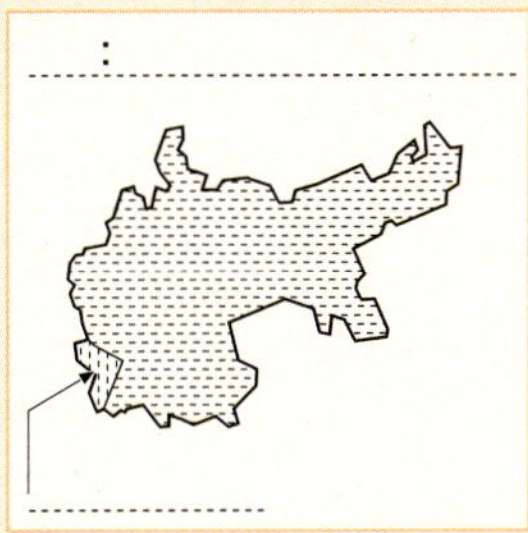

2 Mark the correct answers on the German Empire:

a *The territory enclosed ...*	A *"Greater Germany"*	B *"Little Germany"*
b *Political system was a ...*	A *republic*	B *monarchy*
c *The German Empire was a ...*	A *federal state*	B *central state*

3 In German, the war of 1870–1871 is called the *"Deutsch-Französischer Krieg"*; in English, it is called the "Franco-Prussian War". Explain the difference.

4 The two pictures below show two major events in 19th-century German history. Copy and fill in the chart. Then describe what the two events had in common and what was different.

Features	***Picture on the left***	***Picture on the right***
Colours of flag	...	...
Place	...	...
Time	...	...
People involved	...	...
Events leading up to the situation	...	...
Effects	...	...

8.1 Treaties and tensions[1], 1871–1890

S1 Europe after German unification: Powers and interests

German Empire
- ?
- ?
- ?
- ?
- ?

Kingdom of Great Britain
- profited enormously from its industrialization and overseas trade
- interested in a free trade route to India (through the Straits of Gibraltar, Suez Canal 1869)
- interested in gaining colonies in Africa
- interested in gaining territories in Persia, Afghanistan, northern China
- stayed away from alliances with other powers (splendid isolation)
- protected itself with a powerful navy
- encouraged a balance of power on the continent

Russian Empire
- industrialization was just beginning
- regarded itself as defender of the Slav[2] nationalities in the Balkans (pan-Slavism); helped them in their fight for independence against the Austrian and Ottoman Empires
- interested in gaining territories in Persia, Afghanistan, northern China
- interested in gaining a Mediterranean port and control over Dardanelles, Sea of Marmara and Bosphorus

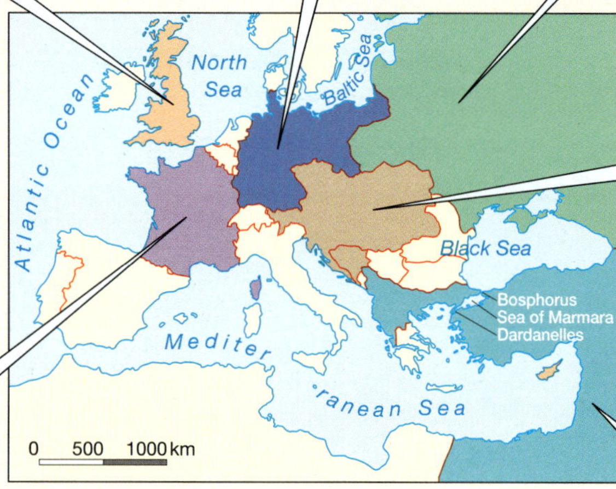

Austro-Hungarian Empire
- industrialization was just beginning
- consisted of[3] many nationalities, ethnic groups and religions (Catholics, Christian Orthodox, Muslims)
- threatened by the Slav movements for independence in its Balkan territories
- interested in keeping the Russians away from the Dardanelles, Sea of Marmara and Bosphorus

Republic of France
- less industrialized than Britain and Germany
- weakened by the Franco-Prussian War, 1870–1871
- desire for revenge on Germany
- interested in winning back the lost territories of Alsace-Lorraine
- interested in gaining colonies in Africa

Ottoman (= Turkish) Empire
- hardly industrialized
- consisted of many nationalities and ethnic groups, especially in the Balkans
- threatened by the Slav movements for independence in its Balkan territories
- losing control over its territories since c. 1800

Bismarck's alliance system[4]

After 1871, Germany expected a French war of revenge[5]. Bismarck, however, tried to avoid war at all costs. He stated that Germany had no wish to gain any further territory.

Bismarck's most important aim was to isolate[6] France in Europe so that France could never go to war. Hence, he negotiated[7] a series of alliances with Russia and Austria to make an alliance impossible between Germany's western neighbour (France) and eastern neighbours (Austria and Russia) with Germany in the middle ("nightmare of coalitions"*). Bismarck formed

- in 1873 the Three Emperors' League[8] of Germany, Austria and Russia;
- in 1879 the Dual Alliance[9] of Germany and Austria against Russia (Rumania and Italy were linked in 1883 and 1888);
- in 1881 the Three Emperors' Alliance[10] (a renewed version of the 1873 League);
- in 1882 the Triple Alliance[11] of Germany, Austria and Italy
- in 1887 the Reinsurance Treaty[12] with Russia (after the Three Emperors Alliance had broken in 1885): Germany promised to stay neutral if Russia was attacked by Austria; Russia would stay neutral if Germany was attacked by France.

1 tension *Spannung*
2 Slav *slavisch*
3 consist of *bestehen aus*
4 alliance system *Bündnissystem*
5 revenge *Vergeltung, Rache*
6 isolate sb./sth. *jdn./etwas isolieren, abgrenzen*
7 negotiate sth. *etwas verhandeln*
8 Three Emperors' League *Dreikaiserbund*
9 Dual Alliance *Zweibund*
10 Three Emperors' Alliance *Dreikaiservertrag*
11 Triple Alliance *Dreibund*
12 Reinsurance Treaty *Rückversicherungsvertrag*

Instability in the Balkans

The rise of nationalism and the "hunger" for independence made the situation in the Balkans very unstable. In 1875, for example, there were uprisings in Bosnia and Herzegovina against the Ottoman Empire.

In 1877, war broke out when the Bulgars (a Slav people) rose up against their Ottoman rulers. Russia supported them and declared war on the Ottoman Empire. When the Russians defeated the Ottoman Empire, Austria and England became extremely alarmed: Austria feared that Russia would also help the Slav nationalities within the Austrian Empire to fight for their independence. England was afraid that the Russian navy would soon gain access[1] to the Mediterranean.

The Congress of Berlin, 1878

Bismarck, who was afraid that Germany might be drawn into the conflict in the Balkans, organized a peace conference in June and July 1878. The fact that this meeting took place in Berlin (Congress of Berlin) was a sign of Germany's new power and Bismarck's prestige.

Bismarck reached a settlement[2] which avoided a war between the European superpowers[3]. The loser was the Ottoman Empire because it lost control over the Balkans. New independent states like Montenegro, Serbia and Romania were created. Because Austria took control over Bosnia-Herzegovina, the rivalry between Russia and the Austrian Empire for influence in the Balkans grew. The Balkans remained[4] a region of great instability in the decades that followed.

1 gain access to sth. *Zugang zu etwas bekommen*
2 settlement *Abkommen, Übereinkunft*
3 superpower *Großmacht*
4 remain *bleiben*

S2 Anton von Werner (1843–1915), "Final meeting at the Congress of Berlin in July 1878", oil painting, 1881

8.2 Africa: When the whites came to Loango

1 baptize *taufen*
2 trading post *Handelsniederlassung*
3 ivory *Elfenbein*
4 plentiful *reichlich, massenhaft*
5 explorer *Forscher*
6 protectorate *Protektorat, besetztes Gebiet, „Schutz"-Gebiet*
7 rubber *Naturkautschuk*
8 timber *Holz*
9 ivory carving *Elfenbeinschnitzerei*

The African Kingdom of Loango (15th–19th century) – A timeline

c 1400 The region of Loango on the west coast of Africa (between the equator and the mouth of the Congo River) is part of the newly founded Kingdom of Congo.

1482 The Portuguese captain Diego Cão discovers the mouth of the Congo River.

1488 The Portuguese establish contact with the Kingdom of Congo. Its King welcomes missionaries, is baptized[1] and sends his son to Portugal to become educated.

16th cent. Portugal establishes trading posts[2] along the coast.

c 1550 The Kingdom of Loango separates from the Kingdom of Congo.

1668 Dutch writer, geographer and historian Olfert Dapper publishes the first detailed description of the Kingdom of Loango in Dutch in Amsterdam. It is translated into German, English and French a decade later.

S5 **Loango, capital of the Kingdom of Loango, engraving from the book *Description of Africa* by Olfert Dapper, Amsterdam, 1668**

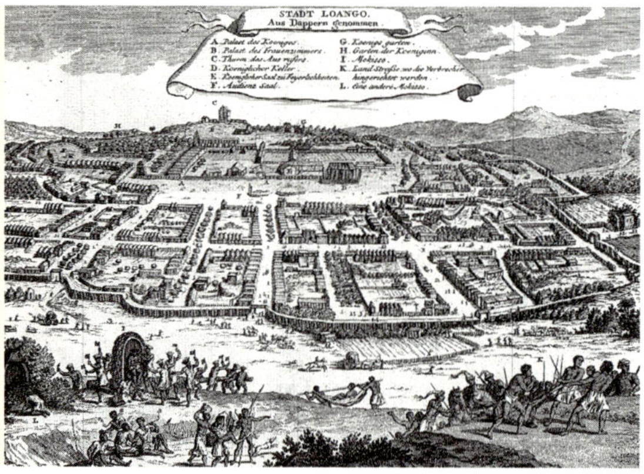

S6 **The ancient Kingdom of Loango**

S7 **Ivory carving[9] from the Loango Coast, 19th century**
Inscribed on reverse: "Congo Missionaries". Height: 8.5 cm.

17th–18th cent. Loango traders import ivory[3] and slaves from the interior of Africa; on the coast the slaves are sold to European slave traders to work on the plantations on the American continent. Since civil wars make slaves plentiful[4], up to 18,000 a year are sold. African traders become extremely wealthy. European luxury goods are imported.

19th cent. When the slave trade is forbidden, the Kingdom of Loango slowly collapses.

1880 French explorer[5] Count de Brazza reaches the region of the Congo River ruled by Chief Makoko of the Bateke people. Makoko signs treaties with France. He places the territory under French protection because he wants to have more trade as well as protection from attacks by other tribes. The French establish Brazzaville as a trading post.

1883 The area of the Kingdom of Loango becomes part of the French protectorate[6] of Middle Congo. French colonial companies force the native population with great brutality to deliver rubber[7], ivory and timber[8].

1910 Middle Congo becomes part of the colony* of French Equatorial Africa with Brazzaville as capital.

8 **a** Look at Unit 1.2, p. 9, and organize the information on slavery in the British colonies in North America (who, where, when, why and how) in an event map (see Appendix, pp. 142–143).
b Then, compare it with what historians know about slavery in the African Kingdom of Loango (timeline). Is there information you did not expect? Give reasons.

9 **Extra research:** Explain the colonial companies' interest in African rubber. Collect information and present your findings to the class (tip: search term "the history of rubber")

10 **Extra research:** Complete the timeline above with information on what has happened in the colony of French Equatorial Africa (and the region of Loango) since 1910.

8.3 Colonial rivalry in the age of imperialism: "The scramble[1] for Africa"

S 8 ***"La France va pouvoir porter librement au Maroc la civilisation, la richesse et la paix"* (Of her own free will France will bring civilization, wealth and peace to Morocco), front page of the French magazine *Le Petit Journal*, November 1911**

Vocabulary help: female person (representing Marianne; *see p. 49, S 3**) – ring of light – Phrygian cap – tricolour stripes – cornucopia[2] (symbolizing wealth) – money runs out of sth. – Moroccan natives – traditional clothing – plough – book – kneel down[3] – look up – humble[4] – joyful – grateful – white colonist pointing to Europe – tropical helmet – native (servant) saluting the European soldier (colonist) – fez*

A new wave of colonization

At the end of the 18th century, Britain had lost its thirteen colonies* in North America (see Unit 1.3–1.5). At the same time, Spain and Portugal had lost most of their colonies in South America, and The Netherlands had difficulties keeping control of the East Indies (today's Indonesia).
A hundred years later, however, a second wave of colonization* took place. Within a short time, c 1880–1900, every corner of the Earth (apart from the Americas) was taken over by European powers. Africa saw the most aggressive colonization. It was divided up between European powers like a cake. This was called "the scramble for Africa".

Motives for European imperialism

The European desire to create overseas empires[5], a movement beginning around 1880 and called imperialism*, had several motives. For the British, the colonies in Africa had to protect the shipping routes between Britain and its most valuable colony, India (see Unit 2.1). Another motive was national prestige. Colonies were seen as national status symbols. Clubs and societies were established which supported imperialism and pushed governments to acquire[6] more colonies. The popular press, best-selling authors and songwriters created enthusiasm for empire building and made a lot of propaganda.

1 scramble *Gerangel, Wettlauf*
2 cornucopia *Füllhorn*
3 kneel down *niederknien*
4 humble *demütig*
5 overseas empire *Überseeimperium*
6 acquire *erwerben*

Some European colonists believed they were bringing civilization to Africa and Asia: not only the benefits[1] of ports and railways, but also a fully developed legal system, an educational system, hospitals and the Christian religion. Others saw future economic advantages in the African colonies. They argued that European nations had to control lands that had raw materials (metals, timber, agricultural products, etc.) which they needed for their industrial economies. They also wanted to open up markets for European manufactured goods.

Key terms

Imperialism
Imperialism was the aggressive policy of the industrialized nations to get control over distant "weaker" countries, especially during the time between c 1880 and 1914. An imperialist state dominated a colony's economic, political and cultural life.

S 9 Excerpt from "Confession of Faith" (1877) by Cecil J. Rhodes (1853–1902)

Rhodes was the owner of de Beers – the world's biggest diamond mine in southern Africa – and Prime Minister of the British Cape Colony from 1890 to 1896:

I say that we are the finest race in the world and that the more of the world we inhabit the better it is for the human race. Just imagine what change there would be if those parts that are at present inhabited by the most inferior[2] human beings were brought under Anglo-Saxon influence. Think of the extra employment a new country added to our dominions[3] would give. [...] The acquisition[4] of the greater part of the world under our rule would simply mean an end to all wars. [...] Africa is lying ready for us, it is our duty to take it.

Abridged and simplified version from: Edgar Otten et al., Spotlight on History, *Volume 1, Cornelsen, Berlin, 1995, p. 67.*

S 10 Thomas Theodor Heine (1867–1948), *"So kolonisiert der Engländer"* (That's how the Englishman colonizes), cartoon in the German magazine *Simplicissimus*, 1905

Vocabulary help: pressing board[5] – capstan[6] – missionary – Bible – give one's blessing[7] – torture[8] sb. – squeeze sth. out of sb.[9] – turn sth. into sth. – force sb. to do sth. – pour sth. down sb.'s throat[10]

1 benefit *Vorteil, Nutzen*
2 inferior *niedere*
3 dominion *Dominion (überseeische Besitzung des British Empire)*
4 acquisition *Erwerb*
5 pressing board *Pressbalken*
6 capstan *Drehkreuz, Presse*
7 give one's blessing *seinen Segen geben*
8 torture sb. *jdn. quälen, foltern*
9 squeeze sth. out of sb. *etwas aus jdm. herauspressen*
10 pour sth. down sb.'s throat *jdm. etwas einflößen*

S 11 Africa around 1880

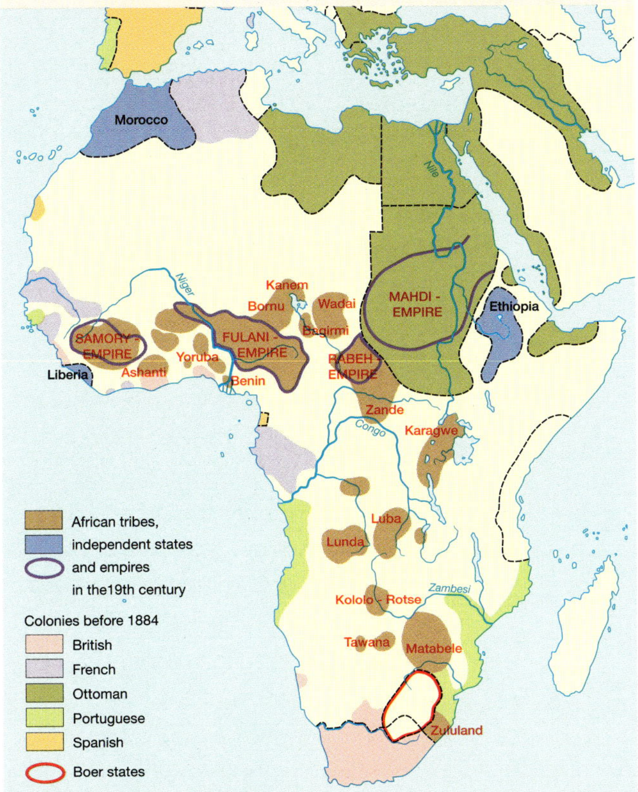

S 12 Colonies and anti-colonial rebellions in Africa before 1914

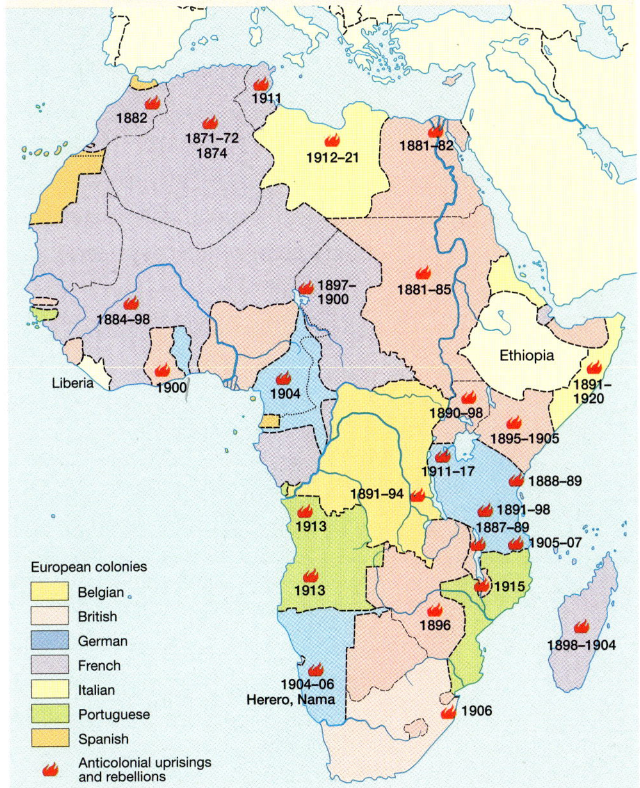

Activate your English

Reading and interpreting historical maps

What can a historical map show?

– *a situation at a certain moment*[1]
– *a situation during a certain period of time*[2]
– *the changes between two moments or epochs*
– *the developments within a certain period of time*

Describing a situation at a certain moment in time

The map shows … and the political boundaries[3] *of …*
We learn about the development of …
We can see that … was divided up between … / the borders were drawn along …

Describing change and development

At first the continent / the area / the territory was …
A century/decade later the Europeans …
Later … / At the beginning / in the middle / at the end of the … century
During this period / the period from … to …, …
In the course of the … century, …
After the … the situation had completely/ hardly changed

Togo
Kamerun
German South-West (Namibia)
German East Africa (Tanzania)

11 Working in pairs:

a Describe the situation shown in the map in S 11 to your partner. For vocabulary help, see **Activate your English** above.

b Look at the map in S 12 and explain the political changes in Africa between c 1880 and 1914. Pay special attention to Germany as an imperialist power.

1 moment *Zeitpunkt*
2 period of time *Zeitspanne*
3 boundary *Grenze, Grenzlinie*

S 13

American cartoon, c 1900

Key terms

Colony

A country or area that is ruled by another, more powerful, country. In former times, the local native population of a colony did not enjoy full rights. Many were forced into slave labour or driven out of their homes. Their land was sometimes taken and given to settlers from the ruling country. Foreign customs[1], religions or legal systems were imposed.

Key terms

Racism

1. A belief which developed in the second half of the 19th century in Europe and which argued
- that humans can be separated into so-called races[2],
- that all people of a race have the same characteristics given by nature,
- that the white race is superior to other races.

2. Racism in the 19th century was heavily influenced by social Darwinism. Following the British philosopher Herbert Spencer (1820–1903), social Darwinists argued that individuals and groups (nations), just like plants and animals, compete[3] with one another for success in life. In this competition only the fittest survive. Social Darwinism justified overseas expansion by nations (imperialism*) during the 1890s because white Europeans were considered more fit in the struggle for survival.

12 Look at the text extract in S 9:
a List Rhodes' arguments on why the Anglo-Saxon race must "take" the world.
b Compare and contrast Rhodes' arguments with the characteristics of racism (see Key term "racism") in a Venn diagram (see Appendix, pp. 142–143).
c Discuss in class whether Rhodes' ideas can be classified as racist.

13 Divide into two groups. One group looks at S 8 and the other at S 10. Analyse the source your group has chosen with the help of the "Study skills" for cartoons (p. 18) or paintings (p. 121). Choose meaningful, appropriate[4] questions for your source. Present your results to the other group.

14 **a** Organize the information on the motives for European imperialism in a mind map (see the text, p. 97; the Key terms, p. 98 and 100; and S 8–S 10).
b In the chart to the right, indicate[5] in the right-hand column why each social group had an interest in imperialism (different groups can have the same interests). If you cannot find information in the text, try to speculate.

Social groups in European countries	***Interests in imperialism***
Military 	...
Government 	...
Enthusiastic population 	...
Business 	...

15 Write a caption for the cartoon in S 13.

16 **Extra research:** Around 1900, the United States of America became the world's leading economy. Did the USA become an imperial nation, too? Give a PowerPoint presentation on the history of US foreign policy up until 1914. (Tip: search the terms "US imperialism" and "US colonialism".)

1 customs *Sitten*
2 race *„Rasse"*
3 compete *konkurrieren*
4 appropriate *passend*
5 indicate *angeben, bezeichnen*

8.4 A conflict in today's Kenya

S 14 **Excerpt from an article in the BBC magazine *Focus on Africa*, 2005**

In 1963, the east African state of Kenya won independence from Britain. The following article describes a conflict in today's Kenya that is closely linked to colonial history:

Source	Tasks
Perhaps nowhere in Kenya is the land divide[1] more graphic[2] than at the Laikipia plateau [...]. On it, lush[3] ranches [...] belong to the descendants[4] of the white settlers. In the reserves[5], where Maasai cows and goats graze[6], the soil is bare[7] and brown. [...] Matters came to a head[8] in August last year when police shot and killed a 70-year-old man and wounded four other Maasai who were grazing cattle on private land they say is theirs. They were members of the Maasai tribes[9] in Laikipia demanding the return of their ancestral territory[10] – 100 years after being driven from the land by British colonialists. [...]	*Describe in note form the land situation in today's Kenya. Describe the demands of the Maasai.*
The land problem has its roots in the colonial past, a process [...] which confered[11] enormous powers to the colonial government to deal with[12] what was then known as Crown land. These laws [by the colonial government] were seen as part of the colonial policies to crowd out[13] Africans [...] from the land market[14], allowing settlers to acquire long leases[15] – many for 999 years – on Crown land. [...] The campaign [of today's Maasai] is based on a treaty signed with the British colonial government in 1904, which gave the colonial power a 100-year lease on their ancestral land. That treaty, claim[16] the Maasai, expired[17] on 15 August 2004.	*Describe the historical roots of the problem.*
It's common knowledge that the treaty [...] took the Maasai's best land and confined[18] them to reserves. These claims[19] are supported by some Kenyan politicians who have repeatedly emphasised[20] that the country's best land remains the domain of the descendants of English colonialists. The white farmers and some Kenyans disagree, saying that the best land is in the hand of politicians. [...] The white ranches have become popular destinations for the West's rich and famous, where owners now operate luxury safari lodges in the growing sector known as eco-tourism. [...] The Kenyan government [...] says the land claim is a Maasai myth. The lease, say the government, was for 999 years and not 100 years.	*List the groups involved and their points of view in today's conflict.*

From: Gray Phombeah, "Hand it back", in: Focus on Africa, *July–September 2005, pp. 31–32.*

17 Analyse the conflict in present-day Kenya by doing the tasks in S 14.

18 In the conflict (S 14) the Kenyan government could

A *take the land, compensate[21] the white owners for the loss and give the land back to the Maasai tribes;*

B *take the land and give it back to the Maasai tribes, with no compensation for the white owners;*

C *do nothing.*

Speculate on the effects of each of these government decisions.

19 What do you think? Discuss what the Kenyan government could or should do.

20 **Extra research:** Collect information in the Internet on the most recent developments in the land dispute in Kenya. (Tip: search the terms "land dispute", "Kenya", and "Maasai".)

1 divide *Teilung, Kluft*
2 graphic *anschaulich*
3 lush *üppig, luxuriös*
4 descendent *Nachfahren*
5 reserve *Reservat*
6 graze *weiden lassen*
7 bare *kahl*
8 come to a head *sich zuspitzen*
9 tribe *Stamm*
10 ancestral territory *Land der Vorfahren*
11 confer sth. *etwas verleihen*
12 deal with sth. *handeln*
13 crowd out sb. *jdn. verdrängen*
14 land market *Grundstücksmarkt*
15 acquire a lease *einen Pachtvertrag bekommen*
16 claim sth. *etwas behaupten*
17 expire *ablaufen*
18 confine to *(hier) in die Grenzen der Reservate zwingen*
19 claim *Anspruch*
20 emphasize sth. *etwas betonen*
21 compensate sb. for sth. *jdn. für etwas entschädigen*

8.5 German colonies in Africa

Germany and the colonial rivalry

Germany arrived very late in "the scramble for Africa" (see Unit 8.3). There were German merchants like the Woehrmanns from Hamburg or adventurers like Carl Peters who set up colonies* as *private* individuals. But there was no *government* interest because, after unification in 1871, Chancellor Bismarck was against colonizing distant parts of the world. It was at the beginning of the 1880s, under pressure from businessmen and nationalists, that Bismarck was forced to change policy.

However, it was almost too late. Most of the world was already under the control of other colonial powers. A German colonial empire could only be established by either taking the colonies from other empires by force, for example from Britain or France, or by taking the last unclaimed[1] regions in Africa (or on other continents).

Many Germans did not feel that Germany after the unification was respected as equal among the other European powers such as England, France or Russia. However, they thought it had earned this respect because it was the strongest military power in Europe. The country was also gradually overtaking Britain as the strongest economic power. Its population was growing rapidly. Its universities and scientists were leading in scientific research. Its culture and educational system were dynamic (see Unit 6.3).

In the age of imperialism*, people judged nations according to whether they were expanding or remaining stable. Since the German Empire had no colonies, many Germans felt it was losing in the competition[2] for influence and world markets.

Finally, the German Empire set up colonies in Togo, Cameroon and South-West Africa (1884), in East Africa (1885–1890), in the Pacific (1884–1899) and in Kiaotchov in China (1898).

S 15 Road construction near Dar-es-Salam in the colony of German East Africa (present-day Tanzania), photograph, c 1900

Vocabulary help: men and women chained to each other – carry loads[3] on their heads – spade[4] – local guard – German supervisor[5] – donkey[6] – looking into the camera – palm tree

1 unclaimed *unbeansprucht*
2 competition *Wettstreit*
3 loads *Lasten*
4 spade *Spaten*
5 supervisor *Aufseher*
6 donkey *Esel*

S 16 **An African teacher and a German school inspector in the German colonial school in Dar-es-Salam, colony of German East Africa, photograph, 1903**

Pupils are being tested in mathematics and Swahili (the native language widely spoken in East Africa).

S 17 **Excerpt from a letter originally in Afrikaans from the Nama chief[1] Hendrik Witbooi to Joseph Fredericks, 27 June, 1892**

Fredericks was chief of the tribe which had sold the land of today's Lüderitz Bay to the German merchant and adventurer Adolf Lüderitz in 1883. When the letter was written, the area was part of the colony of German South-West Africa. The Nama and Herero tribes lived from livestock farming[2]:

The Germans settle in the area without asking for permission, impose their laws on the people who own the land, outlaw their free movement on the roads, take away their right to pasture their animals on their own land and to use their own water, and forbid the locals to hunt their own game.

From: Hendrik Witbooi, Afrika den Afrikanern. Aufzeichnungen eines Nama-Häuptlings, *Wolfgang Reinhard, ed., Dietz, Berlin, 1982, pp. 132–134. Translated by the author.*

S 18 **Hendrik Witbooi on a Namibian banknote, 2006**

S 19 **Excerpt from the pamphlet *Bedarf Deutschland der Kolonien?* (Does Germany need colonies?) by Friedrich Fabri (1824–1891), 1879**

From 1857 to 1884, Fabri was the director of the Barmen Rhine Missionary Society. He never visited any colonies and developed his views only from written sources:

We are convinced [...] that the colonial question has become a matter of life-or-death for the development of Germany. Colonies will have a salutary[3] effect on our economic situation as well as on our entire national progress. Here is a solution for many of the problems that face us. In this new *Reich* of ours there is so much bitterness, so much [...] political wrangling[4], that the opening of a new, promising road of national effort[5] will act as a kind of liberating[6] influence. Our national spirit will be renewed. [...]

In any case, it would be wise for us Germans to learn about colonial skills from our Anglo-Saxon cousins and to begin a friendly competition with them. When the German *Reich* centuries ago stood at the pinnacle[7] of the states of Europe, it was the number one trade and sea power. If the new Germany wants to protect its newly won position of power for a long time, it must [...] delay[8] no longer in the task of renewing the call for colonies.

Translation: Louis L. Snyder, The Imperialism Reader: Documents and Readings on Modern Expansionism, *Princeton, 1962, pp. 116–117. From: www.web.jjay.cuny.edu/~jobrien/reference/ob44.html, 7 August 2005.*

1 chief *Häuptling*
2 livestock farming *Viehzucht*
3 salutary heilsam
4 wrangling *Gerangel*
5 effort *Anstrengung*
6 liberating *befreiend*
7 pinnacle *Gipfel*
8 delay *aufschieben*

S 20 The colonies of the German Empire and their economic importance, 1884–1914

a) German settlers in the colonies, 1884–1913:

Settlers in % of all emigrants from the German Empire, 1871–1914	0.03 %

b) Trade data in 1913:

Raw materials imported from the colonies (in % of all German imports)	1.6 %
Exports to the colonies (in % of all German exports)	0.5 %
Capital investment in the colonies (in % of all German foreign investment)	2.0 %

c) German Empire subsidies[1] to its colonies, 1884–1914 (in million RM[2]):

German Colony	Subsidies
South-West Africa	278.0
Kiaotchov	174.0
East Africa	122.0
Cameroon	48.0
German New Guinea	19.0
Togo	3.5
Samoa	1.5

d) Costs of colonial wars (in million RM):

War in South-West Africa (today's Namibia)	585.0

From: Hilke Günther-Arndt et al. (ed.), Geschichtsbuch, *new edition, vol. 3, Cornelsen, Berlin, 1995, p. 235.*

S 21

Herero tribe members in Namibia commemorate[3] the German genocide[4] on the Herero and Nama in 1904, photograph, 1999

21 **a** Working in pairs or groups, organize the information on German colonization in Africa (see p. 102) in an event map (see Appendix, pp. 142–143).
b Draw lots[5] in each group to decide who will present the results in class.

22 **a** Look at the photographs in S 15 and S 16 and describe what is happening.
b Do you think S 15 and S 16 were arranged beforehand or were snapshots? Give reasons.

23 **a** Look at S 17 and list the Herero chief's complaints about German rule in South-West Africa.
b **Extra Research:** Find information on the Herero genocide in German South-West Africa (today: Namibia; see S 21). Prepare a poster with a headline, short texts, images, etc.
c In recent years, the Herero have demanded financial compensation for the genocide committed by the Germans. Discuss how the German government should react.

24 **a** List the reasons given in S 19 why Friedrich Fabri felt that Germany should have colonies.
b Be a foreign policy expert. Read the information on the German colonization in Africa again (see p. 102) and point out the dangers of the German desire to win colonies.

25 **a** Working in pairs, use the information in S 20 a–d to describe to your partner the economic importance of the German colonies for the German economy. Example:

Statistical information	*Description*
capital investment	*Only two per cent of all the money which Germans invested in businesses in foreign countries was invested in German colonies.*
...	...

b Discuss who profited from the German "national effort" to win colonies:
A *the Africans*
B *German workers*
C *German taxpayers*
D *German companies active in the colonies*
E *the German economy*
F *the German military*
G *others*

26 Imagine you are a textbook author and write a short paragraph titled "The economic benefits of the German colonies for the German Empire".

27 European colonists (see S 8, p. 97) justified colonization with the argument that they were bringing civilization to Africa.
a Working in groups, discuss and note down what, in your opinion, is meant by the term "civilization" (infrastructure? human rights? democratic government? modern medicine? etc.).
b Check whether the sources in this unit support the colonists' argument.

1 subsidy Subvention, *Unterstützungsgeld*
2 RM = Reichmark *Imperial Marks*
3 commemorate *gedenken*
4 genocide *Völkermord*
5 draw lots *auslosen*
6 presence *Anwesenheit*

8.6 The "New Course": German *Weltpolitik*, 1890–1914

On the way to world power: *Weltpolitik* under Wilhelm II

The German Emperor Wilhelm II and his government believed that Germany should play a much larger role in world politics and become a "world power" rather than a "European power" (New Course*). After Wilhelm II dismissed Bismarck in 1890, German foreign policy changed dramatically and became less cautious[1] and more aggressive.

For Wilhelm II, *Weltpolitik** meant overseas colonies and a navy to protect them. The Kaiser chose Alfred von Tirpitz (1849–1930) as the "architect" of his new navy and Tirpitz became State Secretary of the German Navy Office[2] in 1897. Some months later, the German Naval League *(Flottenverein)* was founded. This society made the idea very popular that colonies and a strong navy were necessary for national greatness and prosperity[3]; membership[4] in the League grew to more than one million in 1913.

German *Weltpolitik* and its consequences

Britain's naval superiority[5] and dominance[6] of trade routes gave her great power and wealth. When Germany began build up its navy, Britain felt its position was threatened, and the two countries entered into a naval arms race[7].

Britain also actively looked for other ways to protect itself from the rising power of Germany. As a consequence, Britain and France put aside[8] their own conflicts over trading rights and influence in Africa (see Unit 8.3) and formed the *Entente Cordiale* (Friendly Agreement) in 1904.

When Wilhelm II supported Austria against Russia in the Balkans (see p. 93), Russia reacted and formed an alliance with Britain in 1907. This was extremely dangerous for Germany because Russia was already allied with France in the Dual Alliance from 1892/1894 (see Unit 8.1, p. 92). As a result, Russia joined the *Entente* powers in 1907.

1 cautious *vorsichtig*
2 German Navy Office *Reichsmarineamt*
3 prosperity *Wohlstand*
4 membership *Mitgliedschaft*
5 superiority *Überlegenheit*
6 dominance *Vorherrschaft*
7 naval arms race *Marinewettrüsten*
8 put aside *beiseite schieben*
9 erratic manner *launische, unberechenbare Art*
10 rapprochement *Annäherung*

Biography

Wilhelm II

Wilhelm II (1859–1941) was King of Prussia and Emperor of Germany from 1888 to the end of the German Empire in 1918. His father was Emperor Friedrich III (1888), his grandfather Wilhelm I (1871–1888). He was also a grandson of Queen Victoria. From an early age, he showed great interest in the military. Historians disagree on how much his personality, especially his erratic manner[9], influenced German politics.

He emigrated to the Netherlands in 1918.

S 22 The European Alliance System in 1907

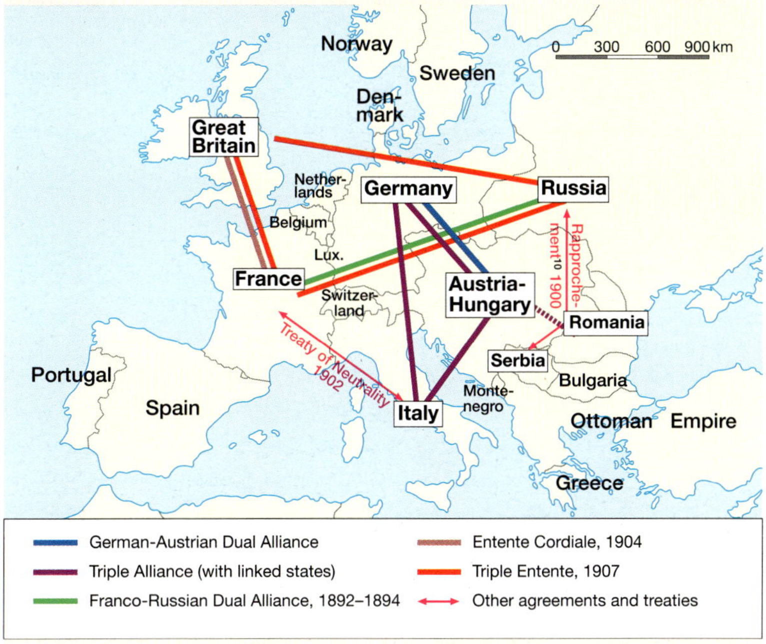

S 23 A close adviser on the personality of Wilhelm II

Bernhard von Bülow, one of Wilhelms' Chancellors, wrote in his Memoirs (1930–1931) what Philipp Count of Eulenberg, a close adviser to Wilhelm II, told him about the Kaiser:

Wilhelm takes everything personally. Only personal arguments will impress him. He likes to lecture[1] others but will not allow himself to be taught. [...] Wilhelm likes to shine and to do and decide everything by himself. [...] To get him to accept an idea one has to pretend that the idea is his own. [...] Never forget that HM [His Majesty] needs to be praised from time to time.

From: Alison Kitson, Germany 1858–1990, *OUP, 2001, p. 54.*

S 24 The building of large battleships in Britain and Germany, 1906–1913

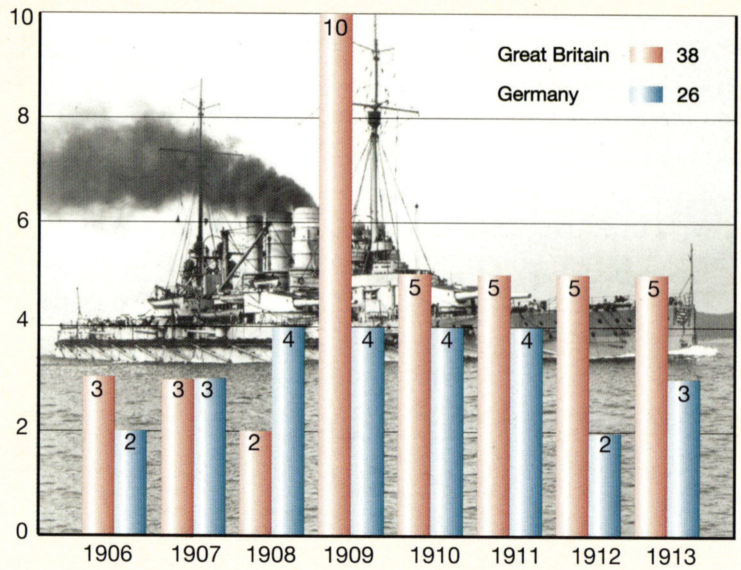

S 25 Points of view on naval policy around 1900

25 a) Alfred von Tirpitz wrote in 1900:

Under the present circumstances[2] there is only one means to protect Germany's trade and colonies: Germany must have a fleet of such strength that in a war even the biggest fleet would run the risk of endangering its own superiority. For this purpose, it is not absolutely necessary that the German fleet is as big as the biggest naval power, because as a rule[3] a big naval power will be unable to concentrate its whole force against us.

25 b) Excerpt from an article in the British Daily Mail, 5 February, 1903:

While great naval power in the hands of Britain cannot constitute a menace[4], in the hands of Germany it will be a great peril[5] to the world, the more so as the recent history of German policy is one of daring[6] aggression and as the want[7] of space at home compels[8] Germany to conquer the colonies of others or perish[9].

From: Spotlight on History, *vol. 1, Cornelsen, Berlin, 1995, p. 83.*

28 List the changes in German domestic and foreign policy after 1888 (see the text, p. 105, and S 24).

29 **a** Read the *Daily Mail's* comment on German naval policy in S 25 b.
b Then read S 25 a and imagine you are Alfred von Tirpitz, who has to write a note to the Kaiser commenting on the *Daily Mail's* comment (S 25 b).

30 **a** Look at the second part of the text on p. 105 and make a table that lists the international consequences of Germany's New Course.
b Sketch a simple map showing the countries in Europe in 1907. Then colour the countries of the two most important alliance systems in 1907 in a simple way and label the map.
c Did the situation of the German Empire at the end of 1907 fulfil Bismarck's "nightmare of coalitions" (see Unit 8.1, p. 92)? Why or why not?

31 Read S 23 and the biography of Wilhelm II on p. 105. Then discuss in class if history, for example the history of a nation, can be influenced or changed by a single person (think of its domestic and foreign policy, its economy, its culture, etc.). Give reasons and examples why or why not.

1 lecture sb. *jdm. eine Standpauke halten*
2 circumstance *Umstand*
3 as a rule *in der Regel*
4 menace *Bedrohung*
5 peril *Gefahr*
6 daring *waghalsig*
7 want *(hier) Mangel*
8 compel sb. *jdn. zwingen*
9 perish *zugrunde gehen*

8.7 The road to war

Europe divided

At the beginning of the 20th century, Europe found itself divided into two rival groups:
– the Triple *Entente** (Britain, France, Russia) and
– the Triple Alliance* (Germany, Austria, Italy).
The policies of these groups began to clash[1] in many parts of the world. Whenever a clash arose, the two groups came close to war. Each international crisis from 1905 to 1913 threatened the security of all the powers and increased the hostility[2] between them.

Franco-German rivalry in Morocco – A timeline

Around 1900, Morocco, situated in the north of Africa, is the last independent nation in North Africa, and is fertile and rich in minerals. Both Germany and France wish to colonize it.

1904 Through its Friendly Agreement with Britain (see Unit 8.6, p. 105), France is given a free hand by Britain to turn Morocco into a French colony.

1905 The German government, angry that German companies are excluded from profitable investment and trade in Morocco, decides to intervene. In March, the *Kaiser* travels to Tangier, where he makes a speech greeting the Sultan of Morocco as an independent sovereign. He promises him German protection if France tries to colonize his state. He also demands a conference to settle the Moroccan question and to test the British-French *Entente*.

1906 International conference at Algeciras, Spain, on the Moroccan question. Germany is only supported by Austria while France is supported by Britain, Russia and the United States. On paper, Morocco is preserved as an independent state whose trade is to be open to all nations; France is not given total control of Moroccan political and financial affairs. However, the conference makes Germany look weak and the *Entente* powers score a diplomatic victory[3].

1906–1907 France wants to have complete control of Morocco and increases its influence.

1911 The Germans react by sending the gunboat *Panther* to Agadir. The British fear that Germany could turn Agadir into a German naval base on the British naval route around Africa to India. So Britain protests and backs up[4] France against Germany. War seems to be inevitable. Because of Britain's support of France, Germany gives in. France (together with Spain) takes control of most of Morocco. Germany is compensated with a part of the French Congo.
Consequences: Germany has suffered a diplomatic defeat and is unwilling to suffer another. The *Entente* governments are alarmed by the aggressive German attitude.

1 clash *zusammenstoßen*
2 hostility *Feindschaft*
3 score a victory *einen Sieg verbuchen*
4 back sb. up *jdn. unterstützen, in etwas bestätigen*

S 26 The Balkans, 1913

S 27 Expenditure on arms, 1870–1913 (in million marks)

State	1905	1913
Russia	1069	2050
France	991	1327
Germany	1064	2111
Austria-Hungary	460	720
Britain	1263	1491

From: Reichsarchiv (ed.), Kriegsrüstung und Kriegswirtschaft, *Anlagenband, p.* 530.

Russo-Austrian rivalry in the Balkans

In 1908, Austria annexed Bosnia and Herzegovina to strengthen its position in the Balkans. This crushed Serbian dreams of creating a "Greater Serbia" – a Serbian nation state which was to include all the Serbs of the ex-Ottoman Empire, the Austro-Hungarian Empire and Serbia in a state called Yugoslavia. Serbia protested against the annexation and asked Russia for support. War was avoided when Russia backed down[1] because the *Entente*-powers England and France were unwilling to become involved in the issue[2] and because Germany promised to give military support to its alliance partner Austria.

Consequences: Russia felt humiliated and was determined that this must not happen again. Immediately after the crisis, the Russian government intensified its armaments programme.

The annexation of Bosnia-Herzegovina made Serbia the irreconcilable[3] enemy of Austria. Tensions increased dramatically after Serbia was able to enlarge its own territory in the two Balkan Wars against the Ottoman Empire in 1912–1913 and in summer 1913. Secret terrorist societies in Serbia intensified their efforts to free the Balkans from Austrian control.

Biography

Bertha von Suttner

Baroness[4] Bertha von Suttner (1843–1914) was an Austrian novelist and the first woman to win the Nobel Peace Prize[5] in 1905. Von Suttner, born in Prague, became a leading activist in the peace movement with her novel *Die Waffen nieder!* (Lay Down Your Arms!) in 1889. Two years later, she founded an Austrian peace group and started a peace newsletter. In 1899 and 1907, she took part in the International Peace Conferences in The Hague. Von Suttner repeated again and again that "Europe is one". For her, uniting Europe was the only way to prevent the world catastrophe which seemed to be coming. All her efforts, however, did not lead to a *détente*[6]. The peace demonstrations organized by European socialist parties were not successful either. Von Suttner died in Vienna in 1914, just weeks before the outbreak of the First World War.

32 Explain why the first part of Unit 8.7 is titled "Europe divided".

33 Group work: Every group chooses either Franco-German rivalry in Morocco or Russo-Austrian rivalry in the Balkans.
A *Franco-German rivalry:* Study the timetable of the Moroccan crisis on p. 107 and list
a the actions and events which contributed to an increase in tensions and
b the actions and events which contributed to a *détente.*
c Present and discuss the results.
B *Russo-Austrian rivalry:* Read about the tensions in the Balkans on pp. 93 and 108 and
a make a timetable that shows the events in 1875, 1877, 1908, 1912–1913 and 1913.
b Explain why, around 1910, the Balkans were called "Europe's powder keg"[7].

34 Look at the statistics in S 27 and explain each European country's motives in expanding its army (see Units 8.3, 8.6 and 8.7).

35 "If a war broke out in Europe, it would naturally become an international war involving all the powers." Comment on and explain this pre-war[8] statement.

36 **a** In class discuss the chances of the following peacekeeping measures around 1910:
A *disarmament*[9] B *arms control*[10] C *ban of colonial conquests*
D *founding of an organization which can serve as mediator*[11] *in international conflicts*
b Discuss other possible peacekeeping measures.

37 Read Bertha von Suttner's biography and check which of the following statements is true or false. Give reasons in each case:
A *No one in Europe was interested in peace around 1900.*
B *Some individuals, organizations and political parties in Europe were interested in peace, but they could not do much against the aggressive policy of their governments or the nationalistic enthusiasm of the general public.*
C *If there had been TV and Internet at the time, the peace movement would have had a better chance of influencing the aggressive nationalism in the populations and governments.*

1 back down *nachgeben*
2 issue *Angelegenheit*
3 irreconcilable *unversöhnlich*
4 baroness *Freifrau*
5 Nobel Peace Prize *Friedensnobelpreis*
6 détente *Entspannung*
7 powder keg *Pulverfass*
8 pre-war *Vorkriegs-*
9 disarmament *Abrüstung*
10 arms control *Rüstungskontrolle*
11 mediator *Vermittler*

Unit revision

Europe in the age of imperialism

Key events

1873 Three Emperors League (Germany, Austria, Russia)
1878 Congress of Berlin
1882 Triple Alliance (Germany, Austria, Italy)
1884 Germany sets up colonies
1888–1918 Wilhelm II, German Emperor
1889 Bertha von Suttner, *Lay Down Your Arms!*
1890 Wilhelm II dismisses Bismarck
1899 Peace conference in The Hague
1904 British-French *Entente Cordiale*
German genocide on the Herero and Nama
1905–1908 Moroccan crisis
1907 Russia joins the *Entente Cordiale*
Peace conference in The Hague
1908 Austria annexes Bosnia-Herzegovina
1912/1913 1st and 2nd Balkan War

Key terms

splendid isolation, pan-Slavism, "nightmare of coalitions", colony, colonization, imperialism, racism, *Weltpolitik*, New Course, Triple *Entente*, Triple Alliance

Key personalities

Wilhelm II
Bertha von Suttner

Activate your English

Alliance systems *(p. 95)*
Conferences and treaties *(p. 95)*
Talking and writing about "international relations" *(Task 6, p. 95)*
Reading and interpreting historical maps *(p. 99)*
Describing "civilization" *(Task 26 a, p. 104)*

1 Discuss whether more key events, personalities and terms are needed to describe the changes in the age of imperialism. Add your suggestions to the lists.
2 Make vocabulary flash cards for the key terms (see Unit 2, p. 31).
3 "What happened in Morocco?" Divide into pairs or groups and create a radio broadcast discussing the events of the Moroccan crisis beginning in 1905. Start with the following statement: *"Europe is now divided into two rival camps. On the one side is …".*
Choose one of the following perspectives from which to write your radio broadcast:
A *a German radio programme in 1906.* B *a French radio programme in 1906.*
In each case, describe the events and discuss the possible consequences for Germany of the division of Europe into two rival camps.
4 Copy the following chart "Germany – strengths and weaknesses at the beginning of the 20th century" and fill in the missing information:

	Strengths	***Weaknesses***
Industry	*Dynamic development of secondary sector; "Made in Germany" becomes a seal of approval[1], …*	…
Government	*Voting rights for all men …*	*No equality for women, …*
Social sphere[2]	*– Rising wages – Bismarck's social security system*	…
Culture	*First-class schools and universities, …*	…
International relations	…	…

1 seal of approval *Gütesiegel*
2 sphere *Bereich*

Unit 9 **The First World War 1914–1918**

9.1 The outbreak of war in 1914

S1 **The assassination[1] of the Austrian Archduke Franz Ferdinand and his wife, engraving and headlines of the Austrian *Kronen-Zeitung*, June 1914**

Franz Ferdinand in Sarajevo

On 28 June 1914, the Austro-Hungarian crown prince Archduke Franz Ferdinand was visiting Sarajevo in Bosnia, an Austro-Hungarian province with a large Serbian population. Among the crowds gathered[2] to greet the royal visitors were six teenage Bosnian Serbs, including 19-year-old Gavril Princip, who planned to kill the archduke. At 10.45 am, when the royal couple passed Princip, he pulled a pistol from his pocket and fired. Within the hour both the archduke and his wife were dead from their wounds. Within four weeks another war had broken out in the Balkans. However, unlike the Balkan wars before it, this local war quickly developed into the First World War. The soldiers involved came not only from Europe but also from France's colonial empire and, serving in the British Army, from Canada, India, Australia and New Zealand.
This war saw the rise of new weapons such as poison gas[3]*, machine guns, landmines and tanks[4]. For the first time, fighting took place not only on land, but also in the air and at sea, and millions of civilians were forced to work in munitions factories and on farms. In total, the war cost the lives of about 10 million soldiers and civilians and about 20 million persons were wounded – the exact number of victims will never be known.

The assassination and its consequences – A timeline

28 June **Austrian Archduke Franz Ferdinand** and his wife are assassinated by **Gavril Princip,** member of the Serbian terrorist group Black Hand, in **Sarajevo, Bosnia.**

6 July Germany encourages Austria-Hungary to act firmly against Serbia, promising its full support, even in a war against Russia ("blank cheque"*).

23 July Austria-Hungary officially blames Serbia for the assassination and gives Serbia an ultimatum* to hand over the assassins.

25 July Russia announces its support for Serbia. Serbia rejects the ultimatum.

1 assassination of sb. *Attentat auf jdn.*
2 gather *sich versammeln*
3 poison gas *Giftgas*
4 tank *Panzer*

28 July Austria declares war on Serbia and bombards Belgrade, the Serbian capital.
31 July Russia begins mobilization[1]* of its army to defend the Serbs.
1 August Germany declares war on Russia.
3 August Germany invades neutral Belgium according to the Schlieffen Plan.
Germany declares war on France.
4 August Britain declares war on Germany (under the British-Belgian treaty of 1839 Britain had agreed to protect Belgium).

The German war plan: The Schlieffen Plan

In 1905, German military commanders realized that if war broke out Germany would have to fight against France to the west and Russia to the east. Germany wanted to avoid this at all costs. General Alfred Graf von Schlieffen therefore worked out a plan. In his view, Germany could only win if it fought France and Russia one after the other. He had seen the Russian army and knew that it would take Russia at least six weeks to prepare for any kind of war. This would give the German troops enough time to defeat France and then turn to the eastern front to fight against Russia. The Schlieffen Plan* was later revised, however the basic plan remained the same:

- a surprise attack on France via Belgium as soon as Russia began to mobilize its army;
- the defeat of France in six weeks;
- the quick movement of troops from the French to the Russian front using Germany's modern railways;
- attack and defeat Russia.

However, the success of the plan depended on Britain which had promised in a treaty in 1839 to protect Belgium. But would it really go to war against Germany to defend Belgium? The German generals believed that Britain was not willing to do this.

S2 **The Schlieffen Plan**

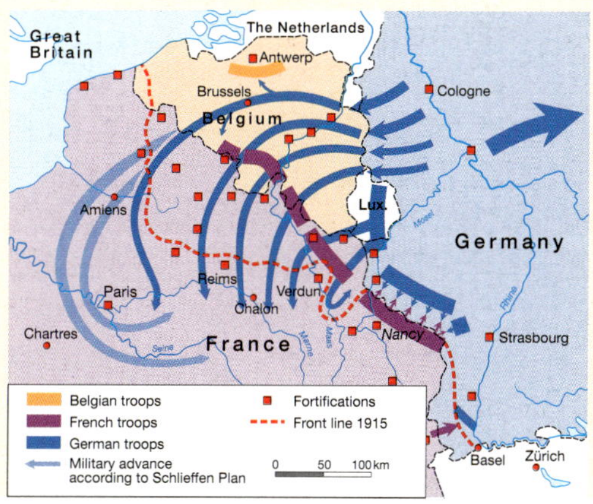

S3 The outbreak of the First World War: A deliberate[2] policy or an "accident"? – Contemporary views

3 a) David Lloyd George (1863–1945), British Prime Minister 1916–1922, wrote in his War Memoirs *(1933):*

The nations slithered over the brink into the boiling cauldron of war[3].

From: David Lloyd George, War Memoirs, *vol. 1, London, 1933. Quoted from: James Joll, "The 1914 Debate Continues: Fritz Fischer and His Critics",* Past and Present, *no. 34, 1966, p. 107.*

3 b) Georges Clemenceau (1841–1929), French Prime Minister 1906–1909 and 1917–1920, said in a speech at the Peace Conference of Versailles on 16 June, 1919:

In the view of the Allied [...] Powers the war which began on 1 August 1914 was the greatest crime against humanity and the freedom of peoples that any nation, calling itself civilized, has ever consciously committed. For many years, the rulers of Germany [...] strove[4] for a position of dominance over Europe. [...] They required that they should be able to tyrannize and dictate to a subservient[5] Europe. [...]
Germany's responsibility, however, is not confined to[6] having planned and started the war. She is not less responsible for the savage and inhuman manner in which it was conducted[7].

From: www.spartacus.schoolnet.co.uk/FWW-clemenceau.htm, 20 April 2006.

1 mobilization *Mobilmachung*
2 deliberate *absichtlich*
3 slither over the brink into the boiling cauldron of war *über den Abgrund in den brodelnden Hexenkessel des Krieges stürzen*
4 strive for *nach etwas streben*
5 subservient *unterwürfig*
6 be confined to *begrenzt auf*
7 conduct a war *einen Krieg führen*

S 4 What historians say about the outbreak of the First World War in 1914

4 a) British historian Alan J. P. Taylor (1906–1990) in 1974:

It was often said before 1914 that one day the weapons of war would go off by themselves. In 1914 this happened. Though there were no doubt deep-seated[1] reasons for disputes[2] between the great powers, the actual outbreak of World War I was provoked almost entirely by the rival plans for mobilization. [...]

[The great powers] were dragged into war by their armies instead of using the armies to further[3] their policies.

From: Alan J. P. Taylor, War by Time-table. Purnell's History of the 20th Century, *vol. 2, Purnell, London, 1974, p. 444.*

4 b) German historian Fritz Fischer (1908–1999) in 1975:

There is no doubt that the war which the German politicians started in July 1914 was not a preventive war[4] fought out of fear and despair. It was an attempt to defeat the enemy powers before they became too strong, and to realize[5] Germany's political ambitions which may be summed up as German hegemony[6] over Europe.

From: Fritz Fischer, War of Illusions: German Policies from 1911 to 1914, *Chatto & Windus, London, 1975, p. 470.*

4 c) British historian Norman Stone (born 1941) in 1996:

Bethmann Hollweg, who was the German Chancellor, went to Russia at the turn of 1911–1912, and he was taken round[7] some of the big factories in the St. Petersburg region. [...] A lot of the German electrical combines[8], for instance AEG, had established themselves in Moscow, and they knew [...] that Russia was becoming a superpower. They all said it. Bethmann Hollweg said, on 8 July 1914, to his private secretary: 'Russia grows and grows, and preys upon[9] us like a nightmare.'

The Germans, in a way, were absolutely right in 1914, when they said: 'If we challenge Russia later, we'll be beaten. [...] But, we've just got a chance to beat them in 1914, so let's do it now.' [...] And, pretty well every competent observer in Germany said: 'The Russians are getting too strong. They've got their alliance with the French. They'll crack us like a nut when the time comes. [...] So, better now than later.'

From: Norman Stone, "Russia – Getting too Strong for Germany" in: The Great War and the Shaping of the 20th Century, *Public Broadcasting Service, www.pbs.org/greatwar/historian/hist_stone_01_russia.html, 20 April 2006.*

4 d) French historian Marc Ferro (born 1924) in 2004:

Man hat gar nicht ernsthaft darüber nachgedacht, weil man den Krieg wollte. Kaiser Wilhelm II wollte ihn, Kaiser Franz Joseph [von Österreich] wollte gegen Serbien Krieg führen, Frankreich wollte den Krieg, um Elsass-Lothringen zurückzuerobern. Die politischen Führungen waren auf Krieg aus, wenn auch aus unterschiedlichen Gründen.

From: "La Grande Guerre, *Interview mit dem französischen Historiker Marc Ferro zum Ersten Weltkrieg", 2004, www.arte-tv.com/de/geschichte-gesellschaft/Der-Erste-Weltkrieg/587320.html, 20 April 2006.*

1 deep-seated *tief sitzend*
2 dispute *Auseinandersetzung*
3 further sth. *etwas vorantreiben, fördern*
4 preventive war *Präventivkrieg*
5 realize sth. *etwas verwirklichen*
6 hegemony *Vorherrschaft*
7 take sb. round *jdn. herumführen*
8 combine *Großkonzern*
9 prey upon sb. *jdm. keine Ruhe lassen*

1 Do the following task in pairs:

a Read the text and timeline on pp. 110–111. Make sure that you know what ultimatum, blank cheque, neutrality and mobilization mean.

b With the help of S6 (p. 113) describe the outbreak of the war to your partner.

c From your knowledge of the events leading to the outbreak of the war, explain the reasons for the actions of the governments, e.g. why Germany supported Austria.

S 5 **Frederic Henry Townsend (1868–1920), "Bravo Belgium", cartoon from the British magazine *Punch*, 12 August 1914**

2 Based on the information you have so far, make an educated guess[1]
  a where and why the Schlieffen Plan might fail and
  b what consequences the failure of the Schlieffen Plan could have for Germany and the course of the war (see the text, p. 111, and S 2).

3 **a** State in your own words how the British and French Prime Ministers (S 3 a–b) explained the outbreak of the First World War.
  b Comment on these explanations.

4 British historian Alan J. P. Taylor wrote that the European countries had "deep-seated reasons for disputes" and French historian Marc Ferro said that the political leaders wanted war, but for different reasons. Make a table which lists the reasons why the different countries wanted to go to war (S 4 and Unit 8.6 and 8.7).

5 Copy the table below and make notes on how the historians explain the outbreak of the war in 1914 in S 4 a–d.

Fischer	***Taylor***	***Stone***	***Ferro***
attempt to defeat the enemies before they became too strong	...	...	...

6 The authors of S 4 a–d have different opinions about the causes of the war. Discuss in class how it is possible for historians to have such different views.

7 Analyse the cartoon "Bravo Belgium" (S 5). Photocopy the cartoon, label it with all the necessary information and write a short caption with the cartoon's message.

1 make an educated guess *eine Hypothese aufstellen*

S 6 **The outbreak of war in 1914 – An event chain**

1 **28 June**
On ... was shot by ...

2 **6 July**
In reaction to ... Germany promised to ... This is called ...

3 **23 July**
Austria reacted to ... by sending / by confronting ...

4 **25 July** Russia declared ...
After the Russian declaration ... Serbia rejected ...

5 **28 July**
After Serbia had ...
Austria declared ...

6 **31 July**
Russia mobilized its ...
to ..., but this ...

7 **1 August** Germany declared ...
Frightened by ... Germany put into operation ...

8 **3 August**
On ... Germany ... and ...

9 **4 August**
On ... Britain ... to fulfil ... in which it had ...

9.2 The course of the war – Part I: The Western Front

War on the Western Front – A timeline

1914 August: War on Western Front begins with German invasion of Belgium. German advance[1] is stopped 40 kilometres away from Paris as several important things go wrong:
- Belgians put up more resistance than expected, which slows down German advance.
- British keep to treaty with Belgium and send troops.
- Russians mobilize more quickly than expected and cross German border; Germans have to send two divisions[2] to try to stop them on Eastern Front.

September: After the Battle of the Marne, both sides take up trench[3] positions; trenches eventually stretch from the Channel coast to the Swiss border; very little change in these positions until mid-1918; both sides are held in a deadlock[4] (trench warfare[5]*).

1915 April: First German attack with poison gas* at Ypres.

1916 February–December: Massive German attack on the French at Verdun; French hold on, led by General Philippe Pétain (1856–1951), despite huge losses.

June–July: New British Commander in Chief Sir Douglas Haig (1861–1928) launches[6] an attack at the Battle of the Somme; 20,000 are killed on the first day; a few kilometres are gained.

1917 April: USA enters war on the side of Great Britain, France and Russia (= *Entente* or Allied Powers).

Autumn: Russian October Revolution (see Unit 9.3); British attack under General Haig at Arras and Ypres, German defences under General Paul von Hindenburg (1847–1934); terrible losses on both sides.

1918 Spring: After Russian-German ceasefire agreement[7] in December 1917 (see Unit 9.3), Germany brings thousands of soldiers by train from the Eastern to the Western Front; General Erich Ludendorff (1865–1937) prepares final effort.

July: British and French at last combine under one Supreme Commander, Marshal Ferdinand Foch (1851–1929), supported by US troops.

11 November: Ceasefire between the Allied Powers and Germany (after German Revolution on 9 November and abdication of Emperor Wilhelm II).

1 advance *Vormarsch*
2 division *Division (10–15,000 Soldaten)*
3 trench *Schützengraben*
4 be in a deadlock *festgefahren, in eine Sackgasse geraten sein*
5 trench warfare *Grabenkrieg, Stellungskrieg*
6 launch an attack *zum Angriff übergehen*
7 ceasefire agreement *Waffenstillstandsabkommen*
8 (un)remarkable *beachtenswert, (unauffällig)*
9 rifle *Gewehr*
10 barbed wire *Stacheldraht*

S7 **New weaponry in the First World War: the machine gun, photograph, c 1915**

The MG 08/15 was the standard German machine gun – one for every regiment as the main defensive weapon. The machine gun crews were the elite infantry units. "08/15" became a German adjective meaning "standardized and unremarkable[8]". In 1914, about 200 MG 08s were produced each month; by 1916, 3000; and a year later, 14,400 per month. One MG had the firepower of 80 rifles[9]. The combination of machine guns and barbed wire[10] was responsible for the largest number of casualties during the First World War.

S 8 **The trench system, modern drawing, 2004**

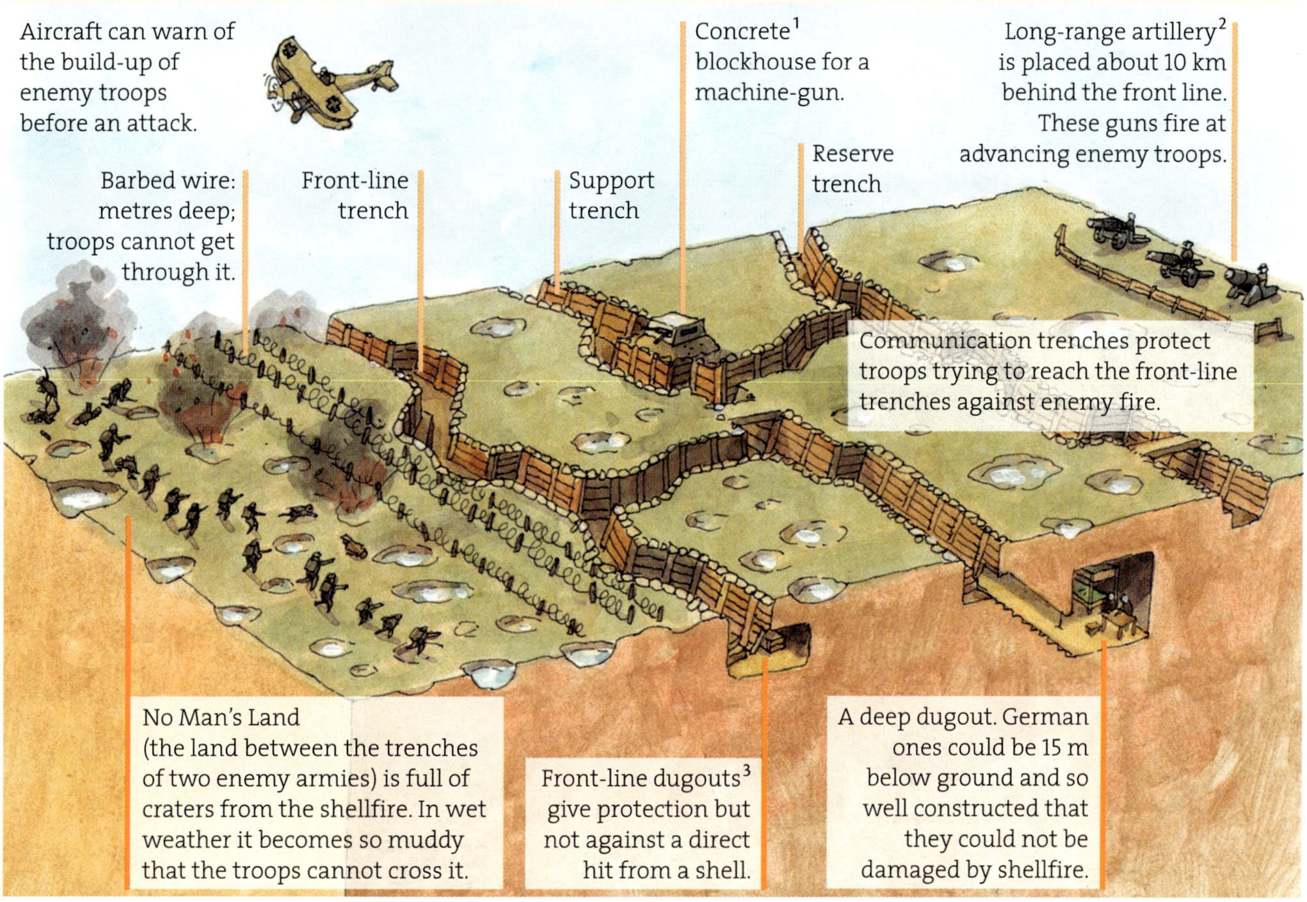

S 9 **German soldiers in a trench at the Western Front, photograph, 1915**

8 Read the timeline on p. 114: Discuss which dates or events you would consider as turning points in the course of the war.

9 **a** Working in pairs, study S 7–S 9 and discuss the problems which attacking troops had. Make notes.

b Imagine you are a textbook author and write a short paragraph on the question of how any battle to win territory could end in the deaths of tens of thousands of soldiers.

10 **Extra research:** The First World War saw the rise of weapons of mass destruction*, one example being landmines. In 1993, an "International Campaign to Ban Landmines (ICBL)" began. Collect information on the history of land mines and the work of the ICBL. Are landmines banned today? Present your results on a poster or as a PowerPoint presentation.

1 concrete *Beton*
2 long-range artillery *Geschütz mit großer Reichweite*
3 dugout *Unterstand*

Analysing a photograph

The camera always lies

From the very beginning of the war, the popular media had to accept the control of the censors to make sure that they did not show high numbers of dead soldiers or the ugly ways the soldiers died. But newspapers in Leipzig and London, Rome, Berlin, Vienna and Paris were still full of pictures. Many of these pictures were snapshots taken by the soldiers themselves with their new easy-to-handle cameras. Although they were not allowed to use or even have cameras at the front, many of them risked their lives to make the most spectacular or the most frightening photographs. But the most well known pictures of the war were taken by the official photographers of the different armies, for example Frank Hurley (see below).

Biography

Frank Hurley

Frank Hurley (1885–1962) was an official photographer for the Australian Imperial Force. He arrived in France at the beginning of the third battle of Ypres in 1917, and soon became known as "the mad photographer" for the risks he took to take photographs even on the front line. Hurley was expected to record exactly what he saw. But the photos he delivered were often manipulated. He staged battle scenes or combined elements taken from different negatives. He even added elements like explosions to create a more dramatic effect: the three aircraft in the sky at the left in "An episode after the Battle of Zonnebeke" (S 10, S 11), for example, are taken from other images.

Photographs as primary sources

In contrast to written primary sources, which have existed for thousands of years, photography is a "young" type of primary source. Photography was invented in the 1830s and it was only in 1880 that the first photo was published in a (US) newspaper. In its early days the photograph was seen as an accurate way of recording information. However, as technology advanced, photographers were able to manipulate images (most recently with digital technology).

S 10 **Frank Hurley, "An episode after the Battle of Zonnebeke: Going over the top", photograph, Ypres, 1917**

S 11 **Frank Hurley, "An episode after the Battle of Zonnebeke: Going over the top", the left-hand part of the photograph in S 10, Ypres, 1917**

S 12 German munitions factory, photograph, 1917

S 13 Women's employment in German industry, 1914–1918

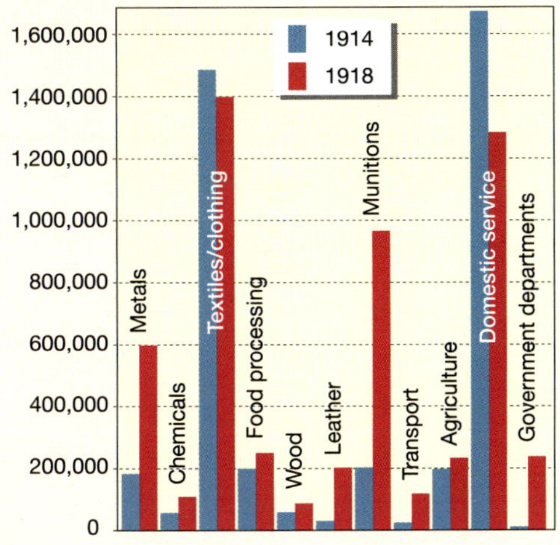

Study skills

Photographer:
Who took the photo? Is the photographer known?
Was the photo commissioned? If so, by whom?
Setting:
When was the photo taken?
Where was it taken?
Purpose:
What was the intended use of the photo?
home decoration – personal use – advertisement – calendar – political campaign – newspaper or magazine – art – public notice – other
Description:
Examine and take notes on people, objects and/or activities that are presented.
Reliability:
Was the photo staged[1] or a snapshot? Did the people realize that they were being photographed?
If it was a commissioned photo: Does this have an effect on the photo?
Has the photo been manipulated? (Have details been added or removed that would change the meaning of the photograph? Has the photo been cropped[2]?)
Evaluating the photo as a historical source:
All sources are "windows to past events and ideas and to people's lives": What can we see and learn "through" the photo? List your conclusions.

11 Study the two versions of Frank Hurley's photographs (S 10, S 11).
a Describe the differences between the two versions. Which one would you have on the front page of a newspaper? Write captions for both photos.
b Discuss how useful Hurley's photos are for historians.

12 Analyse the photo in S 12 with the help of the study skills. Make a note of the questions you cannot answer.

S 14 Women and men in paid employment[3] in Germany, 1907–1939 (in % of female and male population)

Year	Women	Men
1907	30.4	61.1
1925	35.6	68.0
1933	34.2	65.7
1939	36.2	67.7

From: Dietmar Petzina et al. (ed.), Sozialgeschichtliches Arbeitsbuch, *vol. III, C.H. Beck, München, 1978, p. 54.*

13 **a** Before the First World War, women in European countries usually only worked in jobs regarded as "women's work". Discuss what jobs in what industries or industrial sectors women worked in.
b Which of the following statements are supported[4] by S 12–S 14:
A *In the First World War, German industry hired women for jobs which were not regarded as "women's work".*
B *The shortage[5] of men meant that German women workers had to be shifted[6] from one industry or industrial sector to another.*
C *The First World War had no long-term effect on the development of women in paid employment.*

1 staged *gestellt*
2 crop a photograph *eine Photoaufnahme beschneiden*
3 paid employment *Erwerbstätigkeit*
4 support sth. *(hier) etwas belegen*
5 shortage of sth. *Mangel an etwas*
6 shift sth. *etwas verlagern*

9.3 The course of the war – Part II: The Eastern Front

The Russian Army

In 1914, the Russian Army was the largest army in the world. However, Russia's poor roads and railways made the effective transportation of these soldiers difficult. By December 1914, the Russian Army had 6,553,000 men. But they only had 4,652,000 rifles. Untrained troops were ordered into battle without adequate arms or ammunition, and as a consequence, all the Russian military campaigns eventually ended in disaster.

The best-known battle: The Battle of Tannenberg

Allied with France and Britain, Grand Duke Nicholas, the Russian commander, agreed to help relieve[1] the French (under attack from Germany) with an offensive in East Prussia. General Paul von Hindenburg and General Erich Ludendorff were sent forward to meet the Russian advancing troops. They made contact on 22 August 1914. By 29 August, the Russian troops were surrounded. Only 10,000 of the 150,000 Russian soldiers managed to escape. The Germans, who lost 20,000 men in the battle, took over 92,000 Russian prisoners. At home, Hindenburg and Ludendorff were honoured and German propaganda* made them heroes.

The Russian defeat shocked Russia's allies. However, the Russian action had diverted[2] the Germans from their attack on France and allowed the French to counter-attack at the Marne (see S 2, p. 111, and the timeline, p. 114).

Buying peace on the Eastern Front

Harvests were poor in Russia and civilians were starving. Soldiers were alarmed at the news from the front and regiments began to refuse to move to the front line. Increasingly large numbers of men were deserting. By the autumn of 1917, an estimated two million men had unofficially left the Russian army.

After the October Revolution in 1917, Vladimir I. Lenin (1870–1924), the leader of the new communist Russian government, announced an armistice with Austria-Hungary and Germany.

1 relieve sb. *jdn. entlasten*
2 divert sb. from sth. *jdn. von etwas ablenken*

S 15 Fallen memorial of the Russian Tsar Alexander III in Moscow, photograph, February 1917

S 16 Russian territories lost by the Treaty of Brest-Litovsk (1918)

The Treaty of Brest-Litovsk, March 1918

In December 1917, a peace conference between a Russian delegation and German and Austrian representatives began at Brest-Litovsk. For the Russian delegation the difficult task was to try to end Russian participation in the war without losing any territory.

After nine weeks of discussions without agreement, the German Army was ordered to advance into Russia again. In March 1918, when German troops were moving towards Petrograd, the Russian delegation accepted the German ultimatum: Russia recognized the independence of Ukraine, parts of Georgia, Finland, Poland, Belarus and the Baltic states (today Lithuania, Latvia and Estonia). In all, the treaty took away a third of Russia's population, much of its best farming land, half of its industry and nine-tenths of its coal mines.

Almost 15 million soldiers served in the Russian Army during the First World War. An estimated 1.7 million were killed, 2.8 million wounded and 2.4 million taken prisoner.

S 17 **Graves of Russian soldiers in South Russia, photograph, c 1917**

Activate your English

War and peace

declare / go to war	*retreat*
spark off a war/crisis	*ceasefire*
mobilize an army	*armistice*
serve in an army	*defeat*
provoke sth.	*casualties*
invade sth.	*navy*
occupy sth.	*artillery*
annex sth.	*civilian*
conquer sth.	*treat sb. leniently/harshly*
threaten sth.	*send/issue an ultimatum*
give in to demands	*preventive war*
intervene (in sth.)	*reparations*
arm/disarm	*victory*
withdraw troops	*loss*

14 Read the text and give reasons for Germany's military superiority on the Eastern Front.

15 The German army could never totally defeat the Russian army. What military effect did this have?

16 Explain the heading "Buying peace ..." (see the text, p. 118).

17 Look at the timeline on p. 114 and read the text on pp. 118–119: Explain why historians call the year 1917 the turning point of the First World War (see also S 17).

18 **a** Look at the words and phrases for "War and peace" above and add the other members of the word family where possible. For example: *invade sth. – invasion.*

b Working in pairs, organize the words and phrases for "War and peace" in a mind map (see below).

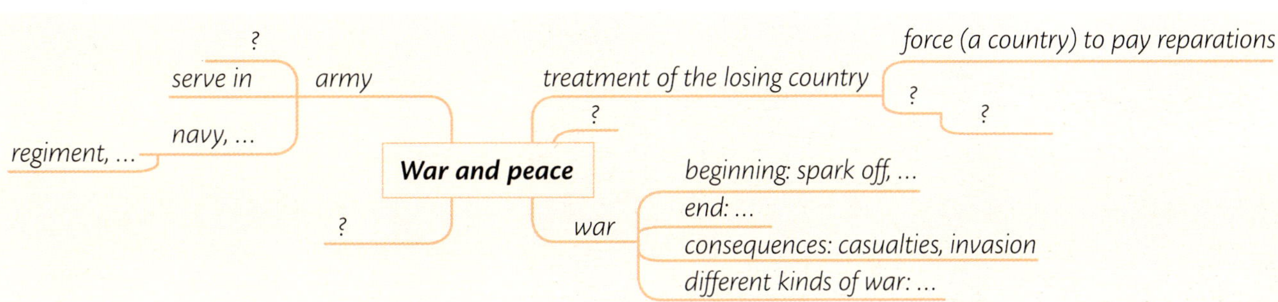

Analysing a painting

S 18 **Otto Dix (1891–1969), *"Kriegskrüppel"* (War Cripples), 150 x 200 cm, oil painting, 1920**

Vocabulary help: disabled war veteran[1] – push a wheelchair – walk with crutches[2] – tremble[3] and shake – wooden leg – shoemaker's shop – dotted line – white head in the cross-hairs[4] – wear an eye patch[5]

Biography

Otto Dix

Otto Dix (1891–1969) began his career as a painter at the Dresden School of Arts and Crafts *(Dresdner Kunstgewerbeschule)*. At the outbreak of World War I, Dix volunteered for the German Army and was trained as a machine gunner. He fought at the Battle of the Somme in summer 1916. After fighting on the Eastern Front in 1917, he returned to France in spring 1918. Dix was wounded several times; one time he nearly died.
Dix was angry about the indifference[6] of civilians towards disabled veterans. To wake them up, he did not paint the soldiers' heroism and bravery but instead shocking pictures of the effects of the war on human bodies. In 1924 his painting "The Trench", showing decomposed corpses[7] in a German trench, was exhibited in the Wallraf-Richartz Museum in Cologne. It created such a public scandal that the mayor[8] of Cologne, Konrad Adenauer, forced the director of the museum to resign.
When in 1933 Adolf Hitler was brought to power in Germany, Dix lost his teaching position at the Dresden School of Arts and Crafts. His paintings "War Cripples" and "The Trench" appeared in the 1937 Nazi exhibition *"Entartete Kunst"* (Degenerate Art). The purpose of the exhibition was to let the Germans know that some forms and pieces of art were not accepted by the new regime. The catalogue especially attacked his painting "War cripples" as "weakening the will of the German people to defend themselves". Later, Nazi authorities destroyed his paintings together with other anti-war paintings.
After the Second World War (1939–1945), Dix returned to Dresden. He died in 1969.

1 war veteran *Kriegsveteran*
2 crutches *Krücken*
3 tremble *zittern*
4 in the crosshairs *im Visier*
5 eye patch *Augenklappe*
6 indifference *Gleichgültigkeit*
7 decomposed corpses *verweste Leichen*
8 mayor *Bürgermeister*

19 **a** Describe the painting in S 18. For vocabulary help, see S 18 and S 19.
b Read Otto Dix's biography for information that helps you understand the painting.
c Formulate the painter's message.

Study skills

Who, when, where?

1. Who painted the picture? What do you know about the artist that helps you to understand or interpret the work of art?
2. When and where was it painted?
3. Was the painting commissioned?

For whom?

4. What effect did the painting have on the audience at the time of its creation?
5. What kind of mood is created? What emotions are evoked?

What and how?

6. What is the subject of the painting? Does the painting tell a story?
7. What was going on in the world at the time that helps us to understand or interpret the work of art? What was the artist reacting to?

Purpose and conclusions

8. What was the purpose of the painting?
9. What do we see and learn "through" the painting?

1 amputated *amputiert*
2 disfigured *entstellt*
3 artificial limb *Prothese*
4 horrific scar *grauenhafte Narbe*
5 crippled *schwer geschädigt, verkrüppelt*

S 19 Germans wounded and crippled in World War I

Wounded	Men returning ...
4,247,000	– amputated[1]
	– disfigured[2]
	– blinded
	– with artificial limbs[3]
	– with horrific scars[4]
	– emotionally crippled[5]

From: Der Große Ploetz, *31. ed., Ploetz, Würzburg, 1991, p. 848*

S 20 War-related deaths of military personnel in World War I

	Deaths in 1000s	Deaths as % of population
Great Britain	715	1.6
British Empire	198	0.1
France	1327	3.4
French colonies	71	0.1
Russia	1811	1.1
Italy	578	1.6
USA	114	0.1
Belgium	38	0.5
Serbia-Montenegro	278	5.7
Romania	250	3.3
Greece	26	0.5
Portugal	7	0.1
Total Allied Powers	*5413*	*0.7*
Germany	2037	3.0
Austria-Hungary	1100	1.9
Turkey	804	3.7
Bulgaria	88	1.9
Total Central Powers	*4029*	*2.6*
Total	*9442*	*1.0*

From: Stephen Broadberry, Mark Harrison, The Economics of World War I: A Comparative Quantative Analysis, *Coventry, 2005, p. 30, www2.warwick.ac.uk/fac/soc/economics/staff/faculty/broadberry/wp/wwitoronto2.pdf, 25 April 2006.*

20 Explain why S 18 and a similar painting by Otto Dix, "The Trench", created a public outcry in 1924. Do they still have the same effect today? Why or why not?

21 In class, evaluate Dix's painting as a "window to the past". What can historians learn "through" it?

22 At the end of the First World War, an enormous number of physically and emotionally crippled German men returned home (S 19, S 20). Speculate on
a the personal consequences (for family life),
b the economic consequences (for family income, the national budget, etc.),
c other consequences.

Project work – Producing an exhibition on the First World War

S21 ***"Im Gedenken"* (We remember), death notice in the *Frankfurter Allgemeine Zeitung*, 7 October 2004**

Im Gedenken an meinen Großvater

Julius von Hinten

Rechtsanwalt

geb. am 15. November 1880 in Rinteln
gefallen als Leutnant bei Cernay-Les-Reims am 7. Oktober 1914

und an meinen Vater

Hans-Hinrich von Hinten

Ass. jur.

geb. am 28. März 1911 in Hamburg
gefallen als Oberleutnant bei Sewastopol/Krim am 8. Mai 1944

Ina-Maria Schreiber geb. von Hinten
61381 Friedrichsdorf

S22 **Results of project work by the 10th class at Mataré Gymnasium in Meerbusch-Büderich, Germany, photograph, September 2005**

23 The death notice[1] shown in S 21 was discovered by pupils during project work on the First World War. Discuss what motivated Ina-Maria to place this expensive death notice in Germany's leading quality paper.

a Does she want to denounce[2] the horrors and madness of war?
b Does she want to praise[3] what her grandfather and father did?
c Can you think of other possible motivations?

24 **Project 1: Visiting a World War I memorial in your town**

If there is a World War I memorial in your town or district, go and study it:

a Collect information about its location, who commissioned it, when it was built and when it opened (see "History skills", p. 89).
b Take pictures of the monument and describe its measurements, the material it is made of and its appearance (see "History skills", p. 89).
c Write down the names of the men who died (if they are listed). Then use census records[4] from your local library or archives to find out the number of people living in your town in 1914 (remember that about half of this number would have been female and about a quarter of the rest were young boys or old men and not eligible[5] for military service). Compare the number you have left over with the number of names on the war memorial. Then work out the proportion of the men of military age from your town who were killed during the war (see, for example, S 20).
d Prepare all your results for an exhibition. For help, see "Study skills", p. 90.

25 **Project 2: Trench warfare**

a Prepare maps, charts, statistics and illustrations of warfare on the Western front.
b Prepare your results for an exhibition. For help, see "Study skills", p. 90.

26 **Project 3: Creating a model for a World War I memorial**

Plan, draw or build your own model for a memorial that commemorates the people who lost their lives in World War I. When you present your model in class, explain your point of view, values and beliefs which you express in the memorial. For help, see "Study skills", p. 90.

1 death notice *Todesanzeige*
2 denounce sb./sth *jdn./etwas anprangern, verurteilen*
3 praise sb./sth. *jdn./etwas loben*
4 census records *Volkszählungsdaten*
5 eligible *wählbar, in Frage kommend*

Unit revision

The First World War (1914–1918)

Key events

1914 8 June: Assassination at Sarajevo
August: Battle of Tannenberg
1916 Feb–Dec: Battle of Verdun
June–July: Battle of the Somme
1917 April: USA enters the war on the side of the Allied Powers
Oct: Russian October Revolution
Dec: Russian ceasefire
1918 March: Brest-Litovsk Treaty
9 Nov: German Revolution; abdication of Emperor Wilhelm II
11 Nov: Armistice between the Allied Powers and Germany

Key personalities

Otto Dix, Frank Hurley

Key terms

ultimatum, blank cheque, propaganda, Schlieffen Plan, mobilization, neutrality, trench warfare, poison gas, weapons of mass destruction

History skills

Analysing a photograph *(pp. 116–117)*
Analysing a painting *(pp. 120–121)*
An exhibition on the First World War *(p. 122)*

Activate your English

War and peace *(p. 119)*

S 23 ***All Quiet on the Western Front*, poster, 1929**

1 Working in pairs, explain to your partner what the key events and key terms mean.
2 Complete the chart below by ticking the correct column to show whether the different causes of World War I were of a political or economic nature, and long-term or short-term problems. The first one has been done for you.

Causes of World War I	Political A	Economic B	Long term C	Short term D
There was a colonial rivalry between the European superpowers.	✔		✔	
In early August 1914, Russia, France and Germany all mobilized their huge armies in an attempt to force the other side to back down.				
Austria declared war on Serbia.				
Germany wanted to gain an overseas Empire like those of Britain and France.				
Rival alliance systems encouraged both sides to behave aggressively in crises.				
United Germany became the biggest industrial power in Europe. German industry had overtaken the British in steel production.				
The heir to the throne of the Austrian Empire was assassinated by Serbian nationalists.				
Europeans were enthusiastic about aggressive nationalism.				
The German Emperor Wilhelm II began a New Course of Weltpolitik.				
There was an arms race long before the outbreak of war.				
The people of the Balkans wanted independence.				

All Quiet on the Western Front *by Erich Maria Remarque, Germany, 1929 (book and film)*
Nineteen-year-old Paul Bäumer and his friends join the German army after listening to the patriotic speeches of their teacher Kantorek. Paul describes the brutal realities of the war and how his soldier friends die one after the other.

Glossary of terms

absolute monarchy: the rule of a country by a monarch, usually a king or a queen. Absolute monarchy is different from a *constitutional monarchy* and from a *republic* →: Absolute monarchs had complete power of rule over the people. They believed that they had a "Divine Right" – a theory which argued that certain kings ruled because they were chosen by God to do so and that these kings were responsible to no person except God. The power of the ruler thus came from God, not the people. To the kings, it was a sin to revolt. Absolute monarchy lasted in France until 1789 and in Russia until 1917.

Ancien Régime: the French term for Old Rule or Old Order. It usually refers to the social and political system in France before the French Revolution in 1789. The King's rule was absolute and society was divided into three estates →.

anti-Semitism: see Key term, p. 86.

balance of power: the theory in politics that the best way of keeping international peace is to distribute power among states equally. The aim is that no state should achieve a dominant position. In the 18th and 19th centuries Britain actively promoted the "balance of power" on the European continent.

Bill of Rights: the ten amendments (or additions) added to the Constitution of the United States → in 1791 which guarantee certain freedoms (religious and political freedom, the right to bear arms, the right to life, liberty and property, protection in criminal trials, etc.).

birth rate: the number of babies born for every 1000 people during a particular period of time.

"blank cheque": the German promise to support Austria-Hungary against Serbia, even in a war against Russia (July 1914).

bourgeoisie: the social class above the workers and peasants and below the nobility; also known as the middle class. For Karl Marx → and the socialists, the bourgeoisie is the class which owns the means of production, whereas the proletariat (working class →) does not own anything.

Bundesrat: the federal council of the German states.

capitalism (also capitalist or free-enterprise system): an economic system in which the means of production (land, buildings, machinery) are in the hands of private companies and individuals, not in the hands of the state. The aim of production is profit for the companies and individuals.

checks and balances: see p. 21.

colonization: the process by which a more powerful and often distant country wins control over a country or area.

colony: see Key term, p. 100.

constitution: a country's highest law upon which all other laws are based. It is the basis for government because it states how the government will be organized. It describes how the government is formed, who makes it up, and how laws are passed and amended. A constitution also defines the limits of the power of the government. In Germany the constitution, called the *Grundgesetz* (Basic Law), includes a catalogue of citizens' basic rights.

constitutional monarchy: monarchy →

Consulate: the new French government introduced by Napoleon → after his *coup d'état* → in 1799.

Customs Union *(Zollverein)*: a union of states in the German Confederation (1815–1866) which abolished tariffs at their borders in 1834.

coup d'état: a sudden, illegal and often violent change of government by (a part of) the military.

death rate: the number of people per 1000 who die during a particular period of time.

democracy: a form of government in which all the people of a country vote to elect their representatives. For Abraham Lincoln (President of the USA, 1861–1865), democracy was a government "of the people, by the people, and for the people". All adults either vote on all affairs directly (direct democracy) or elect representatives who vote for them (representative democracy) and make political decisions, formulate laws and administer programmes for the public good. The elected representatives are members of a national parliament → (e.g. *Bundestag*, Congress, House of Commons, *Assemblée Nationale*). In a democratic state, the majority rules and the rights of minorities are protected by law. The features of democracy are:
- sovereignty of the people
- government based upon consent of the governed
- majority rule
- minority rights
- guarantee of basic human rights →
- free and fair elections
- equality before the law
- due process of law (= *Rechtmäßigkeit staatlichen Handelns)*
- constitutional limits on government

emigration: the act or instance of leaving your own country to go and live permanently in another country.

Ems Telegram: see p. 83.

estate: see Key term, p. 32.

Estates-General: the French legislative body that was first established in 1302 and was made up of members of the three groups, or estates, of French society – the nobility, the clergy, and the commoners. Powerful in the 14th and 15th centuries, the body's importance declined, and it did not meet at all between 1614 and 1789.

factory: a large industrial building where a large number of workers manufacture goods or products. The machines which are used are powered by steam, water or electricity.

Federal Diet *(Bundestag)*: an organization of the 39 states of the German Confederation (1815–1866) which was not an elected but a delegated assembly which made common laws.

federation: a group of states which have joined together, usually because they share a common interest.

"first" Industrial Revolution: Industrial Revolution →

Greater Germany: see p. 63.

human and civil rights: basic rights which many societies since the American and French Revolutions have believed all people should have.

imperialism: see Key term, p. 98.

indentured servant: in former times, a person who signed a contract to work for an employer in another country. The employer then paid for that person's passage to the new country. During the 17th century, most of the white workers in Maryland and Virginia came from England as indentured servants. They sold themselves to an agent or ship captain before leaving Britain who then sold them to a buyer in the colonies →. Most indentured servants in the colonies were young, single males in their teens or twenties. They typically worked for somebody for seven years; in most cases as household servants or unskilled workers on farms and plantations. In theory, the person only sold his or her labour. In practice, however, indentured servants were basically slaves. The treatment of the servant was harsh and often brutal. The system developed because of the labour shortage in the colonies. The tobacco plantations in Virginia needed a lot of workers. The local Indian population was unwilling to work there, so the plantation owners "bought" poor English adults who were slowly replaced by African slaves (slavery, slave trade →).

Industrial Revolution: the period of fundamental technological, economic and social change which began in Britain in the late 18th century and spread throughout the world. This revolution completely changed the ways in which the world produced its goods. Factories → with large numbers of workers and/or machines driven by water or steam power replaced the traditional craftsmen with their simple machines and tools who worked in their homes or in small workshops. New industries developed quickly as a result of a number of new inventions in the textile industries. The Industrial Revolution also changed the way in which people lived. Before, people lived in villages and small towns, working the land. As farm machinery replaced workers in agriculture and new jobs were created in the textile factories, people moved from the countryside to the towns (urbanization →). Farming played a smaller and smaller role in the national economies. In Germany, the "First" Industrial Revolution began in the 1840s with the construction of railways. About 1900, the "Second" Industrial Revolution followed with new electrical, car and chemical industries.

industrialization: the fundamental technological, economic and social change caused by the Industrial Revolution →.

Jacobins: the most radical political group of the French Revolution. The group's leader was Maximilien de Robespierre →, who began the Reign of Terror in 1793–1794.

Junker: a member of the Prussian landowning nobility.

liberalism: see Key term, p. 48.

Little Germany: see p. 63.

mass production: the manufacture of standardized products in large amounts. The aim is to increase production per worker and thus to make products less expensive.

mobilization: the preparation of a country's armed forces for a conflict.

monarchy: a system of government in which a country is ruled by a monarch, usually a king or a queen. In the period of the French Revolution, all European states had some form of monarchy (absolute monarchy → or constitutional monarchy →). Today, European countries which still have a monarch as head of state are constitutional monarchies. This means that the power of the king or queen is controlled by a set of laws and basic principles.

Native American: a member of any of the races of the original people living in America (before the arrival of European settlers). Originally referred to as Indians by European settlers.

nation: a group of people with a common language, culture and history, who live in a particular area under one government. Some nations exist without states, for example, the Kurds.

Princip, Gavril (1894–1918) A Bosnian Serb and a member of a terrorist group, he assassinated Archduke Franz Ferdinand → in 1914. He was sentenced to 20 years in prison. Under hard conditions he died of tuberculosis on 28 April 1918. *p. 110*

Robespierre, Maximilien (1758–1794) French lawyer and one of the best-known leaders of the French Revolution. He was the leader of the Jacobin club → and an influential member of the Committee of Public Safety. He was mainly responsible for the Reign of Terror between 1793 and 1794. His arrest and execution in 1794 put an end to the terror. *pp. 38, 42*

Roland de la Platière, Jeanne Marie (1754–1793) See Biography, p. *42*.

Sand, Karl Ludwig (1795–1820) German student activist. He studied theology in Jena and founded a student association in Erlangen. After killing Kotzebue → he was sentenced to death and executed outside Mannheim's city walls. He was buried in the same cemetery as Kotzebue. Their graves are about 200 metres apart. *p. 53*

Schlieffen, Alfred von (1833–1913) German field marshal. He developed the *Schlieffen Plan*. *p. 111*

Schurz, Carl See Biography, *p. 65*.

Sieyès, Emmanuel-Josephe Abbé See Biography, *p. 33*.

Steuben, Friedrich von (1730–1794) German officer. He fought on the American side in the American War of Independence. He helped to teach military discipline in the Continental Army through his drilling techniques. He died in Steubenville, N.Y. To honour von Steuben parades are held in New York, Chicago and Philadelphia during the month of September. *p. 16*

Suttner, Bertha von (1843–1914) See Biography, *p. 108*.

Talleyrand, Charles Maurice de (1754–1838) Foreign Minister of France, chief representative of France at the Congress of Vienna. *p. 52*

Tirpitz, Alfred von (1849–1930) German admiral and politician. As Secretary of State for the Navy he had a strong influence on German foreign policy before the First World War. *p. 106*

Victoria, Queen (1819–1901) See Biography, *p. 24*.

Washington, George (1732–1799) See Biography, *p. 20*.

Watt, James (1736–1819) British engineer. He improved the Newcomen steam engine → by constructing a steam machine with a separate condenser; in 1781 he developed the rotary motion of the piston. This new steam engine could be used to drive many different types of machinery. A unit of power called the watt was named after him. A watt (W) is equal to 1/746 of a horsepower, or one volt times one ampere. *p. 25*

Wellington, Duke of (1769–1852) British general and politician. From 1808 to 1812 he fought successfully against Napoleon → in Portugal and Spain and became his greatest rival. Together with Prussian forces he defeated Napoleon in Waterloo in 1815. *p. 45*

Werner, Anton von (1843–1915) German painter. A favourite among Prussian kings, he painted themes of the Prussian military, German nationalism → and upper-class society. *pp. 80, 93*

Wilhelm I (1797–1888) King of Prussia, 1861–1888; first Emperor of Germany, 1871–1888. *pp. 80, 82–85*

Wilhelm II (1859–1941) See Biography, *p. 105*.

Witbooi, Hendrik (1835–1905) Chief of the Nama tribe of Namibia. He organized resistance against German colonial → control over Namibia. His efforts among the Herero and Nama tribes led to the Herero Wars. In total, about 65,000 Herero (80 per cent of the total Herero population) and 10,000 Nama (half of the total Nama population) were killed between 1904 and 1907. *p. 103*

English-German vocabulary

A

abandon sth. [ə'bændən] *etwas aufgeben*
abdication *Abdankung*
abdicate *abdanken*
abolish sth. *etwas abschaffen beseitigen*
abolition *Abschaffung, Auflösung*
absolute monarchy *absolutistische Monarchy*
access ['ækses] *Zugang*
accept sth. *etwas anerkennen, akzeptieren*
accomplishment *Leistung*
account *Bericht*
accurse sb. / sth. *jdn. / etwas verfluchen*
accuse sb. [ə'kju:z] *jdn. beschuldigen*
achieve sth. *etwas erreichen*
achievement *Errungenschaft*
acquire sth. *etwas bekommen, erwerben*
acquisition *Erwerb*
act *Gesetz*
adaptation *Bearbeitung, Anpassung*
adequate ['ædɪkwət] *angemessen*
administer sth. *etwas verwalten*
adopt sth. *etwas annehmen, verabschieden*
adoption *Annahme, Verabschiedung*
advance *Vormarsch, Vorrücken, Fortschritt*
advance sth. *etwas (be)fördern, voranbringen*
affluence *Wohlstand, Überfluss*
agree with sth. / sb. *einer Sache / jdm. zustimmen*
aim *Ziel, Absicht*
aircraft *Flugzeug*
alliance *Bündnis*
alliance system *Bündnissystem*
allow sth. *etwas erlauben*
ally *Verbündeter/in, Allierter/in*
Alsace-Lorraine [æl'sæs lə'reɪn] *Elsass-Lothringen*
alternating current (ac) *Wechselstrom*
ambassador *Botschafter/in*
ambitious *ehrgeizig*
analogy *Analogie, Entsprechung, Übereinstimmung*
ancestor *Vorfahr/in, Ahn/in*
ancestral *Ahnen-, Vorfahren-*
Ancien Regime [ɒn'siæn reɪ'ʒi:m] *Ancien Regime*
annex sth. *etwas annektieren*
Anti-Socialist Law *Sozialistengesetze*
Anxious ['æŋkʃəs] *ängstlich*
appear *erscheinen*
appoint sb. *jdn. ernennen*
appointment *Ernennung*
appropriate [ə'prəʊpriət] *geeignet, passend*
approve sth. *etwas genehmigen, billigen*
approximately [ə'prɒksɪmətli ☆ ə'prɑ:k-] *annähernd, ungefähr*
area *Gebiet*
arise *entstehen*
arm yourself / sb. *sich/jdn. bewaffnen*
armistice ['a:mɪstɪs] *Waffenstillstand*
armour ['a:mə] *Rüstung*
arise *entstehen*
arrogant *arrogant, hochnäsig*
artificial limb *Prothese*
artillery *Artillerie*
artist's signature *Künstlersignatur*
aspire to sth. [- '-] *etwas anstreben*
assassinate sb. [ə'sæsɪneɪt] *ein Attentat auf jdn. verüben, jdn. umbringen*
assassination of sb. [əsæsɪ'neɪʃn] *Attentat auf jdn.*
assembly *Versammlung*
assumption *Vermutung*
attend sth. [- '-] *etwas besuchen*
audience ['ɔ:diəns] *Adressaten*
Austro-Prussian War *Preußisch-Österreichischer Krieg*
authority *Autorität, Erlaubnis*
auto worker *Automechaniker/in*
availability *Verfügbarkeit*

B

back down *nachgeben*
back sb. up *jdn. unterstützen, in etwas bestätigen*
balance of power *Gleichgewicht der Mächte*
Balkan War *Balkankriege*
Baltic Sea *Ostsee*
bank clerk *Bankangestellter/in*
bankrupt *bankrott*
baptize sb. *jdn. taufen*
bar *Gitter*
barbed wire *Stacheldraht*
bare *kahl*
baroness *Freifrau*
basis ['beɪsɪs] *Grundlage*
battle *Schlacht*
Battle of the Nations *Völkerschlacht*
bee *Biene*
benefit from sth. *Nutzen ziehen aus etwas*
bias ['baɪəs] *Tendenz, Voreingenommenheit, Neigung*
Bill of Rights *Grundrechtekatalog*
birth rate [reɪt] *Geburtenrate*
blank cheque *Blankoscheck*
Bohemia [bəʊ'hi:miə] *Böhmen*
boil *brodeln*
bookkeeper *Buchhalter/in*
boundary *Grenze, Grenzlinie*
breech-loading needle rifle ['raɪfl] *Zündnadelgewehr*
Brest-Litovsk Treaty *Frieden von Brest-Litowsk*
bring about sth. *etwas hervorbringen, etwas zur Folge haben*
be on the brink of sth. *kurz vor etwas stehen*
Brunswick *Braunschweig*
build-up *Aufbau*
bulleted list *Aufzählung (mit Aufzählungszeichen am Zeilenanfang)*
burden *Last*
burnt-down *abgebrand*
bury sb. ['beri] *jdn. beerdigen*
bustle ['bʌsl] *Gewimmel*
butcher ['bʊtʃə] *Schlachter/in*

C

cancer *Krebs*
candle *Kerze*
capstan *Drehkreuz, Presse*
caption *Bildunter/überschrift*
capture sth./sb. ['kæptʃə] *etwas einnehmen, jdn. gefangen nehmen*
Carlsbad Decrees *Karsbader Beschlüsse*
carpenter *Tischler/in*
carriage ['kærɪdʒ] *Kutsche*
carry sb. *jdn. tragen*
cart *Karren*
cartoon *Karikatur*
cast steel rifled cannon *Gussstahlkanone*
casualty *Verwundeter*
Catalogue of civil liberties *Grundrechte*
catch up with sb. *jdn. einholen*
Catholic Emancipation Act ['kæθlɪk] *Katholikenemanzipation*
cattle *Vieh, Rinder*
cauldron ['kɔ:ldrən] *Hexenkessel*
cause *Ursache*
cause-and-effect diagram *Ursache-Wirkungs-Schema*
cautious ['kɔ:ʃəs] *vorsichtig*
ceasefire *Waffenruhe*
ceasefire agreement *Waffenstillstandsabkommen*
cemetery *Friedhof*
census *Volkszählung*
census records *Volkszählungsdaten*
census suffrage *Zensuswahlrecht*
Central Powers *Mittelmächte*
chain *Kette*
chain sb. *jdn. anketten*
challenge sb. *jdn. herausfordern*
chancellor *Kanzler/in*
character *Charakter, Gesinnung*
cheer sb. *jdm. zujubeln*
cheerful *freundlich, heiter*
cheers *prost; danke; tschüss*
chemist ['kemɪst] *Chemiker*
chest *Brust(korb)*
chief *Haupt-, Häuptling*
circa *zirka*
circumstance *Umstand*
citizen ['sɪtɪzn] *Bürger*
Civil Code ['sɪvl] *Gesetzbuch*
civil rights ['sɪvl] *Bürgerrechte*
civil servant ['sɪvl] *Beamter/in*
civilian [sə'vɪliən] *zivil; Zivilist/in*
civilizing ['sɪvəlaɪsɪŋ] *zivilisatorisch*
claim *Anspruch*
claim sth. *etwas behaupten*
clash *zusammenstoßen*
clearing *Waldlichtung*

clergy ['klɜːdʒi] *Geistlichkeit, Klerus*
clergyman ['klɜːdʒimən] *Geistlicher/in, Kleriker/in*
client ['klaɪənt] *Kunde / Kundin, Auftraggeber/in*
cloth *Stoff*
coach *Kutsche, Waggon*
coal-tar *(Steinkohlen-)Teer*
cockade *Abzeichen*
colonization *Kolonisierung*
colony ['- - -] *Kolonie*
column ['kɒləm ☆ 'kɑːləm] *(Heeres-) Kolonne*
combine ['- -] *Großkonzern*
come to a head *sich zuspitzen*
commemorate [kə'meməreɪt] *gedenken*
commercial [kə'mɜːʃl] *Handels-, kommerziell, gewerblich*
commercial code [kə'mɜːʃl] *Handelsgesetz*
commission sth. *etwas bestellen*
commit a crime *ein Verbrechen begehen*
Committee for Public Safety *Wohlfahrtsausschuss*
common lands *Allmende*
compare sth. *etwas vergleichen*
compel sb. [kəm'pel] *jdn. zwingen*
compensate sb. for sth. ['- - -] *jdn. für etwas entschädigen*
compete *am Wettbewerb teilnehmen, konkurrieren*
competition *Wettstreit*
compile sth. *etw. erstellen, zusammenstellen*
complain *sich beschweren*
complaint *Beschwerde*
compromise ['kɒmprəmaɪz ☆ 'kɑːm-] *Kompromiss*
conclusion *Schlussfolgerung*
concrete ['- -] *Beton*
condition *Bedingung, Umstand*
conduct sth *etwas führen*
Confederation of the Rhine *Rheinbund*
confer sth. *etwas verleihen*
confident *vertrauensvoll*
confine sth. to sth. *etwas begrenzen auf etwas*
Congress ['- -] *Kongress*
Congress of Vienna ['kɒŋgres ☆ 'kɑːŋ-] *Wiener Kongress*
connection *Verbindung*
conquer sth. ['kɒŋkə ☆ 'kɑːŋ-] *etwas erobern*
conscience ['kɒnʃəns ☆ 'kɑːn-] *Gewissen*
consent [kən'sent] *Zustimmung*
consequence ['- - -] *Folge, Konsequenz*
consider sth. *etwas betrachten*
consist of sth. *bestehen aus etwas*
constitution *Verfassung*
constitutional *verfassungsgemäß*
construction worker *Bauarbeiter/in*
consulate ['kɒnsjələt ☆ 'kɑːnsə-] *Konsulat*
context *Kontext, Zusammenhang*
contract ['- -] *(geschäftlicher) Vertrag*
contrast sth. [kən'trɑːst ☆ -'træst] *etwas gegenüberstellen*
contrast ['kɒntrɑːst ☆ 'kɑːntræst] *Gegensatz*
contribute sth. *etwas beitragen*
convey sth. *etwas vermitteln*
convince sb. *jdn. überzeugen*
corpse *Leiche*
cornucopia *Füllhorn*
corvées ['kɔːveɪ] *Frondienste*
cotton *Baumwolle*
counter-revolutionary *Gegenrevolutionär/in*
coup d'état [ˌkuː dei'tɑː] *Staatsstreich*
court *königlicher Hof*
cradle *Wiege*
craftsman *Handwerker*
cramped *beengt*
crippled *geschädigt, verkrüppelt*
criticize sb. *jdn. kritisieren*
crop(s) *Feldfrucht; Ernte*
crop failures *Ernteausfälle*
crop rotation *Fruchtfolge*
crop sth. *etwas beschneiden*
in the crosshairs *im Visier*
crowd *Menge*
crowd sb. out *jdn. verdrängen*
crown sb. *jdn. krönen*
cruel ['kruːəl] *grausam*
crush sth. *etwas niederschlagen, zerdrücken*
crutch *Krücke*
currency *Währung*
customs *Sitten, Zoll*
customs officer *Zollbeamter/in, Zöllner/in, Mautner/in*
Customs Union *Zollverein*

D

damage sth. / sb. *etwas schaden, jdm. Schaden zufügen*
damp *Feuchtigkeit*
daring ['deərɪŋ] *waghalsig*
deadlock *Sackgasse*
deal with sth. *mit etwas zu tun haben, handeln*
death rate ['deθ ˌreɪt] *Todesrate*
death notice *Todesanzeige*
debts [dets] *Schulden*
decent ['diːsnt] *anständig, annehmbar*
declaration [ˌdeklə'reɪʃn] *Erklärung*
Declaration of Independence [ˌdeklə'reɪʃn] *Unabhängigkeitserklärung*
Declaration of the Rights of Man [ˌdeklə'reɪʃn] *Menschenrechtserklärung*
declare sth. *etwas erklären*
decline *Niedergang*
decode sth. *etwas entschlüsseln*
decrease *sinken, zurückgehen; Sinken, Rückgang, Abnahme*
deep-seated *tief sitzend*
defeat *Niederlage*
delay sth. *etwas aufschieben*
delegate ['delɪgət] *Abgeordneter, Beauftragter*
deliberate [dɪ'lɪbərət] *absichtlich*
deliver sth. *etwas liefern*
demagogical [ˌdemə'gɒgɪkl ☆ -gɑːg-] *demagogisch, hetzerisch*
democracy [di'mɒkrəsi ☆ -'mɑːk-] *Demokratie*
democrat ['- - -] *Demokrat/in*
denounce sb. / sth *jdn. / etwas anprangern, verurteilen*
depict sth. *etwas darstellen, abbilden*
descendant [dɪ'sendənt] *Nachfahr/in*
desperate ['despərət] *trostlos*
détente [ˌdeɪ'tɑːnt] *Entspannung*
determine sth. [dɪ'tɜːmɪn] *etwas bestimmen*
development *Entwicklung*
device *Gerät*
differ *sich unterscheiden*
dignified *würdevoll, würdig*
direct sth. *etwas leiten*
disagree *ablehnen*
disarm *entwaffnen*
disarmament *Abrüstung*
discriminate against sb. *jdn. diskriminieren, benachteiligen*
disease [dɪ'ziːz] *Krankheit*
disfigured *entstellt*
disgrace sb. / sth. *jdn. / etwas entehren*
disguise sth. [dɪs'gaɪz] *etwas verdecken*
dismiss sb. *jdn. entlassen*
dismissal *Entlassung*
disobedience [ˌdɪsə'biːdiəns] *Ungehorsam*
disposal *Entsorgung*
dispute [dɪs'pjuːt] *Auseinandersetzung*
dissatisfied with sth. *unzufrieden mit etwas*
dissolve [dɪ'zɒlv ☆ -'zɑːlv] *auflösen*
distribution [ˌdɪstrɪ'bjuːʃn] *Verteilung*
divert sb. from sth. *jdn. von etwas ablenken*
divide *Teilung, Kluft*
divine right *Recht von Gottes Gnaden*
divorce *sich scheiden lassen*
dole sth. out to sb. *etwas an jdn. verteilen*
dominance *Vorherrschaft*
dominion *Dominion*
donkey *Esel*
dotted line *gepunktete Linie*
double sth. *etwas verdoppeln*
draft *Entwurf*
draft sth. *etwas entwerfen*
draw lots *auslosen*
drawing *Zeichnung*
dress as sb. / sth. *sich wie jmd. / etwas kleiden*
driver *Kutscher/in*
drop *Rückgang*
Dual Alliance *Zweibund*
duchy ['dʌtʃi] *Herzogtum*
dues *Abgaben*

dugout *Unterstand*
Dutchman *Holländer*
dye-stuff *Farben*

E

eagle *(Reichs)adler*
earn sth. [ɜːn] *etwas verdienen*
economic sector *Wirtschaftssektor*
on the edge of sth. *am Rande von etwas*
educated guess *Hypothese*
effect on sth. *(Aus)wirkung auf etwas*
effort ['efət] *Anstrengung*
Electoral College *Wahlmänner*
elementary school *Volksschule*
eligibility [ˌelɪdʒə'bɪləti] *Wählbarkeit*
eligible ['elɪdʒəbl] *wählbar, in Frage kommend*
emigration *Auswanderung, Emigration*
emperor *Kaiser*
emphasize sth. *etwas betonen*
empire *Kaiserreich, Weltreich*
employ sb. *jdn. beschäftigen*
employer *Arbeitgeber/in*
empress *Kaiserin*
Ems Telegram *Emser Telegramm*
endure sth. *etwas ertragen*
enemy *Feind*
engraving *Stich, Druckgrafik*
Entente governments [ɒn'tɒnt ☆ ɑːn'tɑːnt] *Ententemächte*
entrepreneur [ˌɒntrəpre'nɜː ☆ ˌɑːn-] *Unternehmer*
envious ['enviːəs] *neidisch*
epaulet ['epəlet] *Schulterklappe, Epaulette*
epoch ['iːpɒk ☆ 'epək] *Epoche*
equality *Gleichheit*
equilibrium [ˌiːkwɪ'lɪbriəm] *Gleichgewicht*
erratic *launisch, unberechenbar*
establish sth. *etwas einrichten, errichten, verordnen*
estate *Stand (im Pl. auch Ländereien)*
Estates-General *Generalstände*
estimate ['estɪmeɪt] *schätzen*
etching *Radierung*
evaluate sth. *etwas einschätzen, beurteilen*
event chain *Ereigniskette*
event map *Ereignisdiagramm*
evidence *Beleg, Beweis*
exaggerate (sth.) [ɪg'zædʒəreɪt] *(etwas) übertreiben*
excerpt ['eksɜːpt] *Auszug, Ausschnitt*
exclude sb. *jdn. ausschließen*
exclusion *Ausschluss*
execution [ˌeksɪ'kjuːʃn] *Hinrichtung*
Executive Branch [ɪg'zekjətɪv] *Exekutive*
exhaust [ɪg'zɔːst] *erschöpfen*
exhibition [ˌ– – '– –] *Ausstellung*
exhibit [– '– –] *Ausstellungsstück*
expect sth. *etwas erwarten*
expire *ablaufen*
exploit sb. *jdn. ausbeuten*
exploitation *Ausbeutung*
explorer *Forscher/in*
export ['ekspɔːt] *Export, Ausfuhr*
extent *Ausmaß*
eye patch *Augenklappe*

F

factory *Fabrik*
Factory Acts *Fabrikgesetz*
fail *scheitern*
fail to do sth. *versäumen, etwas zu tun*
fall behind *zurückfallen*
favourable *günstig, vorteilhaft*
fear *Angst*
feature ['fiːtʃə] *Merkmal*
Federal Diet ['daɪət] *Bundestag*
Federal Statistical Office *Statistisches Bundesamt*
federation *Föderation, Staatenbund*
fee *Gebühr*
fence *Zaun*
fertile ['fɜːtaɪl ☆ 'fɜːrtl] *fruchtbar*
Festival on the Wartburg *Wartburgfest*
fez *Fes*
filth *Schmutz*
finished goods *Fertigwaren*
First Estate *Erster Stand*
flee *flüchten*
flow chart *Fließdiagramm*
flyer *Flugblatt*
force *Kraft, Armee*
foreground *Vordergrund*
foreman *Vorarbeiter/in*
foreshadow sth. *etwas vorausahnen lassen*
found sth. *etwas gründen*
frame sth. *etwas einrahmen*
Franco-Prussian War *Deutsch-Französischer Krieg*
fraternity *Brüderlichkeit*
freedom of assembly *Vereinigungsrecht*
French Indian War *Siebenjähriger Krieg*
fulfill sth. *etwas erfüllen*
further sth. *etwas vorantreiben, fördern*
fuss (about sth.) *Getue (um etwas)*

G

gain sth. *etwas bekommen, gewinnen*
gallop *Galopp*
gap *Lücke*
gather *sich versammeln*
general *allgemein*
genocide ['dʒenəsaɪd] *Völkermord*
German Confederation *Deutscher Bund*
German-Danish War *Deutsch-Dänischer Krieg*
German Empire *Deutsches Kaiserreich*
German Naval League *Deutscher Flotten-verein*
German Navy Office *Reichsmarineamt*
give in to sth. *etwas nachgeben*
give one's blessing *seinen Segen geben*
give rise to sth. *führen zu etwas, Anlass geben zu etwas*
gloom *gedrückte Stimmung, Trübsinn*
go on trial for sth. *angeklagt sein*
go up *heraufgehen*
goods *Güter*
government spending *Regierungsausgaben*
gradual ['grædʒuəl] *allmählich, langsam*
grain *Getreide*
grammar school *Gymnasium*
Grand Duke [djuːk ☆ duːk] *Großherzog*
granite rock ['grænɪt] *Granitstein*
grant sth. *etwas gestatten*
graphic *anschaulich*
graphic novel *Comicroman*
graze *weiden lassen*
Greater Germany *Großdeutschland, „großdeutsche Lösung"*
greet sth. *etwas begrüßen*
grievance *Beschwerde, Klage*
gross national product *Bruttosozialprodukt*
ground floor *Erdgeschoss, Parterre*
grow up *erwachsen werden*
guard [gɑːd] *Wache*
gutter *Gosse, Rinnstein*

H

hairdresser *Friseur/in*
halo ['heɪləʊ] *Heiligenschein, Glorienschein*
handloom weaver *Handweber*
hardly *kaum*
harm sb. *jdm. schaden, jdn. verletzen*
harvest *Ernte*
hatred ['heɪtred] *Hass*
have a say *Mitspracherechte haben*
have blind spots *„auf einem Auge blind sein"*
head tax *Personensteuer*
heal (sth.) *(etwas) heilen, wiedergutmachen*
hearse [hɜːs] *Leichenwagen*
Hebrew ['hiːbruː] *hebräisch*
hegemony [hɪ'dʒeməni ☆ -moʊni] *Vorherrschaft*
helmet *Helm*
hereditary [hə'redɪtri ☆ -teri] *angeboren, erblich, Erb-*
hide sb. / sth. *jdn. / etwas verstecken*
hire sb. *jdn. einstellen*
hoe *Hacke*
holy *heilig*
Holy Roman Empire of German Nation *Heiliges Römisches Reich Deutscher Nation*
horrific [– '– –] *grauenhaft*
horse-drawn coach *Pferdekutsche*
hostile ['hɒstaɪl ☆ 'hɑːstl] *feindselig*
hostility *Feindschaft*

House of Representatives *Repräsentantenhaus*
human rights *Menschenrechte*
humble *demütig*
humiliate sb. **[hjuːˈmɪlieɪt]** *jdn. demütigen*
humorous **[ˈhjuːmərəs]** *witzig, humorvoll*

I

illegal **[- ˈ- -]** *ungesetzlich, illegal*
immigration *Immigration, Einwanderung*
immortality *Unsterblichkeit*
imperial **[- ˈ- - -]** *kaiserlich*
imperial orb *Reichsapfel*
Imperial Mark *Reichmark (RM)*
impose sth. etwas auferlegen
impression *Eindruck*
improvement *Verbesserung*
increase *(an)steigen, (an)wachsen; Anstieg*
independence *Unabhängigkeit*
indentured servant *Dienstverpflichteter/in*
indicate sth. *etwas angeben, bezeichnen*
indifference *Gleichgültigkeit*
industrial enterprise *Industrieunternehmen*
inferior *niedere*
influential *einflussreich*
information technology specialist *Informatiker/in*
inhabitant *Einwohner/in*
initiate sth. *etwas einleiten*
injure sb. *jdn. verletzen*
injustice **[ɪnˈdʒʌstɪs]** *Ungerechtigkeit*
insult sb. **[- ˈ-]** *jdn. beleidigen*
insurance **[ɪnˈʃʊərəns ☆ -ˈʃʊr-]** *Versicherung*
insurance agent **[ɪnˈʃʊərəns ˈeidʒənt ☆ -ˈʃʊr-]** *Versicherungskaufmann*
insurrection *Aufruhr, Aufstand, Erhebung*
integrate sb. *jdn. integrieren, einschließen*
intention **[ɪnˈtenʃn]** *Absicht, Intention*
interest (on debts) *Kreditzinsen*
interested in sb. / sth. *an jdm. / etwas interessiert*
intervene *eingreifen, intervenieren*
introduce sb. / sth. *jdn. / etwas einführen*
invade *einmarschieren*
invalidity **[- - ˈ- - -]** *Berufsunfähigkeit*
investigation *Untersuchung*
invitation *Einladung*
involuntary **[- ˈ- - - -]** *unfreiwillig*
involved in sth. *an etwas beteiligt*
ironic **[aɪˈrɒnɪk ☆ -rɑːn-]** *ironisch*
irreconcilable **[ɪˈrekənsaɪləbl]** *unversöhnlich*
isolate sb. / sth. **[ˈaɪsəleɪt]** *jdn. / etwas isolieren, abgrenzen, absondern*
issue **[ˈɪʃuː,** BE also **ˈɪsjuː]** *Problem, Angelegenheit, Streitpunkt*
ivory **[ˈaɪvəri]** *Elfenbein*
ivory carving *Elfenbeinschnitzerei*

J

Jacobin **[ˈdʒækebɪn]** *Jakobiner/in*
join *sich zusammenschließen*
join sth. together *etwas verbinden, vereinigen*
Judicial Branch **[dʒuˈdɪʃl]** *Jurisdiktion*
just *gerecht*
justice **[ˈdʒʌstɪs]** *Gerechtigkeit*
justify sth. *etwas rechtfertigen*

K

keep sb. from sth. *jdn. vor etwas bewahren*
kneel down **[niːl]** *niederknien*

L

label **[ˈleɪbl]** *Beschriftung*
label sth. **[ˈleɪbl]** *etwas beschriften, kennzeichnen*
labour force *Arbeitskräfte*
labourer *Arbeitskraft, Arbeiter/in*
lack of sth. *Mangel an etwas*
land market *Grundstücksmarkt*
last *dauern*
launch an attack **[lɔːntʃ]** *zum Angriff übergehen*
laurel **[ˈlɒrəl ☆ ˈlɔːrəl]** *Lorbeer*
laurel wreath **[ˈlɒrəl riːθ ☆ ˈlɔːrəl]** *Lorbeerkranz*
law *Gesetz*
law-abiding **[ˈlɔː əbaɪdɪŋ]** *gesetzestreu*
lawyer **[ˈlɔːjə]** *Rechtsanwalt / -anwältin*
lease **[liːs]** *Pachtvertrag*
lecture sb. **[ˈlektʃə]** *jdm. eine Standpauke halten*
led to sth. *zu etwas führen*
left-hand (corner) *linke (Ecke)*
legend **[ˈledʒənd]** *Sage*
Legislative Branch **[ˈledʒɪslətɪv ☆ -leɪtɪv]** *Legislative*
length *Stück*
liberating *befreiend*
liberty *Freiheit*
liberty cap *Freiheitsmütze* (→ Phrygian cap)
life expectancy *Lebenserwartung*
limit sth. *etwas begrenzen, beschränken*
line *Verszeile*
lion **[ˈlaɪən]** *Löwe*
list of grievances *Beschwerdeliste, Klageliste*
lithograph *Lithografie*
Little Germany *Kleindeutschland, „kleindeutsche Lösung"*
livestock farming *Viehzucht*
load *Last*
lock sb. out *jdn. aussperren*
lodging house *Wohnheim*
long-term *langfristig*
long-range *mit großer Reichweite*
long-term *langfristig*
loom *Webstuhl*
lorry driver *Kraftwagenfahrer/in*
lower class *Unterschicht*
lush **[lʌʃ]** *üppig, luxuriös*

M

majority decision *Mehrheitsbeschluss*
manner *way*
manufactured goods *Industriegüter*
manufacturer *Hersteller, Erzeuger*
manufacturing *(verarbeitende) Industrie*
manuring **[məˈnjʊərɪŋ ☆ -nʊr-]** *Düngen*
March Demands *Märzforderungen*
March Ministries *Märzministerien*
mayor *Bürgermeister/in*
means of production *Produktionsmittel*
measure sb. / sth. *jdn. / etwas messen*
medal **[ˈmedəl]** *Orden, Ehrenzeichen*
mediator *Vermittler/in*
medieval **[mediˈiːvəl]** *mittelalterlich*
membership *Mitgliedschaft*
memoir **[ˈmemwɑː]** *Lebenserinnerung*
memorial *Denkmal*
menace **[ˈmenəs]** *Bedrohung*
mentally inferior *geistig unterlegen*
merchant *Kaufmann / Kauffrau*
Middle Ages *Mittelalter*
middle class *Mittelschicht*
militia **[məˈlɪʃə]** *Bürgerwehr, Miliz*
mill *Mühle, Fabrik*
moment **[ˈ- -]** *Zeitpunkt*
monarchist **[ˈmɒnəkɪst ☆ ˈmɑːn-]** *Monarchist, Königsanhänger*
Moroccan Crisis *Marokkokrise*
motion **[ˈməʊʃn ☆ ˈmoʊʃn]** *Antrag (in einer Sitzung)*
muddy *schlammig, matschig*

N

National Assembly *Nationalversammlung*
nation-state *Nationalstaat*
Native American *Ureinwohner Amerikas, Indianer/in*
naval arms race *Marinewettrüsten*
navy *Marine*
need *Bedürfniss*
negotiate sth. *etwas verhandeln*
New Course *Neuer Kurs*
new generation *Nachwuchs*
nightmare *Albtraum*
No Man's Land *Niemandsland*
noble *adlig*
Nobel Peace Prize *Friedensnobelpreis*
noble(man) *Adliger*
nobility *Adel*
North German Confederation *Norddeutscher Bund*
notable *bemerkenswert, bedeutend*
notably *insbesondere, hauptsächlich*

noticeably *merklich, deutlich*
notorious *berüchtigt*

O

oak *Eiche*
oath *Eid*
obey sb. [ə'beɪ] *jdm. gehorchen*
object to sth. [əb'dʒekt] *etwas einwenden*
obligatory [ə'blɪgətri ☆ -tɔːri] *verpflichtend*
occupation *Beruf; Beschäftigung; Besetzung*
occupy sth. *etwas besetzen*
office *Amt, Büro*
oil painting *Ölgemälde*
opinion *Meinung*
opinion poll *Meinungsumfrage*
oppose sb. / sth. *sich wenden gegen jdn. / etwas; sich jdm. / etwas entgegenstellen*
oppression *Unterdrückung*
ordinary *normal, gewöhnlich*
origin ['ɒrɪdʒɪn ☆ 'ɔːr-, 'ɑːr-] *Ursprung*
Ottoman Empire *Osmanisches Reich*
outcome *Ergebnis, Ausgang, Resultat*
outlaw sth. *etwas verbieten*
outline sth. *etwas umreißen, grob beschreiben*
overcome sth. *etwas überwinden*
override sth. *etwas aufheben*
overthrow *Umsturz (einer Regierung)*
own sth. *etwas besitzen*
owner *Besitzer/in*

P

package of measures *Maßnahmenbündel*
paid employment *Erwerbstätigkeit*
painting *Gemälde*
pamphlet *Broschüre, Prospekt, Streitschrift*
pan *Schüssel*
pan-Slavism *Panslavismus*
paralyze sb. / sth. *jdn. / etwas lähmen*
paraphrase sth. *etwas umschreiben*
parliament of professors *Professorenparlament*
Parliamentary Reform Acts *Wahlrechtsreformen*
pass a law *ein Gesetz verabschieden*
passenger ['pæsɪndʒə] *Fahrgast, Reisender*
pauper labour ['pɔːpə 'leɪbə] *Billigarbeiter*
pauperism ['pɔːpərɪzm] *Pauperismus, Armut*
paving stone *Pflasterstein*
peace conference *Friedenskonferenz*
peace settlement *Friedensvereinbarung*
peak *Spitze, Höhepunkt*
peasant ['peznt] *(Klein)bauer/in*
pedestal *Sockel, Unterbau*
pence *Penny*
peril *Gefahr*
period of time *Zeitspanne*
perish *zugrunde gehen*
personify *personifizieren, vermenschlichen*
persuade sb. [pə'sweɪd] *jdn. überzeugen*
petition [pə'tɪʃn] *Bittschrift*
phenomenon [fə'nɒmɪnən ☆ -'nɑːm-] *Erscheinung*
Phrygian cap ['frɪdʒiən] *Phrygische Mütze*
pictorial broadsheet *Bilderzeitung*
pigeon ['pɪdʒn] *Taube*
Pilgrim Fathers *Pilgerväter*
pinnacle ['pɪnəkl] *Gipfel*
pious ['paɪəs] *fromm, (streng)gläubig*
pit *Grube*
plantation *Plantage*
plebiscite ['plebɪsɪt, -saɪt] *Plebiszit, Volksabstimmung*
plentiful *reichlich, massenhaft*
plough [plaʊ] *Pflug*
plumber ['plʌmə] *Installateur/in*
plumed hat *Federhut*
point of view *Standpunkt*
point sth. out *etwas zeigen*
poised *bereit*
poison gas *Giftgas*
pole *Stange, Mast*
poor relief *Armenhilfe, Fürsorge*
popular sovereignty *Volkssouveränität*
pottery *Tongeschirr*
pound (lb) *Pfund*
pour sth. down sb.'s throat *jdm. etwas einflößen*
powder keg *Pulverfass*
powder magazine *Pulverfass*
praise sb. / sth. *jdn. / etwas loben*
predict sth. *etwas vorhersagen*
presence ['prezns] *Anwesenheit*
preside *Vorsitz führen*
pressing board *Pressbalken*
pressure ['preʃə] *Druck*
prevent sth. *etwas verhindern*
preventive war *Präventivkrieg*
pre-war *Vorkriegs-*
prey upon sb. *jdm. keine Ruhe lassen*
pride in sth. *Stolz auf etwas*
primary source *Primärquelle*
Prime Minister *Ministerpräsident/in*
prince *Prinz, Fürst*
principal *Haupt-, hauptsächlich*
principality *Fürstentum*
prison sentence *Gefängnisstrafe*
process sth. *etwas weiterverarbeiten*
proclaim sb. / sth. *jdn. / etwas ausrufen, verkünden, erklären*
productivity growth *Produktivitätswachstum*
profess sth. *sich zu etwas bekennen*
promote sth. *etwas fördern, vorantreiben*
proper *eigentlich, schicklich, passend*
property *Besitz*
proportion of sth. [- '- -] *Anteil an etwas*
in proportion to sth. [- '- -] *im Verhältnis zu etwas*
propose sth. *etwas vorschlagen, einbringen*
props *Requisiten*
prosperity *Wohlstand*
protect sb. *jdn. schützen*
protection *Schutz*
protectorate *Protektorat, besetztes Gebiet*
Protests of Silesian Weavers *Schlesischer Weberaufstand*
provide sth. *etwas anbieten, bereitstellen*
provisional *provisorisch, vorläufig*
provoke sth. *etwas hervorrufen, provozieren*
Prussian State Assembly *Preußischer Landtag*
Public Health Acts *Gesundheitsgesetz*
publish sth. *etwas veröffentlichen*
purpose ['pɜːpəs] *Zweck, Absicht*
put aside sth. *etwas beiseite schieben*

Q

quadruple sth. *etwas vervierfachen*
question sth. *etwas hinterfragen, prüfen*

R

rabbit *Hase*
race *„Rasse"*
racism *Rassismus*
rail *Schiene*
railroad (AE) *Eisenbahn*
railway (BE) *Eisenbahn*
railway bridge *Eisenbahnbrücke*
railway net *Eisenbahnliniennetz*
raise sth. *etwas aufbringen*
rapier ['reɪpiə] *Degen*
rapprochement [ræ'prɒʃmɒ̃ ☆ ˌræproʊʃ'mɑːn] *Annäherung*
raw material *Rohstoff*
reason *Vernunft*
recognize sth. *etwas (an)erkennen*
record *Aufzeichnung*
refer to sth. *sich beziehen auf etwas*
refusal [rɪ'fjuːzl] *Weigerung*
reign [reɪn] *Herrschaft*
Reign of Terror [reɪn] *Terrorherrschaft*
rein *Zügel*
Reinsurance Treaty [ˌriːɪn'ʃʊərəns] *Rückversicherungsvertrag*
reject sth. *etwas zurückweisen, ablehnen*
relate to sth. *sich auf etwas beziehen*
relative *Verwandter*
relaxed *entspannt*
reliability [rɪˌlaɪə'bɪləti] *Glaubwürdigkeit, Zuverlässigkeit*
reliable [rɪ'laɪəbl] *verlässlich*
relieve sb. *jdn. entlasten*
remain *bleiben*
remarkable *beachtenswert*
remove sb. *jdn. abberufen*
rental condition *Pachtbedingungen*
reorganization *Umgestaltung*
reparations *Reparationen*
repeal sth. *etwas aufheben, abschaffen*
representative *Abgeordneter/in*
reputation [ˌrepju'teɪʃn] *Ruf*

require sth. *etwas (er)fordern*
resent sb. / sth. [ri'zent] *sich (sehr) über jdn. / etwas ärgern*
reserve [ri'zɜːv] *Reservat*
reside [rɪ'zaɪd] *leben, wohnen*
resist sth. *etwas widerstehen*
resistance *Widerstand*
resolve sth. [rɪ'zɒlv ☆ -'zɑːlv] *etwas lösen*
respond *reagieren*
restore sth. *etwas wiederherstellen*
result *Ergebnis, Resultat*
result in sth. *in etwas münden, zu etwas führen*
retail *Einzelhandel*
retreat *Rückzug*
revenge *Vergeltung, Rache*
Revolutionary Wars *Revolutionskriege*
riding stick *Reitgerte*
rifle *Gewehr*
right to work *Recht auf Arbeit*
right-hand (corner) *rechte (Ecke)*
riot ['raɪət] *Aufruhr, Krawall*
ripe *reif*
rise by *um etwas (an)steigen*
root *Wurzeln*
rubber *Naturkautschuk*
Ruhr Valley *Ruhrgebiet*
rule *Regel*
Russian October Revolution *Russische Oktoberrevolution*

S

sabre ['seɪbə] *Säbel*
sailing ship *Segelschiff*
salesperson *Verkäufer/in*
salutary *heilsam*
sash *Schärpe*
satiated ['seɪʃieɪtəd] *gesättigt*
savage ['sævɪdʒ] *wild*
Saxony *Sachsen*
scale *Maßeinheit*
scar *Narbe*
sceptre ['septə] *Szepter, Herrscherstab*
score sth. *etwas erringen, verbuchen*
scramble *Gerangel, Wettlauf*
Sea of Marmara *Marmarameer*
seal of approval *Gütesiegel*
Second Estate *Zweiter Stand*
secondary *zweitrangig*
secondary source *Sekundärquelle, Sekundärtext*
secretary of the interior *Innenminister/in*
Selesia [sə'liːziə] *Schlesien*
sentence sb. *jdn. verurteilen*
separation of powers *Gewaltenteilung*
serious ['sɪəriəs] *ernsthaft*
servant *Diener/in*
serve as sth. *dienen als etwas*
serve sb. *jdm. dienen*
service *Service, Dienstleistung*
setback *Rückschlag*
setting *Umfeld, Umgebung, Rahmen, Bühnenbild*
settlement *Abkommen, Übereinkunft; Besiedlung, Siedlung*
settler *Siedler/in*
Seven Years War *Siebenjähriger Krieg*
sewer ['suːə, BE also 'sjuːə] *Abwasserkanal*
sewerage ['suːərɪdʒ] *Kanalisation*
shape sth. *etwas formen, prägen*
sharp *stark*
shellfire *Artilleriefeuer*
shield *Schild*
shift sth. *etwas verlagern*
shoot sb. dead *jdn. erschießen*
shortage of sth. *Mangel an etwas*
short-service system *kurzer Wehrdienst*
short-term *kurzfristig*
showcase *Modell*
side with sb. *Partei ergreifen*
sign sth. [saɪn] *etwas unterzeichnen*
significant [- '- - -] *bedeutend*
similar *gleich, vergleichbar*
sitter *Modell*
skilled worker *Facharbeiter/in*
Slav *slavisch*
slave trade *Sklavenhandel*
slavery *Sklaverei*
slight *langsam, leicht*
sling sth. *etwas schmeißen*
smash sth. *etwas zerschlagen*
social question *Soziale Frage*
Social Security Laws *Sozialgesetzgebung*
social security system *Sozialversicherungssystem*
Socialist Workers' Party *Sozialistische Arbeiter Partei*
society *Gesellschaft, Vereinigung*
source *Quelle*
source of power *Energiequelle*
sovereign ['sɒvrɪn ☆ 'sɑːvrən] *Souverän*
spa town *Kurort*
spacious ['speɪʃəs] *geräumig*
spade *Spaten*
spark *Funke*
sphere [sfɪə] *Bereich*
spinning mule *Spinnmaschine*
spirit *Geist*
spokesman *Sprecher*
spouse *(Ehe)gatte, (Ehe)gattin*
squeeze sth. out of sb. *etwas aus jdm. herauspressen*
St Paul's Church *Frankfurter Paulskirche*
stagecoach *Postkutsche*
staged *gestellt*
Stamp Act *Stempelgesetz*
stanza *Strophe eines Gedichtes*
starvation *Hungertod*
starve *hungern, verhungern*
state budget *Staatshaushalt*
steady *gleichmäßig, stetig*
steam engine *Dampfmaschine*
steam locomotive *Dampflok*
steamship *Dampfschiff*
steerage ['stɪərɪdʒ] *Zwischendeck*
stirrup *Steigbügel*
Straits of Gibraltar *Straße von Gibraltar*
strength *Kraft*
stress sth. *etwas betonen*
striking *auffallend*
strive for sth. *nach etwas streben*
struggle for sth. *Kampf um etwas*
struggle for culture *Kulturkampf*
submit sth. *etwas einreichen*
subservient *unterwürfig*
subsidy *Subvention, Unterstützungsgeld*
substitute *Ersatz*
sudden *plötzlich*
suffer *leiden*
suffrage *Wahlrecht*
suicide *Selbstmord*
suited *geeignet*
summon sb. *jdn. einberufen*
Sunday suit *Sonntagskleidung*
sunrise industries *Zukunftsindustrien*
superiority *Überlegenheit*
superpower *Großmacht*
supervisor *Aufseher/in*
supply *Versorgung, Nachschub*
support sb. *jdn. / etwas unterstützen, belegen*
Supreme Court *Oberstes Gericht*
supreme judge *oberste/r Richter/in*
surplus *Überschuss*
surveyor [sə'veɪə] *Landvermesser/in*
swear [sweə] *schwören*
sweep sth. up *etwas auffegen*
sweeping *überwältigend*
sword [sɔːd] *Schwert*

T

tablet *Tafel*
take sb. round *jdn. herumführen*
tank *Panzer*
tape measure *Metermaß*
target *Ziel(-richtung)*
tariff *(Durchgangs-)Zoll*
tax *Steuer*
tenant farmer *Pachtbauer/in*
tension *Spannung*
territories west of the Rhine *linksrheinische Gebiete*
territory *Territorium, Land*
therefore *deshalb, also*
thesis ['θiːsɪs] *Doktorarbeit*
Third Estate *Dritter Stand*
threat [θret] *Drohung*
threaten sb. ['θretn] *jdn. bedrohen, jdm. drohen*
Three Emperors' Alliance *Dreikaiservertrag*
Three Emperors' League *Dreikaiserbund*

Three-Class Election System *Dreiklassen-wahlrecht*
threefold *dreifach*
thus *so, somit, daher, folglich*
timber *Holz*
tiny **['taɪni]** *winzig*
tithe **[taið]** *(Kirchen-)Zehnt*
topic *Thema*
torment sb. *jdn. quälen*
torture sb. *jdn. quälen, foltern*
track *Gleis*
trade *handeln; Handel, Gewerbe*
trade union *Gewerkschaft*
trading post *Handelsniederlassung, -station*
traitor *Verräter/in*
transport *Verkehrswesen*
treacherous **['tretʃərəs]** *verräterisch*
treason **['tri:zn]** *Hochverrat*
treasure **['treʒə]** *Schatz*
treaty **['tri:ti]** *Vertrag (zwischen Staaten)*
Treaty of Paris **['tri:ti]** *Pariser Vertrag*
tree diagram **['daɪəgræm]** *Baumdiagramm*
tremble *zittern*
trench *Schützengraben*
trench warfare *Grabenkrieg, Stellungskrieg*
trial **['traɪəl]** *Prozess, Gerichtsverfahren*
trial by jury **['traɪəl]** *Verhandlung vor einem Geschworenengericht*
tribe *Stamm*
trigger cause *Auslöser*
trigger off sth. *etwas auslösen, einleiten*
triple sth. *etwas verdreifachen*
Triple Alliance *Dreibund*
Triple Entente *Triple Entente*
try sb. (in court) for sth. *jdn. wegen etwas vor Gericht stellen*
twofold *zweifach*
tyranny **['tɪrəni]** *Tyrannei, Gewaltherrschaft*

U

unclaimed *unbeansprucht*
unconstitutional *verfassungswidrig*
undo sth. *etwas zunichte machen*
unfavourable *ungünstig, unvorteilhaft, negativ*
unification *Vereinigung*
universal *allgemein*
Universal Student's Union *Burschenschaft*
unjust *ungerecht*
unremarkable *unauffällig*
unskilled worker *Hilfs-, ungelernte Arbeiter/in*
urban **['ɜ:bən]** *städtisch*
urbanization **[ˌɜ:bənaɪ'zeɪʃn]** *Verstädterung, Urbanisierung*

V

Venn diagram *Schnittmengendiagramm*
verse **[vɜ:s]** *Strophe eines Liedes*
veto sth. **['vi:təʊ ☆ -toʊ]** *Einspruch gegen etwas einlegen*
victory *Sieg*
view *Sicht*
viewer *Betrachter/in*
village council *Gemeinderat*
violate sth. **['vaɪəleɪt]** *etwas missachten, übertreten*
vote *wählen; Wahl, Abstimmungsergebnis*
vote on sth. *über etwas abstimmen*
vote out sb. *jdn. abwählen*
voyage *Reise*

W

wage *Lohn*
wall decoration *Wandschmuck*
war chariot *Kriegswagen*
war cripple *Kriegskrüppel*
warrant *richterliche Anordnung, Haftbefehl*
Wars of Liberation *Befreiungskriege*
waste collection *Müllabfuhr*
watercolour *Aquarell*
wave sth. *etwas schwenken*
wheat *Weizen*
wheelchair *Rollstuhl*
whereupon *woraufhin*
weapons of mass destruction *Massenvernichtungswaffen*
wig *Perücke*
withdraw *zurückziehen*
wooden clogs *Holzschuhe*
working class *Arbeiterklasse*
workshop *Handwerksbetrieb*
wrangling *Gerangel*

Y

yarn *Garn*
yet *jedoch, aber*

Z

zenith *Zenith, Höhepunkt*

Abbreviations and symbols

AE	(mainly or exclusively) American English
BE	(mainly or exclusively) British English
cf.	Lat. *confer* = compare
ed.	editor
e.g.	Lat. *exempli gratia* = for example
etc.	Lat. *et cetera* = and so on
Lat.	Latin
l., ll.	line, lines
p., pp.	page, pages
sb.	somebody
sth.	something
☆	American pronunciation follows
→	see Appendix

Regular differences in American pronunciation – as for instance the [r] after vowels – have not been given.

Historical dictionary

(Analysing, discussing and arguing)

A

jdn. abberufen remove sb.
abdanken abdicate
Abgaben dues (*Pl.*)
Abgeordnete/r Member of Parliament, representative
Abkommen agreement, settlement
etwas ablehnen disagree with sth., reject sth.
Abnahme decrease
Abrüstung disarmament
etwas abschaffen abolish sth., repeal sth.
Abschaffung abolition, repeal
Absicht aim, intention
absichtlich deliberate
über etwas abstimmen vote on sth.
jdn. abwählen vote sb. out
Adel nobility
(Reichs-)Adler eagle
adlig noble
Adliger noble(man)
allgemein general, universal
allmählich gradual
Allmende common lands
also therefore
etwas anerkennen recognize sth.
Angaben data, information
etwas angeben indicate sth.
angeklagt sein go on trial for sth.
Angelegenheit matter, issue
zum Angriff übergehen launch an attack
Anlass geben zu etwas give rise to sth.
Annäherung rapprochement
etwas annektieren annex sth.
jdn. / etwas anprangern denounce sb. / sth.
Anspruch claim
um etwas ansteigen rise by sth. *(eine Zahl oder eine Menge)*
Anstieg increase
etwas anstreben aspire to sth.
(prozentualer) Anteil percentage
Anteil an etwas proportion of sth.
Arbeiter/in labourer
Arbeitgeber/in employer
Arbeiterklasse working class
Arbeitskräfte labour force
sich (sehr) über jdn. / etwas ärgern resent sb. / sth.
Armee army, force
Armenhilfe poor relief
Aufbau build-up
etwas aufbringen raise sth.
etwas auferlegen impose sth.
auffallend striking
etwas aufheben (außer Kraft setzen) overrule, override sth.; *(widerrufen)* abolish sth.
auflösen dissolve
Aufseher/in supervisor
Aufstand revolt, insurrection
jdn. ausbeuten exploit sb.
Auseinandersetzung dispute
Ausfuhr export
etwas auslösen trigger sth. off
Auslöser trigger cause
Ausmaß extent
jdn. ausschließen exclude sb.
Auswanderung emigration
Auswirkung auf etwas effect on sth.

B

Balkan the Balkans
Bauarbeiter/in construction worker
(Klein-)Bauer/-bäuerin peasant
Baumwolle cotton
beachtenswert remarkable
Beamter/-tin civil servant
Beauftragte/r delegate
bedeutend notable, significant
jdn. bedrohen, jdm. drohen threaten sb.
Bedrohung threat, menace
Bedürfniss need
etwas begrüßen welcome, greet sth.
etwas behaupten claim sth.
etwas beiseite schieben put aside sth.
etwas beitragen contribute sth.
etwas bekommen get, gain sth.
jdn. beleidigen insult sb.
Bereich sphere
bereit poised
Beschwerde grievance
jdn. benachteiligen discriminate against sb.
Bericht account; report
etwas besetzen occupy sth.
etwas besitzen own sth.
etwas beurteilen evaluate sth.
jdn. beschäftigen employ sb.
etwas beschränken limit sth.
jdn. beschuldigen accuse sb.
sich beschweren complain
Besiedlung settlement
Besitz property
Besitzer/in owner
bestehen aus sth. consist of sth.
etwas bestimmen determine sth.
an etwas beteiligt involved in sth.
etwas betonen emphasize sth., stress sth.
Betrachter/in viewer
sich / jdn. bewaffnen arm yourself / sb.
jdn. vor etwas bewahren keep sb. from sth
Beweis evidence
sich auf etwas beziehen refer to sth.
bleiben stay, remain
Brüderlichkeit fraternity
Bündnis alliance
Bürger/in citizen
Bürgerrechte civil rights
Bürgerwehr militia

C

Chemiker/in chemist

D

daher thus
Dampflok steam locomotive
Dampfmaschine steam engine
Dampfschiff steamship
dauern last
Denkmal memorial
deshalb therefore
dreifach threefold
deutlich noticeably
Deutsch-Französischer Krieg Franco-Prussian War
dienen als etwas serve as sth.
jdm. dienen serve sb.
Diener/in servant
Dienstleistung service
Dritter Stand Third Estate
Druck pressure

E

jdn. / etwas einberufen conscript, call up sb.; convene, summon sth.
Eindruck impression
einflussreich influential
eingreifen intervene
einmarschieren (in etwas) invade (sth.)
etwas einrichten establish sth.
Einspruch gegen etwas einlegen veto sth.
jdn. einstellen hire sb.
Eisenbahn railway (BE) = (AE) railroad
Eisenbahnbrücke railway bridge
Einwanderung immigration
Einwohner/in inhabitant
jdn. entlassen dismiss sb.
entspannt relaxed
Entspannung détente
entstehen arise
Entwicklung development
Epoche epoch
etwas erfüllen fulfill sth.
Ergebnis outcome, result
jdn. ernennen appoint sb.
ernsthaft serious
Ernte crops
Ernteausfall crop failure

etwas erobern conquer sth.
Errungenschaft achievement
jdn. erschießen shoot sb. dead
Erster Stand First Estate
etwas ertragen endure sth.
Erwerb acquisition
Exekutive Executive Branch

F

Fabrik factory, mill
(gelernte/r) Facharbeiter/in skilled worker
Federhut plumed hat
Feind enemy
Feindschaft hostility
feindselig hostile
flüchten flee
Flugblatt flyer
Folge consequence
folglich thus
jdn. foltern torture sb.
etwas fördern further sth., promote sth.
Forderung demand
Forderungen stellen present demands
Forscher/in explorer
Freiheit liberty
Friedenskonferenz peace conference
Friedensvereinbarung peace settlement
Friseur/in hairdresser
Frondienste corvées
etwas führen conduct sth.
zu etwas führen give rise to sth., result in sth.

G

Garn yarn
Gebiet area
etwas gedenken commemorate sth.
geeignet suited
Gefahr peril
jdn. gefangen nehmen capture sb.
im Gegensatz zu jdm. / etwas in contrast to / with sb. / sth.
jdm. gehorchen obey sb.
Geistlicher clergyman
Geistlichkeit clergy
Generalstände Estates-General
gerecht just
Gerechtigkeit justice
jdn. wegen etwas vor Gericht stellen try sb. (in court) for sth.
Gerichtsverfahren trial
Gesellschaft society
Gesetz act, law
ein Gesetz verabschieden pass a law
Gesetzbuch Civil Code
gesetzestreu law-abiding
etwas gestatten grant sth.
gestellt staged, posed
Getreide grain
Gewaltherrschaft tyranny
Gewaltenteilung separation of powers
Gewehr rifle
Gewerbe trade
Gewerkschaft trade union
gewöhnlich ordinary
Giftgas poison gas
gleich equal
Gleichheit equality
gleichmäßig steady
grausam cruel
Grenze boundary
„großdeutsche Lösung“ Greater Germany
Großmacht superpower
etwas gründen found sth.
Grundrechte (in Entwurf der deutschen Verfassung von 1848) Catalogue of civil liberties
Grundrechtekatalog (der US-Verfassung) Bill of Rights
günstig favourable
Güter goods
Gymnasium grammar school

H

Handel commerce, trade
mit / in etwas handeln deal / trade with / in sth.
Handelsstation trading post
Handweber/in handloom weaver
Handwerker/in craftsman / -woman / -person
Handwerksbetrieb workshop
Hass hatred
Haupt-, chief, principal
Häuptling chief
hauptsächlich (Adj) main, principal; *(Adv)* mainly, principally, especially
Heiliges Römisches Reich Deutscher Nation Holy Roman Empire of German Nation
jdn. herausfordern challenge sb.
Herrschaft reign
Hersteller manufacturer
etwas hervorbringen bring about sth.
etwas hervorrufen provoke sth.
(ungelernte/r) Hilfsarbeiter/in unskilled worker
Hinrichtung execution
Höhepunkt zenith, peak
Holz wood, timber
humorvoll humorous, funny

I

Imperialismus imperialism
Industriegüter manufactured goods
Industrieunternehmen industrial enterprise
Informatiker/in information technology specialist
insbesondere notably
Installateur/in plumber
jdn. integrieren integrate sb.
an jdm. / etwas interessiert interested in sb. / sth
ironisch ironic

J

Jakobiner/in Jacobin
jedoch yet, however
Jurisdiktion Judicial Branch

K

Kaiser/in emperor / empress
Kaiserreich empire
Kampf um etwas struggle for sth.
Kanalisation sewerage
Kanzler/in chancellor
Karikatur cartoon
Kaufmann merchant
kaum hardly
sich wie etw. / jmd. kleiden dress as sb. / sth.
„kleindeutsche Lösung“ Little Germany
Kolonie colony
Kolonisierung colonization
Kompromiss compromise
Königsanhänger monarchist
Kraft strength
Kraftwagenfahrer lorry driver
Krankenschwester nurse
Krawall riot
jdm. den Krieg erklären declare war on sb.
jdn. kritisieren criticize sb.
jdn. krönen crown sb.
Kunde client
kurzfristig short-term
Kutsche carriage, coach
Kutscher driver

L

Land territory
langfristig long-term
Last burden, load
Lebenserwartung life expectancy
Legislative Legislative Branch
leiden suffer
etwas leiten direct sth.
linke (Ecke) left-hand (corner)
jdn. / etwas loben praise sb. / sth.
Lohn wage
Lorbeerkranz laurel wreath
etwas lösen resolve sth.

M

Mangel an etwas lack of sth.
Marine navy
Massenproduktion mass production
Massenvernichtungswaffen weapons of mass destruction

Mehrheitsbeschluss majority decision
Meinung opinion
Menge crowd
Menschenrechte human rights
jdn. / etwas messen measure sb. / sth.
etwas missachten violate sth.
Mitgliedschaft membership
Mitspracherechte haben have a say
Mittelschicht middle class
Müllabfuhr waste collection

N

Nationalismus nationalism
Nationalstaat nation-state
Nationalversammlung National Assembly
neidisch envious
neutral neutral
niedere inferior
Niedergang decline
Niederlage defeat
Nutzen ziehen aus etwas benefit from sth.

P

Panzer tank
Partei party
Pflasterstein paving stone
Pilgerväter Pilgrim Fathers
plötzlich sudden
Postkutsche stagecoach
Privileg privilege
von jdm. / etwas profitieren profit from sb. / sth.

Q

Quelle source

R

Rache revenge
Rassismus racism
Reagieren auf etwas respond to sth.
Recht auf Arbeit right to work
rechte (Ecke) right-hand (corner)
etwas rechtfertigen justify sth.
Rechtsanwalt/-wältin lawyer, solicitor
Reform reform
Regel rule
reichlich plentiful
Reise trip, voyage
Reisender passenger
Resultat result, outcome
Revolution revolution
Richter judge
Rohstoff raw material
Rückgang decrease, drop
Rückschlag setback

S

jdm. / etwas schaden harm sb., damage sth.
etwas schätzen estimate sth.
scheitern fail
Schlacht battle
Schmutz dirt, filth
Schulden debts
Schutz protection
jdn. schützen protect sb.
Schwert sword
Segelschiff sailing ship
Sekundärtext secondary source
Sicht view
Sichtweise perspective
Siedler/in settler
Sieg victory
sinken decrease
Sklaverei slavery
somit thus
Sozialversicherungssystem social security system
Spinnmaschine spinning machine
Staatenbund federation
Staatshaushalt state budget
Staatsstreich coup d'état
Stamm tribe
Stand (im Pl. auch Ländereien) estate
Standpunkt point of view
stark sharp
steigen increase
Stellungskrieg trench warfare
Steuer tax
Stoff cloth
Stolz auf etwas pride in sth.
nach etwas streben strive for sth.

T

Territorium territory
Thema topic
Tischler/in carpenter
jdn. tragen carry sb.
mit etwas zu tun haben deal with sth.

U

Überlegenheit superiority
etwas übertreiben exaggerate sth.
jdn. überzeugen convince sb.; persuade sb.
Umstand circumstance
Umsturz (einer Regierung) overthrow
Unabhängigkeit independence
unfreiwillig involuntary
Ungehorsam disobedience
ungerecht unjust
Ungerechtigkeit injustice
ungesetzlich illegal
ungünstig unfavourable
Unterdrückung oppression
Unternehmer/in entrepreneur
sich unterscheiden von / in etwas differ from / in sth.
Unterschicht lower-class
jdn. / etwas unterstützen support sb.
Untersuchung investigation
unterwürfig subservient
etwas unterzeichnen sign sth.
unzufrieden mit etwas dissatisfied with sth.
Ursache cause

V

etwas verabschieden pass sth. *(z. B. ein Gesetz)*; adopt sth. *(z. B. einen Haushalt)*
Verbesserung improvement
etwas verbieten outlaw sth.
etwas verdreifachen triple sth.
etwas vereinigen join sth. together
Vereinigung unification
Verbindung connection
ein Verbrechen begehen commit a crime
Verbündeter ally
etwas verdecken disguise sth.
etwas verdienen earn sth.
Verfassung constitution
verfassungsgemäß constitutional
verfassungswidrig unconstitutional
vergleichbar similar
im Verhältnis zu etwas in proportion to sth.
etwas verhandeln negotiate sth.
etwas verhindern prevent sth.
verhungern starve
Verkäufer/in salesperson
Verkehrswesen transport
jdn. / etwas verkünden proclaim sb. / sth.
verlässlich reliable
jdn. verletzen injure sb.
Vernunft reason
etwas veröffentlichen publish sth.
verpflichtend obligatory
sich versammeln gather
Versammlung assembly
versäumen, etwas zu tun fail to do sth.
Versicherungskaufmann/-frau insurance agent
Versorgung supply
Verstädterung urbanization
jdn. / etwas verstecken hide sb. / sth.
etwas an jdn. verteilen dole sth. out to sb.
Verteilung distribution
(geschäftlicher) Vertrag contract
Vertrag (zwischen Staaten) treaty
jdn. verurteilen sentence sb.
etwas vervierfachen quadruple sth.
Verwandte/r relative
Verwundete/r casualty
Vieh cattle
Vereinigungsrecht freedom of assembly
Völkermord genocide
Volksabstimmung plebiscite
Volksschule elementary school

Volkssouveränität popular sovereignty
etwas voranbringen advance sth.
Vorherrschaft dominance, hegemony
Vorkriegs- pre-war
vorläufig provisional
etwas vorschlagen propose sth.
Vorsitz führen preside

W

Waffenruhe ceasefire
Waffenstillstand armistice
Wahl vote, election
wählbar eligible
jdn. / etwas wählen vote for sb. / sth.
Wahlrecht suffrage
Webstuhl loom
Weigerung refusal
sich wenden gegen jdn. / etwas oppose sb. / sth.
Wettrüsten arms race
Wettstreit competition
Widerstand resistance
etwas wiederherstellen restore sth.
Wirtschaftssektor economic sector
witzig humorous, funny
Wohlstand affluence, prosperity
woraufhin whereupon
würdevoll dignified

Z

(Kirchen-)Zehnt tithe
etwas zeigen point sth. out
Zeitalter age
Zeitpunkt moment
Zeitspanne period of time
Zensuswahlrecht census suffrage
Ziel aim
Ziel(-richtung) target
zivil; Zivilist/in civilian
(Durchgangs-)Zoll tariff
Zöllner/in customs officer
zugrunde gehen perish
jdm. zujubeln cheer sb.
etwas zurückweisen reject sth.
zurückziehen withdraw
sich zusammenschließen join
zusammenstoßen clash
einer Sache / jdm. zustimmen agree with sth. / sb.
Zustimmung agreement, consent
Zweck purpose
zweifach twofold
Zweiter Stand Second Estate
jdn. zwingen force, compel sb.

Charts and diagrams

Cause-and-effect diagrams

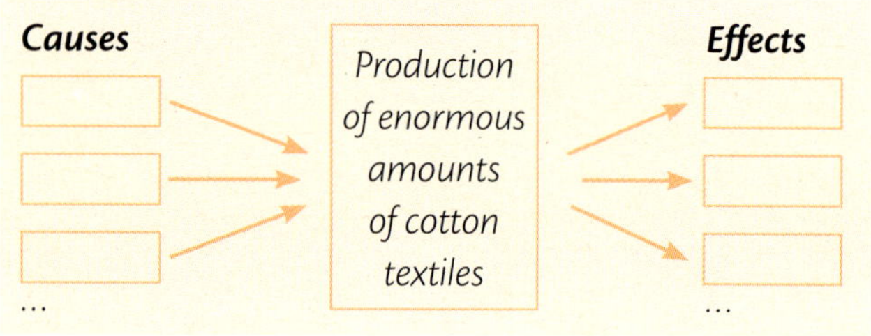

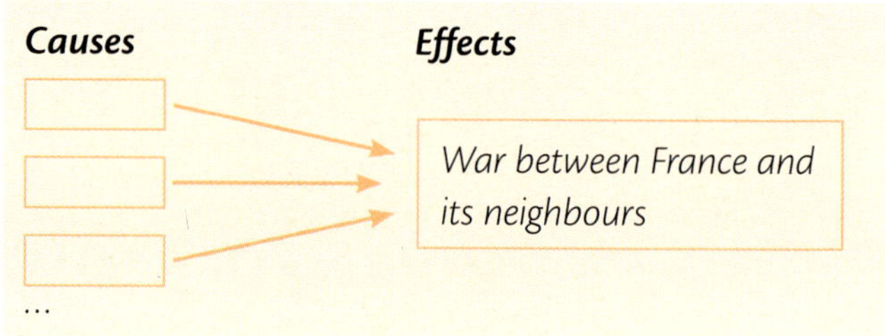

Flow chart

Congress of Vienna
- no national unity in Germany
- no democratic governments in the German states

Vocabulary: *fail to – (not) lead to*

1 →

German Confederation
- …
- …

Vocabulary: *establish – form – create*

2 ↙

University students
- …
- …

Vocabulary: *respond to – demand*

3 →

August von Kotzebue
- …

Vocabulary: *assassinate*

4 ↙

Metternich and leaders of the Confederation
- …
- …

Vocabulary: *convince – argue – introduce – impose*

5 →

Carlsbad Decrees
- … illegal for professors to …
- … illegal for students to …
- … illegal for everybody to …

Vocabulary: *make it / be / become illegal to – not allowed to – allow to*

Event chain

1 **28 June**
On … was shot by …

→ 2 **6 July**
In reaction to … Germany promised to …. This is called …

→ 3 **23 July**
Austria reacted to … by sending/confronting …

↓ 4 **25 July** Russia declared …
After the Russian declaration … Serbia rejected …

← 5 **28 July**
After Serbia had …
Austria declared …

← 6 **31 July**
Russia mobilized its … to …, but this …

↓ 7 **1 August** Germany declared …
Frightened by … Germany put into operation …

→ 8 **3 August**
On … Germany … and …

→ 9 **4 August**
On … Britain … to fulfil … in which it had …

Mind map

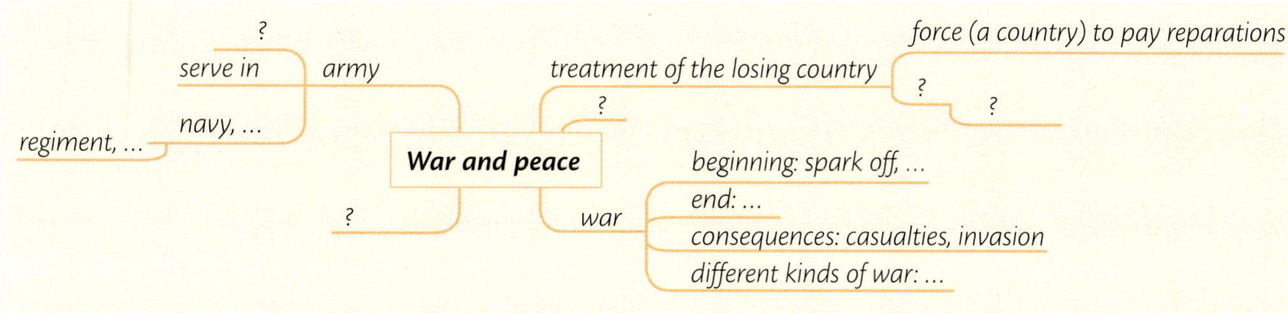

Biography organizer

Venn diagram

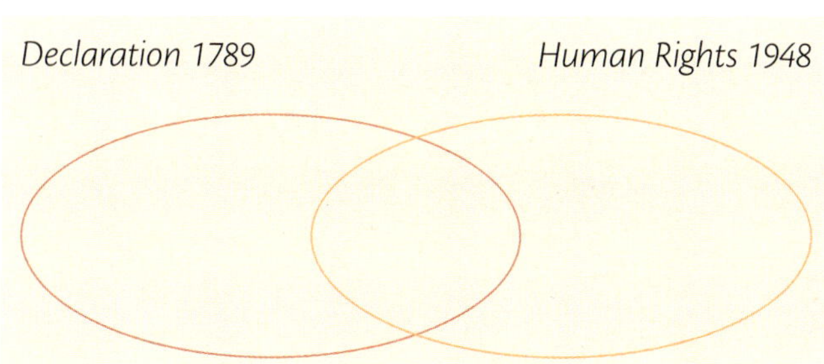

Tri-Venn diagram

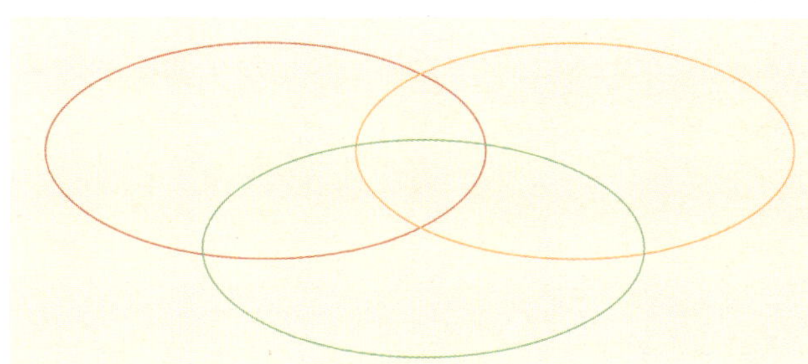

Tree diagram

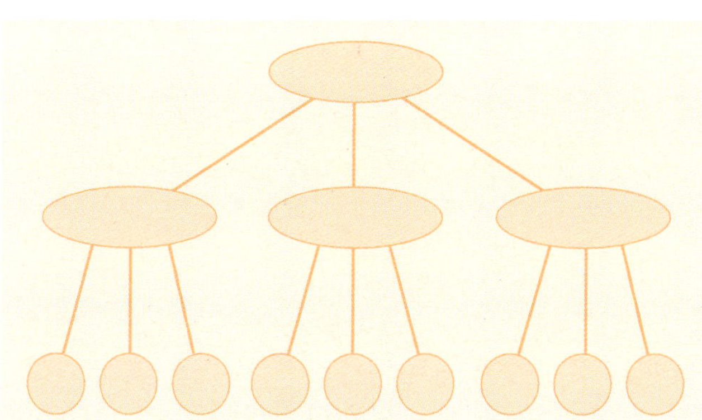

Event map

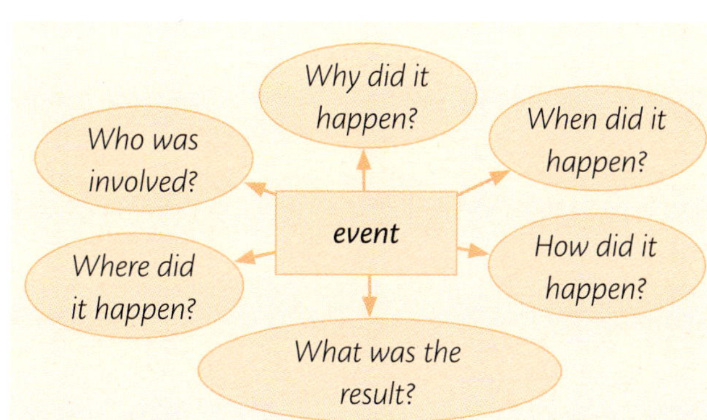

Acknowledgements

akg-images: U2 l. o., 11, 15, 16, 20 r., 25 / S3, 29 / S14, S15, 31, 32 (Erich Lessing), 34, 37, 40, 42 / S11, 43 / S13, 45, 47, 49 / S2, 53, 57, 65 / S10, 77 r., 97, 105, 110, 120 / S18 (© VG Bild-Kunst, Bonn 2006), 124 o. l (Erich Lessing), 125 r. o., 126 l. o., r., 127 r. u., 128 o. l., r., 130 l.; Bildarchiv Preußischer Kulturbesitz: Titelbild r., U2 r. u., U3 l. o., 58, 80, 82, 91 u. r., 93, 94, 103; bpk / Kunstbibliothek, SMB / Knud Petersen: 6; Illustration Thomas Binder (nach einer Vorlage von Chris Rothero): 115 / S8; Bridgeman Art Library: U2 r. o., 127 r. o.; Bridgeman Giraudon: 38; CINETEXT: 43 / S14; Cliché Bibliothèque nationale de France, Paris: 36; © CORBIS: 65 / S11; aus: Chronicle of Britain: 129 r.; aus: Neil Demarco, Britain and the Great, Oxford Univ. Press, 1992: 129 l. u.; Deutsches Historisches Museum, Berlin: U3 l. u., 98 (© VG Bild-Kunst, Bonn 2006); Deutsches Technikmuseum, Berlin: 75 / S12, 79 / S12; dpa: 63, 104; Frankfurter Allgemeine Zeitung, 7. 10. 2004: 122 / S21; Germanisches Nationalmuseum, Nürnberg: 83; aus: Germany 1858–1990, Oxford advanced history: 81; aus: Graudenz / Schindler, Über 1000 Jahre Geschichte in Wort, Bild und Karte. Die deutschen Kolonien, Weltbild Verlag: 102; Historische Bibliothek des CHRISTIANEUMS Hamburg: 88; Historisches Archiv Krupp: 77 / S16, 124 r. u.; Historisches Museum, Frankfurt am Main: 62, 75 / S10, 91 u. l., 124 l. u.; © Hulton-Deutsch Collection / CORBIS: 114.; Christine Keitz, Berlin: 59 / S2; Mary Evans Picture Library, London: 25 / S5; Massachusetts Historical Society, Boston: 13; Musée Lambinet, Versailles: 42 u. r.; National Library of Australia: 116 / 10, S11; Objektsammlungen des DM, Foto: Deutsches Museum: 75 / S11; Photothèque des Musées de la Ville de Paris: 49 / S3; picture-alliance / akg-images: 84; picture-alliance / dpa / © dpa-Bildarchiv: 119; picture-alliance / dpa / © dpa-Fotoreport: 108; Reiss-Engelhorn – Museum, Kunst- und Stadtgeschichtliche Sammlungen, Mannheim (Jean Christen): 67; Wolfgang Rieger, Köln: 90; Sammlung Riepe, Haan: 96 / S5; Sandscapes Travel Services – Namibia: 103 / S18; Spiegel-Verlag, Hamburg: 64; Stiftung Stadtmuseum Berlin: 48; SV-Bilderdienst: U3 r. o., r. u., 103 / S16, 115, 117 / S12; Wilhelm Stöckle, Filderstadt: 86; The Bridgeman Art Library: 24 / S1, 26; The British Library, London: 24 u., 130 r.; The British Museum, London: 42 u. l., 129 l. o.; The Cartoon Bank, New York: 23; The Granger Collection: 124 r. o.; The National Archives, Kew Richmond: 30; ullstein – Archiv Gerstenberg: 55, 68; ullstein bild: Titelbild l., 77 / S15, 78, 127 l.; ullstein – Granger Collection: U2 l. u., 7, 9, 10, 14 / S11, S12, 19, 20 / S16, 65 o. l., 125 l. u., 126 l. u.; ullstein – KPA: 25 / S2, S4, 125 l. o.; ullstein – Schwartz: 89; ullstein – Tappe: 120 r. u.; Universitäts- und Landesbibliothek Düsseldorf: 44; Annegret Weeke, Düsseldorf: 122 / S22; www.filmsite.org: 123 / S23; www.greatwar.nl/frames/default-hurley.html 116 o. r; www.lermuseum.org: 113; www.michaelstevenson.com: 96 / S7; www.saburchill.com: 100 / S13

Nicht in allen Fällen war es uns möglich, die Rechteinhaber der Abbildungen ausfindig zu machen. Für eventuell entstandene Fehler oder Auslassungen bitten wir um Verständnis. Berechtigte Ansprüche werden selbstverständlich im Rahmen der üblichen Vereinbarungen abgegolten.